Witchcraft in Early North America

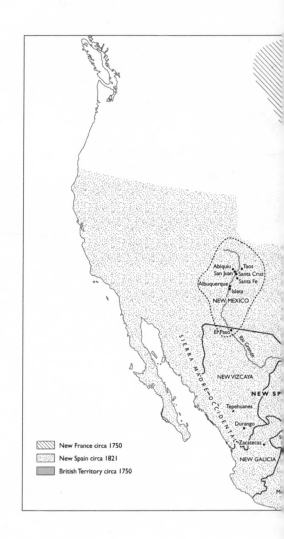

Abiquiu • Taos
San Juan • Santa Cruz
• Santa Fe
Albuquerque • Isleta
NEW MEXICO

El Paso • Rio Grande

NEW VIZCAYA

NEW SP

Tepehuanes •

• Durango

• Zacatecas •

NEW GALICIA

M

SIERRA MADRE-OCCIDENTAL

New France circa 1750
New Spain circa 1821
British Territory circa 1750

Quebec

St. Lawrence River

Montreal
Kahnawake

MASSACHUSETTS (MAINE)
Falmouth
Saco
NEW HAMPSHIRE
Danvers Topsfield
Ossernenon Groton Salem
NEW Boston
YORK MASSACHUSETTS
Hartford RHODE ISLAND
CONNECTICUT
NEW NETHERLANDS

PENNSYLVANIA Philadelphia
Pittsburgh NEW SWEDEN
DELAWARE
Muncie
Washington, D.C.
MARYLAND
Charlottesville
Williamsburg
VIRGINIA Virginia Beach
Norfolk

NORTH
CAROLINA

SOUTH
CAROLINA

Charles Town

GEORGIA Savannah

St. Augustine

FRANCE

Ohio River

Mississippi River

ouis

ew Orleans

American Controversies Series
Series Editor: Douglas R. Egerton, Le Moyne College

Students love debate. They love contention, which they see all about them in modern society. Yet too many monographs or biographies erase the controversies that existed in earlier decades. Slavery and institutionalized sexism, for example, strike modern readers as being so clearly wrong that they cannot understand why rational Americans endorsed slavery or thought it foolish to enfranchise women. How could a politician as brilliant as Thomas Jefferson believe that forced assimilation was the best policy for Native Americans? Why did Americans allow Hitler to become so powerful before confronting him? Why were many of the so-called Greatest Generation indifferent to social justice at home? How did the Vietnam War become such a political and cultural powder keg? Hindsight is often the enemy of understanding, and what strikes us as obvious was often anything but simple to earlier generations.

This series deals with major controversies in American history. The events depicted in this series were either controversial at the time (such as militant abolitionism) or have sparked modern historiographical controversies. (Did slave conspiracies actually exist, for example? Why did witch trials in Salem spiral out of control in 1692?) Each volume in the series begins with an extensive essay that explains the topic, discusses the relevant historiography, and summarizes the various points of view (contemporaneous as well as modern). The second half of the volume is devoted to documents, but each is annotated and preceded by a brief introduction. By contextualizing each document, this series pulls back the curtain, so to speak, on the process of writing history, even as the essays, letters, laws, and newspaper accounts that follow allow important American actors to speak in their own voices. Most of all, by examining both sides in these debates, and by providing documents that see each issue from different angles, the American Controversies Series will bring history alive—and enliven history classrooms.

Volumes Published

Slavery and Sectional Strife in the Early American Republic, 1776–1821
Gary J. Kornblith

Antebellum Women: Private, Public, Partisan
Carol Lasser and Stacey Robertson

Witchcraft in Early North America
Alison Games

Witchcraft in Early North America

Alison Games

ROWMAN & LITTLEFIELD PUBLISHERS, INC.
Lanham • Boulder • New York • Toronto • Plymouth, UK

Published by Rowman & Littlefield Publishers, Inc.
A wholly owned subsidary of The Rowman & Littlefield Publishing Group, Inc.
4501 Forbes Boulevard, Suite 200, Lanham, Maryland 20706
http://www.rowmanlittlefield.com

Estover Road, Plymouth PL6 7PY, United Kingdom

British Library Cataloguing in Publication Information Available

Library of Congress Cataloging-in-Publication Data

Games, Alison, 1963-
  Witchcraft in Early North America / Alison Games.
     p. cm.
  Includes bibliographical references and index.
  ISBN 978-1-4422-0357-0 (cloth : alk. paper) — ISBN 978-1-4422-0359-4 (electronic : alk. paper)
  1. Witchcraft—United States—History. I. Title.
  BF1573.G36 2010
  133.4'30973—dc22   2010014423

♾ ™ The paper used in this publication meets the minimum requirements of American National Standard for Information Sciences—Permanence of Paper for Printed Library Materials, ANSI/NISO Z39.48-1992.

Printed in the United States of America

Contents

Preface

Like many of my colleagues who teach classes in early American history, whether the U.S. history survey or courses on the colonial period, I have always made time to talk about witchcraft. For the most part, I have assigned books that explore the outbreak at Salem in 1692 or witchcraft in New England more broadly. As a result, the story of witchcraft in my classes tended to emphasize the experiences of European colonists and settlers in North America and to keep my students focused on the eastern seaboard, replicating a familiar narrative of American history that privileges the English colonies. But in 2002, I joined forces with my Georgetown colleague Amy Leonard, a specialist in early modern European history, to teach a class on witches and witchcraft in Europe and the Atlantic world. We anchored our class in Europe and then examined the collisions of witch beliefs that transpired beyond Europe, in Africa and the Americas. The class made it obvious to me that witchcraft was a unique and valuable way to understand how Europeans, Africans, and Americans made sense of each other in the sixteenth, seventeenth, and eighteenth centuries. I wondered if it might be possible to develop a book on the subject that I could use in my own North American history classes. I envisioned a text that used witchcraft to explore the colonial encounters and occupations that transformed much of the continent, that moved away from the English colonies, that reached into French and Spanish territories, that integrated Native Americans and Africans, and that might be helpful to colleagues eager to find ways to incorporate the many different inhabitants of the whole continent in their own classes. *Witchcraft in Early North America* is the result of that investigation.

Witchcraft in Early North America covers the period from 1616, the year of an Indian revolt in a northern province of New Spain, through the first decade of the nineteenth century, the years of the Shawnee and Seneca witch hunts in the United States. The book's geographic focus is North America, ranging from the northern provinces of the Spanish Viceroyalty of New Spain (in other words, northern Mexico and the territory contained in the modern state of New Mexico) through the British colonies on the eastern seaboard, French (and Spanish) Louisiana, and southeastern Canada. My goal in the introduction is to help readers understand the people the book examines and the wide array of witch beliefs they held. It thus explores European, African, and Indian witch beliefs in turn, trying to understand, as much as possible, these separate belief systems before each group encountered the other. It then examines how those beliefs changed when these people met, through conquest, enslavement, colonization, and trade, in North America. I explore how witchcraft beliefs manifested themselves in three different colonial jurisdictions (New Mexico, New France, and the British colonies), in addition to looking at the witchcraft beliefs and expression of Africans and their descendants in North America. The introduction also devotes considerable space to outbreaks, setting the familiar episode at Salem in 1692 in a broader North American context. It argues that much of what historians regard as exceptional about Salem ends up looking characteristic of outbreaks across North America when we take a continental approach. The discussion of North American outbreaks includes not only a close assessment of Salem, but also separate discussions of confession, possession, and the Indian witch hunts of the early nineteenth century. The introduction concludes with an exploration of skepticism.

A second goal of the introduction is to introduce students to the historiography of witchcraft—that is, the different ways in which historians have interpreted the subject over time. Scholars who examine witchcraft analyze it through the history of law, medicine, disease, religion, family, community, sexuality, economy, race, psychology, gender, politics, and popular culture. It is a subject characterized by methodological diversity, and thus witchcraft offers an ideal entry into how historians work to understand the past. The primary documents in Section II will encourage students to weigh historians' interpretations and to develop their own.

Readers are likely to understand the primary sources more easily if they read the introduction first, and indeed the two sections of this volume have been designed to be interdependent. The documents represent an array of source material, including missionary reports, trial transcripts, laws, newspapers, letters, church records, and travel accounts. The documents focus on six core topics: First Impressions, Resistance and the Devil, English Witch Beliefs Cross the Atlantic, New Worlds, Possession, and Outbreaks. The documents delineate a wide variety of perspectives and experiences, although rarely are Indians and Africans and enslaved people able to speak for themselves. Students will have to read closely to get beyond European perceptions and viewpoints, and they will also have to wrestle with some archaic language, especially in some legal documents. While I have made some silent editorial changes, for the most part I have left English spelling unchanged from its original seventeenth-century form. Readers might find it helpful to read documents out loud if the spelling confuses them, and if they do so, they might enjoy imagining how the language sounded to those who heard it centuries ago.

I made extensive use of all facets of the Georgetown University libraries in the course of this project. I am especially grateful to the efficient sleuths in the interlibrary loan office, the invisible people who circulate books so expeditiously around the Washington Research Library Consortium, the solicitous staff at the circulation desk who knew when a book arrived from remote storage or another library on the subject of witchcraft that it was for me, and John Buchtel in Special Collections. David Hagen photographed material from Georgetown's Special Collections and worked some digital magic on an image from the Library of Congress. I also thank Steven Tabor at the Huntington Library, Anne-Marie Walsh at the Folger Shakespeare Library, Susan Danforth at the John Carter Brown Library, and Mary Haegert and John Overholt at Harvard University for their help with images. Robert D. Martínez gave me permission to use his translation of Fray Toledo's letter about the possessions at Abiquiu, and I thank him for his generosity. I was fortunate that this project found a home in Rowman and Littlefield's American Controversies series, and I am grateful to Niels Aaboe, Karen Ackermann, Michelle Cassidy, and especially Elisa Weeks for their assistance. Bill Nelson made the map.

I have picked the brains of many friends and colleagues in the past two years as I worked on this book. I thank Rose Beiler, Judy Bieber, Elaine Crane, Steve Hackel, Cindy Nickerson, Carla Pestana, and Jim Williams for their assistance. In the History Department at Georgetown, one never lacks for patient, helpful, and generous readers. I sometimes wonder how historians in less collegial departments manage to write books. I am grateful to the many colleagues who read the introduction for me. I thank Tommaso

Astarita, Katie Benton-Cohen, David Collins, Chandra Manning, Adam Rothman, and John Tutino. I have learned more about witchcraft (and all sorts of other interesting and important things) from Amy Leonard than she can imagine. Special thanks to Karin Wulf (who has been reading my work for twenty years) for her extensive editorial advice. My animal familiars have provided constant companionship. Doug Egerton read drafts of this book with care and enthusiasm and offered many helpful suggestions as I planned and worked on the project. I may have failed to follow all of the suggestions these kind friends and readers made, but this book is vastly better for their careful and helpful intervention.

SECTION I

WITCHCRAFT IN EARLY NORTH AMERICA
An Introduction

Witchcraft in Early North America
An Introduction

What is a witch? Students of American history usually have a quick answer to that question: A witch was one of those poor accused women who were hanged at Salem, Massachusetts, in that town's infamous outbreak of 1692, one such as Sarah Good, whose "wicked spitfull manner," her "base and abusive words," and her "muttering" may have condemned her in her neighbors' eyes far more than her diabolical actions (see document 19).[1] But it turns out that witches were everywhere in North America. And witches were not only terrified English colonists. Witches could be Huron shamans, Pueblo healers, enslaved conjurers, and Jesuit priests. As Europeans, Americans, and Africans converged in North America, so, too, did their ideas about witchcraft. Witches, everyone agreed, were people who performed harmful acts and threatened community order. But when societies and cultures collided on the North American continent in the seventeenth and eighteenth centuries, there was an irrevocable shift in people's assumptions about what harmful acts entailed, who was most likely to be committing them, and how one might preserve communities ravaged by disease and conquest or formed anew out of strangers.

Witchcraft might seem quaint and exotic to many readers, but to the people who are the subject of this book, it was a major preoccupation and concern. Witchcraft explained the unfathomable: prolonged drought, epidemics, deadly storms, earthquakes. Central Africans believed that witches (in the form of greedy and self-aggrandizing rulers) might even cause wars. The past was a time of far greater insecurity in meeting basic needs than most readers of this volume know today. Modern North Americans can alter their environment with ease, overcoming the constraints of the natural world. When it is cold, we can turn on heat, thanks to a massive infrastructure that delivers gas, oil, and electricity to homes in even the most rural regions. In sweltering summers, we reverse the action, chilling the air around us with fans or air conditioning. As night falls, we turn on lights, fending off scary creatures that dwell in the dark unknown and enjoying activities once reserved only for daylight—work, reading, recreation, and safe travel. We shrink distances with the telephone, the Internet, and the airplane, bringing the whole world within our reach with technology. We even traverse time, viewing planets, stars, and distant solar systems of the past through magnificent telescopes. We stave off sickness and delay death with a fantastic array of diagnostic tools, potent chemical cocktails, and palliative care. North Americans live amid unprecedented food security, with few people dependent on a single harvest to survive. In short, in the twenty-first century we have many tools and services at our disposal to challenge and circumvent the dictates of the natural world.

Yet it is in many ways too simple to assert that those who believed in witchcraft were people who, lacking our technology, could not explain or transform their world in any other way. The same people who believed that one drought was caused by witchcraft did not think that all droughts were. Although some mariners on a terribly rough and stormy passage across the Atlantic might find a witch in their midst, most voyages, even those plagued by hurricanes, shipwrecks, and death, did not produce witchcraft accusations. Christian parents might understand a child's death as the punishing hand of God or the unfortunate quirk of fate or just one of the many cruel sicknesses that carried away as many as half of all children before they reached the age of five. The Puritan minister Cotton Mather (1663–1728), who lived in Massachusetts, watched in helpless agony as eight of his fifteen children died before they reached the age of two—and he inhabited what was believed to be a salubrious region.[2] This was a lethal age, and people lived with death and chronic pains and aches in ways mercifully unknown to most of us. Magic might lift these pains and torments, and it might also cause them. People who could manipulate material objects and harness special powers in the supernatural world might effect good or evil. In other words, people believed in witchcraft not because there were so many inexplicable events in their world, but because they lived in a world that contained witches.

In Europe, as many as 90,000 people were prosecuted as witches between 1420 and 1780, and as many as 45,000 of those were likely executed.[3] In this same period, Europeans crossed the Atlantic and claimed, occupied, invaded, settled, and exploited the Americas. Christopher Columbus's successful transatlantic voyage in 1492 marked the inauguration of a new era. European states sought to project their power in the Americas, eager to extract wealth from American resources (natural and human) and to deploy that wealth in struggles for dominion in Europe.

North America figured prominently in this process. The Spanish moved north from the valley of Mexico (where they toppled the Aztec Empire in 1519) across the Rio Grande, establishing their first settlements in the region we know as New Mexico in 1598. The French approached the continent from across the North Atlantic; they followed short-lived experiments in the 1530s with a serious commitment to fur trading in the early seventeenth century, settling in the St. Lawrence valley after 1608. The English ran fisheries in Newfoundland and established numerous colonies to the south in the seventeenth century. By the late seventeenth century, tiny pockets of European settlement dotted the continent. These enterprises were accompanied by intermittent conflicts with indigenous inhabitants. Europeans, moreover, forcibly transported Africans to the Americas and appropriated their labor and their progeny. Witchcraft in North America emerged out of this crucible, one with multiple belief systems; with complex power dynamics; and with stunning social, economic, and demographic transformations. In this book, I invite readers to examine witch beliefs as a unique approach to how cultural beliefs and practices collided. Witchcraft was one important way in which people made sense of their turbulent and changing world.

Colonization and conquests changed witchcraft beliefs and their expression. Witchcraft always provided a mechanism for revenge: victims alleged that the accused had killed their cattle, sickened their child, hindered their sexual performance, or ruined their crops. Any community harbored infinite possibilities for such conflicts. But colonial societies introduced new elements of coercion and cruelty. North America became a place of expanded evil. Indians who linked sickness with malevolence lived in a transformed world, with far more witches in it than had been the case before the arrival of Europeans. (What else could explain the deadly epidemics that swept away entire villages?) Enslaved Africans found their ideas about evil power similarly altered by the expansion of malevolent forces in American slave societies. Christian Europeans believed in the Devil as surely as they believed in God, and the Devil had loyal helpers—witches—especially in North America, a land European theologians regarded as the last bastion of Satan. In a world so fraught with tension, epidemics, conflict, and exploitation, it is little surprise that the chronology of witchcraft in North America differed considerably from that of Europe, where witch hunts petered out by the end of the seventeenth century. In contrast, witchcraft continued to be a fundamental aspect of how Europeans and Africans (and their descendants), Indians, and people of mixed race made sense of each other and of their world into the early nineteenth century, and a major outbreak occurred in eighteenth-century New Mexico.

Preexisting notions about a witch's gender and race and even economic status shifted in new colonial societies. In England, Spain, and France, women were more likely than men to face accusations of witchcraft. But in North America, witches were both men and women. The transition came in part because Europeans, especially Spaniards, linked witchcraft to Indians, to Africans, and to people of mixed race—and as this connection developed, witchcraft lost its special association with women and was attached more to race and caste.[4] In 1626, the first formal allegations of witchcraft reached New Mexican authorities; they involved an Indian woman and her mestiza (or mixed race) daughter. In that same year, across the continent, troubled Virginians charged one of their neighbors with witchcraft in the first known case in the English colonies. She was an Englishwoman, and in this respect typical of witches who landed in English colonial courts. English colonists continued to associate women with witchcraft, but wealthier women were more likely to face allegations than had been true in Europe.

While witch beliefs traveled across the Atlantic with Africans and Europeans, the context in which witchcraft accusations and trials functioned often did not. The manifestation of witch beliefs and trials is thus intertwined with the specific context of migration and colonization in North America. European migrants brought, for the most part, only fragments of their home societies with them. The ecclesiastical structures that shaped understandings about the Devil, the trained witch-hunters, the libraries of legal tomes that informed jurists, the long-standing personal relationships: all of the complex systems that enveloped witch beliefs, accusations, and trials could not be reproduced in America. Migration strained and sometimes shattered belief systems. Some Europeans had ideas about magical practices that were connected to specific geographical features—caves, waterfalls, mountains, forests, swamps. So, too, did Africans. West-Central Africans, for example, believed the forest to be a sacred space, where they buried the dead and where spirits might inhabit rocks or trees. Forests were also a source of herbs for healing and magical charms.[5] In new environments, key ingredients might be unattainable. Both Africans and Europeans were severed—by choice or by force—from the natural world that hosted supernatural spirits. For Americans, sacred places were sometimes deliberately assaulted by Spanish invaders, who placed cathedrals where temples had stood, in a time-honored strategy of conquerors. They did just that in Mexico City, where they built their great cathedral on the sacred grounds of the Aztecs' Templo Mayor.

Witchcraft gives us a raw and unfiltered—indeed, sometimes excruciating—glimpse at the lives of real men, women, and children who lived centuries ago. When we read a transcript of a witch trial, we find ourselves flung into the midst of community life. We learn of old injuries, tangled relationships, broken hearts, political ambitions, terrifying assaults, children long deceased but mourned with as much anguish as if they had died just the day before, families in conflict over generations, petty disputes over baubles and trifles, and heart wrenching loss and betrayal. We meet, for example, husbands who defended their wives when they were accused of witchcraft (see documents 8, 10, and 20), husbands who suspected their wives were witches (see document 19), and one husband whose alleged infidelity drove his distraught wife to accuse three women of witchcraft (see document 12). As a subject of historical inquiry, witchcraft enables us to glimpse a distant and often alien culture with startling intensity and intimacy. This book pulls together documents from different parts of North America, by Spanish, French, and English settlers, about Indians, enslaved Africans, and European colonists. These documents touch on slavery and servitude, family and the individual, sickness and death, the law and the church, reflecting the ways that ideas about witchcraft permeated the entire fabric of society.

Beliefs: Europeans

To make sense of why some people looked like witches while others did not, and why some regions contained numerous trials and others virtually none, we need to understand the witch beliefs that Europeans, Africans, and Americans held at the time of contact and settlement. The discussion starts with European beliefs for two main reasons. First, most of what we know about African and American witch beliefs comes from records generated by Europeans, so it is essential to understand what Europeans believed in order to make sense of what they thought they saw. Second, Europeans created the legal systems in which witch beliefs and accusations found traction in North American courts and through which most evidence of witchcraft has survived.

Europeans believed that a witch was a person who committed a crime using harmful magic. For example, a witch might cause a person or animal to sicken or die by chanting a spell or by sticking pins in a figure. A spell might similarly incite a storm or ruin crops or cause a drought (see document 9). A witch might thwart the hunt, as two men claimed Goodwife Wright did in Virginia in 1626 (see document 8). Witches might also cause men to become impotent. The Latin term for such crimes was *maleficium* (the plural is *maleficia*), and jurisdictions everywhere had statutes that banned and punished them (see documents 6 and 7). Even if a witch was also guilty of blasphemy (showing disrespect for God), her or his case normally appeared in secular courts by the middle of the sixteenth century, not ecclesiastical ones. A witch did not always need to perform any specific action to cause harm; damage could ensue if a witch only *wished* harm on someone. While magic might also be performed for beneficial ends—to heal the sick, to comfort the afflicted, to bring about good fortune, to recover lost or stolen items—by the sixteenth century European laws had defined even this so-called "white" magic as a form of witchcraft and thus also illegal and punishable by death in some jurisdictions. Witchcraft activity surged in Europe in the 1560s and 1570s, with trials in Germany and the Low Countries and new statutes in England and Scotland. Trial activity intensified from 1580 to 1630, followed by a very protracted decline between 1630 and 1770.

A rich folklore developed around witchcraft. Accused witches in Europe might be accompanied by creatures called familiars, including cats, rats, and toads (see figure 1). The more unpleasant and offensive the animal, the more it was "loathed by all people, who generally have a Natural Antipathy against that sort of Vermin," the more likely witches—with their unnatural sensibilities—were to find affinity with it.[6] Some witches transformed themselves into animals. In Estonia, accused witches confessed to acts of maleficia while they were werewolves; one woman testified in 1623 that she had been a werewolf for four years. Other witches worked closely with their familiars, sometimes assuming their shape in order to carry out their crimes. Still others put creatures to work in their spells. Shepherds in Normandy were especially likely to be accused of performing maleficia with the assistance of toad venom. In Iceland, witches, mostly male, worked their magic with the aid of runes, characters from the old Germanic alphabet used in Scandinavia and believed to have magical properties.[7]

One essential component of European witch beliefs was inextricably linked to Christian theology, and that was the idea of a special relationship between witches and the Devil. The Christian religious system contains two arch rivals: a supreme deity of all power and knowledge whom Christians call God, and a competitive fallen angel, Lucifer, who is the main source of evil in the world. Lucifer reigns in Hell and is also known as Satan or the Devil. Christians believed then (and many still do) that God and Satan were consumed by an eternal struggle for power, one that manifested itself in part in Satan's efforts to thwart God's plans and to win away Christians to assist him in his diabolical machinations. These recruits were witches.

Figure 1.   English witches calling to their familiars.
Source: Matthew Hopkins, *The discovery of witches* (London, 1647). By Permission of the Folger Shakespeare Library.

Sorcerers, in contrast, used magic, but did not rely on the assistance of evil spirits. That was the defining feature of the witch—that he or she joined with Satan and with his assistance performed evil acts in the world. In North America, however, this distinction eroded, and European observers used the terms *witch* and *sorcerer* and *wizard* and *demon* interchangeably to describe those (universally Native Americans) whom they saw as engaging in malevolent practices (see documents 1 and 2). Europeans also distinguished "high" magic from "low" magic, another blurred line that ensnared some unfortunate practitioners. High magic included alchemy (transforming metals) and divination (finding out secret or hidden information through astrology and other methods). Although witchcraft statutes banned divination (see document 6), practitioners of high magic were infrequently charged with witchcraft; however, those who had unnatural knowledge of the future or about the location of lost objects might well be accused of witchcraft. So Goodwife Wright's accusers claimed in court in Virginia in 1626. Rebecca Grey testified that Wright predicted the deaths of numerous people (see document 8).

This connection between witchcraft and the Devil emerged over centuries and was solidified in the middle of the fifteenth century, and then circulated in a range of published tracts, all more easily dispersed in the wake of Johannes Gutenberg's invention of movable type in 1439. The most famous such tract, *Malleus Maleficarum (The Hammer of the Witches)*, was written by two Dominican friars, James Sprenger and Heinrich Kramer, both inquisitors in the Holy Roman Empire and the first men to be commissioned by the pope to hunt witches. It provided graphic accounts of witches' behavior, describing their crimes, their sexual relations with the Devil, their demonic progeny, and their devious ways, and it helped elaborate a complex demonology for readers. Published in 1487, it was widely disseminated in Europe among educated elites, and during the Reformation was popular with Protestants, too.[8]

Witches made a pact with the Devil and agreed to serve him. Thus, witchcraft was also diabolism, or worship of the Devil. Europeans emphasized that witches had made a free choice in their service to the Devil. The particulars of this relationship varied by region, but there were some common features. Witches signaled their allegiance to the Devil by signing a book with their signature or, more typically in this era of pervasive female illiteracy, their mark. In the course of doing so, witches acquired a distinctive mark on their bodies. It was allegedly impervious to pain and unable to express blood, and it featured prominently in witch trials as bodies were examined, pricked, and prodded for evidence of the tell-tale sign (see documents 9 and 10). Witches often flew through the air, sometimes many thousands of miles, to meet with other witches at Sabbaths, as witches' assemblies were called. Witches in the Labourd (on the French and Spanish border and the site of a major witch hunt in 1609–1610), a region whose inhabitants made their living from the sea and especially from the fisheries in Newfoundland, confessed to flying across the ocean to Newfoundland at night.[9] Sometimes witches rode on beasts, and sometimes they rode on sticks, with the broom the most common form of nocturnal transport. The larger the gathering, the farther witches needed to fly to reach it. There, witches engaged in all sorts of unusual sexual and social practices. They had orgies, danced naked, and even killed and consumed unbaptized babies. Some Sabbaths included blasphemous practices, including reciting prayers backward, or performing a mock Eucharist (see figure 2). Tortured witches also confessed to having sex with the Devil and bearing his offspring.

Educated, elite men, often the lawyers, judges, and church officials who prosecuted witchcraft in court, expected to hear about diabolical practices, and often they could only get their suspicions confirmed under torture. (Torture

Figure 2. This image of a witches' Sabbath features multiple aspects of European witch beliefs; witches fishing for toads, cooking up spells on a fire of human skulls, feasting on the hearts of unbaptized infants, riding brooms through the sky, and performing a variety of other nefarious deeds.

Source: From Pierre de Lancre, *Tableau de l'inconstance des mauvais anges et demons* (Paris, 1612). By Permission of the Folger Shakespeare Library.

was an integral feature of the judicial system on the European continent, which was based on Roman law; in contrast, the English common law system used torture infrequently.) Accused witches, on the other hand, tended to confess more easily to core elements of popular beliefs about maleficia, animal familiars, and charms and potions. Anna Roleffes (known as Tempel Anneke), tried in Brunswick in the Holy Roman Empire in 1663, confessed to several practices that she clearly regarded as harmless white magic, including a divination ritual designed to help her find stolen goods, and making a concoction of berries, salt, leaves, hops, and sage to cure sick sheep. Rituals required words to give them power, as any Christian knew, and so Tempel Anneke called on God. Sometimes she needed a more elaborate prayer. If, for example, one was blessing a man, she explained to the court, one might say, "John and the Holy Evangelists, they pluck a branch in Paradise."

Tempel Anneke was understandably confused about her ability to use words and actions together. Rituals and sacraments endorsed by the Catholic Church and performed by priests did, indeed, seem magical. Priests transformed wine into blood and bread into flesh. Clerics uttered prayers and suggested that their words could be heard and acted upon by a remote deity. In all these actions, human activity intersected with the divine. Is it any wonder worshipers might believe that their spells were nothing but prayers? Tempel Anneke's potions sounded harmless, and her words Christian, but her interrogators knew better. When they consulted physicians about her herbal concoctions, the doctors denied that the medicines could cause any benefit, so any cure could only be achieved through magic and thus through the aid of the Devil. Tempel Anneke adamantly denied this charge. Under torture, however, when the torturer took her to a new interrogation chamber in the jail's cellar, blindfolded her, and tightened a leg screw, Tempel Anneke confessed to apparitions from a "black man" who threatened to avenge Tempel Anneke on those who insulted her. With leg screws then fastened on both shins, eyes covered, encased in darkness, and with no advocate by her side, only the company of her torturer who exhorted her to acknowledge her crimes and end her ghastly misery, Tempel Anneke confessed to making a pact with the Devil to serve him twelve years, to having sex with him on her bed, to becoming pregnant with salamanders as a result of this intercourse, and to bewitching people and causing injury. She confessed on October 22; just over two months later, on December 30, she was beheaded, and then her body was burned.[10]

As a woman, Tempel Anneke was typical of most executed witches in Europe, where women represented 75 percent of executed witches in most regions.[11] This sex ratio was especially pronounced in England, where some 93 percent of accused witches in the county of Essex were women. There was, however, considerable range within Europe. In Iceland, for example, only 10 percent of accused witches were women; in Poland, 96 percent were.[12] There could also be great variation within a single nation. Take France. In the Department of the Nord, a territory in the far north of the country, 81 percent of accused witches were women. But in one part of Normandy, the Pays de Caux, men were especially likely to be accused of witchcraft, and the region was the "epicenter of male witchcraft in western Europe."[13] Of 381 people accused of witchcraft in Normandy between 1560 and 1660, 278 (73 percent) were men, and 103 (27 percent) were women.[14] Seventeen men from this region—and one woman—were executed as witches. The occupations of the accused were male occupations: half of the accused were shepherds, and the next most frequent occupational category was clergy. Thus, in many places witchcraft might be commonly associated with women (a sex-linked crime) but not associated *only* with women (and thus not a sex-specific crime).

In England, so obvious was the connection between women and witchcraft that when the magistrates of Newcastle, having hired a witch-hunter from Scotland, sent their crier through town, he called on the people of Newcastle to bring forward their complaints "against any *woman* for a Witch." In the wake of this roundup, fourteen women and one man were condemned and hanged. Moreover, the Newcastle authorities were more likely to believe that attractive women were innocent and elderly women guilty (see figure 3). The witch-hunter's method involved sticking pins in alleged witches. When he proposed to do so to one woman, "personable and good like," the magistrates objected. The witch-hunter persevered and found her guilty in a cruel and humiliating ritual in which he stripped her clothes to her waist and plunged pins in her thighs. The magistrates nonetheless intervened, and she was finally cleared.[15]

What was it about women? Attitudes toward women and especially about women's bodies and sexuality persuaded people that women were predisposed toward witchcraft. Medical ideas, derived from Aristotle, regarded men and women as binary opposites; women were wet and cold, men were warm and dry. Women's genitals were likewise the reverse of men's. Aristotelian medical theories, moreover, held that the male body was the norm; the female body was a corrupt variant. Commentators universally discussed women's sexuality in a negative fashion. Women were insatiable creatures, naturally prone to lust and deviance. Their carnality led them to witchcraft: witch-hunting manuals, most notably the *Malleus*, which drew on these ancient ideas about women, emphasized the sexual relationship between Satan and his human agents, and it was easy enough for believers to associate women's

Figure 3.   The depiction of this woman conveys many elements of English ideas about witches; she is old, impoverished (or so her bare feet suggest), unattractive (signaled by the hooked nose), and accompanied by bird familiars. She travels on a board on a river, not by broom through the air.

Source: *A most certain, strange, and true discovery of a witch* (London, 1643). Houghton Library, Harvard University. 24246.62

lust with their attraction to the Devil, who could fulfill their sexual needs as no mortal man could.[16] Thus, in those societies where people believed that a witch's body contained telltale marks of her relationship with Satan, those marks were invariably found in woman's genitals, her "very hidden places," as one legal manual for English justices in the 1630s put it.[17] Women's bodily defects and their immoral natures were accompanied by their greater credulity. Women were frail and impressionable, more likely to be superstitious than men. And their weakness also encouraged them to resort to occult arts to seek revenge on those who wronged them.[18] The *Malleus* codified these ideas, assembling a devastating critique of women's natures and yoking women inextricably to witchcraft.[19] The documents in Section II offer many opportunities to read trials of women and to examine the role that gender played in the charges against them (see especially documents 8, 9, 10, 12, 19, 20, 21, 23, and 24).

Because witchcraft was a crime, its detection and punishment were governed by the prevailing rules of evidence and procedure in different jurisdictions. But witchcraft was also an exceptional crime—*crimen exceptum,* one to which the normal practices did not apply. Because witchcraft was so difficult to prove using the normal rules of evidence, jurists applied different standards. Thus, for example, courts applied torture in places where it was otherwise not regularly employed as a key element of witchcraft trials in order to compel the accused to confess. Severe torture was essential because the Devil could help accused witches withstand pain. Courts even had a word for this assistance—*taciturnitas* (keeping silent). It referred to the ability of a witch to endure the agonies of torture without confession.[20] People who were otherwise not normally allowed to give testimony in court, including children, women, and felons, were often able to do so in witchcraft trials. In Sweden, for example, thousands of children testified during a major witch hunt between 1668 and 1676, although in Swedish legal practice, children under the age of fifteen were not normally allowed to testify. During the outbreak, this principle was set aside and child witnesses were calculated as the equivalent of fractions of adults; in this reckoning, a five-year-old child equaled one-tenth of a witness, and thus by adding together many children, the courts met the legal obligation to have two witnesses for witchcraft convictions.[21] Those whose testimony might otherwise be disregarded in English courts—excommunicated people, children, unreliable servants, runaways—could testify against witches.[22] Some jurisdictions also allowed ordeals to serve as proof of guilt or innocence. Such "ordeals" were legacies of early medieval legal practices and rooted in Celtic and Germanic law, in which, for example, people could demonstrate their innocence by their ability to recover miraculously from carrying a hot iron in their bare hands. In the case of the water ordeal, featured in the trial of Grace Sherwood in Virginia in 1706 (see document 10), a guilty party floated, while the innocent sank.

In many respects, these deviations from normal legal procedures contradicted other prevailing trends in the legal culture of the era. In these centuries, law became transformed in ways that would seem familiar to Americans in the twenty-first century. Courts became more centralized, thus applying standard policies and punishments to guilty parties. Courts expected witnesses to *see* the crimes of which they spoke; juries were not supposed to have an active interest in the outcome of trials; confessions were not to be compelled by force; witnesses, likewise, should not endure pressure to provide testimony.[23]

Where courts banned torture, executions tended to be less frequent and accused witches rarely confessed to diabolical practices. The relative absence of torture in the Netherlands, where less than 150 people were executed out of a population of 1 million, for example, might explain the low number of executions there. In England, juries (not judges) tended to determine a witch's guilt or innocence, and they tended to be lenient. The English also rarely employed torture: it was used once (illegally) during the English Civil War. In Scotland, torture was employed more frequently (but still illegally). There were some significant panics in Scotland in the sixteenth century, and a large witch hunt in England in the 1640s, but there was never anything like the massive hunts that occurred in central Europe. The kingdoms of England and Scotland experienced perhaps 5,000 prosecutions for witchcraft during the era of the witch hunt, and probably half of those were in Scotland, with perhaps 1,500 to 2,500 executions.[24]

Another key to acquittal was the rise of centralized states, as people with a greater distance from the personal conflicts that expressed themselves in witch accusations tended to bring greater skepticism not to witchcraft in general but rather to the particular features of any given case. The lack of centralization in the Holy Roman Empire, composed of a collection of individual political entities, is one explanation that historians have offered for the high number of accusations, trials, and especially executions there (20,000–25,000), in contrast, for example, to France, where the Parlement of Paris, the kingdom's main judicial body, gradually gained control over reviews of regional jurisdictions' decisions about guilt and overturned local sentences. Between 1588 and 1624, the Parlement ended up dismissing 36 percent of cases, and confirmed only 24 percent.[25] By 1640, the Parlement no longer prosecuted witches, and this termination of prosecutions extended to the whole kingdom in an edict in 1682. There were perhaps only 1,000 executions in France. Likewise, although ecclesiastical courts employed torture in Spain and Italy, executions there were infrequent, largely because the Inquisition was a centralized institution. In the kingdoms of Spain and the Italian states, there were about 10,000 prosecutions altogether, many for minor offenses, with very few executions. Iberian and Italian authorities, for the most part, had little interest in allegations of Devil worship, the most serious offense witches committed. Most crimes there pertained to love magic (the use of spells and divination, for example, to attract a lover, or to seek revenge) and healing, behaviors that were believed to be heretical, but not capital crimes.

All of these beliefs and practices concerning witchcraft, finally, were entangled in the major religious transformation of the period, the Protestant Reformation and the Counter-Reformation. In 1517, a monk named Martin Luther launched what became a major religious upheaval after he posted ninety-five critiques of the Catholic Church on the doors of the cathedral at Wittenburg. New churches emerged in the wake of this protest. Protestants (as the followers of Luther's initiative came to be called) established new churches and defined codes of conduct for believers, and they were especially concerned with reforming personal behavior (whether banning card playing and other games or regulating sexual conduct) and ensuring orthodox beliefs (making sure, for example, that worshipers understood church doctrine).

The line between religion and superstition was a fuzzy and shifting one, especially in this period when all churches, Protestant and Catholic, were clamping down on behavior. Across and even within religious traditions, there was little agreement on what might be superstitious or even pagan practices. English Puritans, for example, rejected the celebration of Christmas or the many feast days and seasonal rituals that were practiced in the Protestant Church of England. They refused to use the months' names, which they regarded as pagan, and instead used only the number. They sought to live by God's laws as they strictly interpreted them, and this aspiration affected even their witchcraft statutes, which turned, as the Connecticut colony's 1642 law did, to Leviticus, Exodus, and Deuteronomy for inspiration (see document 7).

Yet these were people whose own habits might strike modern readers as bizarre and laden with superstition. The Puritans believed that God's will was unknowable, yet that his hand was everywhere. Their predestinarian theology convinced them that God had already consigned them to Heaven or Hell, regardless of their actions on this earth. They accompanied this uncompromising doctrine with a belief that God gave men and women clues to read so that they might make educated guesses about the likelihood of their salvation—although they always accepted the real possibility that they might well guess wrong. These two beliefs—that God was present in all aspects of life and that God might have left clues to the eager believer about salvation—made Puritans intensely aware of the world around them. No natural event, no odd coincidence, no accident, passed without some study of God's hand. Thus, for example, a gathering of ministers paused during a meeting in Cambridge, Massachusetts, in 1648 because a snake had slithered into the chamber. What did that mean? What was God trying to tell them? After some deliberation, the ministers concluded that the snake was Satan, and he sought to disturb their gathering, although they were also certain that God knew of Satan's plan, since nothing happened without God's knowledge.[26] Natural events, such as storms or floods or late spring snows or prolonged drought might reveal God's power as well. A people who believed just as firmly in Satan as they did in God could equally find Satan's hand, vying with God for power.[27]

Enhanced regulation of personal conduct and religious expression was only one aspect of the reformations that accompanied church schism and creation in this era. A second important feature was the emergence of political rivalries that were expressed through religious opposition. Europeans divided into warring camps, Protestant and Catholic, even though the composition of those camps shifted continuously throughout the sixteenth century. By the end of the sixteenth century, England had emerged as a major Protestant kingdom, setting itself in opposition to Spain, a bastion of Catholicism. The struggles between these kingdoms for power in Europe leaked into North America, and part of this competition was the battle for souls to convert to their respective faiths. Zeal for conversion interacted with witchcraft beliefs in important ways, in both Europe and North America, emphasizing ideas about the Devil, heightening concerns about the failed orthodoxy of new converts (and thus tempering evangelical fervor), and producing impassioned converts who sometimes expressed their enthusiasm through possession.

These beliefs about what witches did, the importance of the Devil to witches' powers, and the forensic strategies essential to discern and punish malefactors suggested a frame of reference within which Europeans could understand what they encountered in Africa and America. It is difficult to discern genuine indigenous ideas about witchcraft among non-European people in Africa and the Americas in the era of European expansion largely because our sources come from those Europeans—mostly priests—who described indigenous rituals and observed them in the context of their own clearly defined witch beliefs. These sources hinder efforts to move beyond hyperbole and to reveal what Africans and Indians were actually doing—let alone what they believed and what cultural logic lay behind their rituals. Europeans were predisposed to believe that Satan existed everywhere, that everywhere he had his followers, and that unfamiliar practices might well be diabolical. Historians can at best piece together non-Christian ideas about witchcraft. One crucial commonality, however, is that Native Americans and Africans did not tend to have an idea of Satan as a single, fixed entity, the focus of all evil in the world and forever doing battle with God. Thus one central feature of European witch beliefs—the concept of a pact between a witch with free will and the Devil—had no meaning for non-Christians. Like Europeans, however, Africans and Americans agreed that disease and misfortune might be caused by witches.

Beliefs: West and West-Central Africans

Africans who were captured and forcibly transported to North America in the seventeenth and eighteenth centuries came primarily from a few key regions of Africa: West Africa (especially Senegambia [where The Gambia and Senegal are today], Sierra Leone [modern day Guinea-Bissau, Sierra Leone, Guinea, Liberia, and Ivory Coast], the Gold Coast [modern day Ghana], and the Bight of Biafra [modern day Cameroon, Gabon, and southeastern Nigeria]) and West-Central Africa (especially Angola and Congo).[28] What do we know about their beliefs, and how do we know it? Historians trying to understand African witch beliefs in previous centuries rely heavily on observations generated by Europeans, who found their way to West and West-Central Africa most commonly as traders. Merchants frequently recorded information on religious practices, although they were often mocking and derisive of these traditions. In some of those places, traders were accompanied by missionaries who also studied religious practices in order to enhance their ability to convert people. In the kingdom of Kongo (located in present-day western Congo and northern Angola), where the king converted to Christianity in 1491, priests played an important role in educating people about Catholicism, and they provide some of our best sources for religious beliefs there. Elsewhere, ministers and priests were banned from proselytizing.

Africans regarded sickness and death as misfortunes caused by spirits and supernatural powers who worked through human agents. Witchcraft, then, functioned as a common explanation for misfortune, just as it did for Europeans. Witchcraft was part of a collection of secret religious powers, including divining, conjuring, and healing, that could restore harmony to a community or to an individual. These rituals could also be used to punish offenders. In the kingdom of Kongo, witches—*ndokis*—were selfish and greedy people who used powers harnessed from the other world to achieve their goals (in European thinking, comparable to those witches who worked magic with the aid of the Devil). But the same powers could also be used for good ends. An individual might thus have the power both to cause harm and to uncover and counteract it. Witches, then, were not solely or inherently evil (as European authorities believed them to be by the seventeenth century) but rather had the ability to effect good *or* evil. And witches could be men or women.[29]

European men who worked at coastal trading posts were especially fascinated by fetishes and the use of poisons. The word *fetish* derives from a Portuguese term, *feitiço*, which traders used to describe the charms and amulets they saw in West Africa. The meaning of the term expanded to include a wide range of practices, not just the material charms themselves.[30] Those like the trader Willem Bosman, who observed and commented on African religious practices, noted the pervasive use of poison in such rituals (see document 13). Robert Elwes, a merchant at the Royal African Company fort in Egya in 1687, and John Carter, at Whydah in 1686, related stories of others being poisoned and, in Carter's case, of threats of poison against him. When a sergeant at Winneba fell ill "with vomiting and strange paines" in August 1697, the trader there was sure he had been poisoned.[31]

As these traders' remarks suggest, charms were part of practices that ranged from punishing enemies to ferreting out the truth behind a crime. They were employed in two aspects of African religious practice that endured (often in altered form) in the Americas and that Europeans in some jurisdictions identified as witchcraft, most notably conjuring and divination. In the kingdom of Kongo, for example, specialized practitioners called *ngangas* worked with amulets, *minkisis*. The charms had important symbolic power. A nganga who put a stone inside a charm might intend the ritual to remove a tumor, in the same way that a feather could convey the flight required for a charm to look for and identify a criminal. One Capuchin missionary readily identified these practices as "magic" in 1643 and believed that in these rituals the ngangas "speak with the devil, as if they were insane and possessed." At the same time, Catholic priests understood the power of these ritual specialists and their amulets, and tried to appropriate it for themselves: in Kongo priests adopted the title nganga and translated *minkisi* as "holy."[32]

Rituals varied, of course, across Africa. Among the Igbo, who lived in the Bight of Biafra, within modern-day Nigeria, and who comprised the largest single contingent of slaves bound for the colony of Virginia in the eighteenth century, diviners (called *obea*) performed sacrifices (real and symbolic) in order to seek help from the many invisible spirits of the Igbo world.[33] In the late seventeenth century, the French slave trader Jean Barbot described the gris-gris (charms) he saw in Senegal, and said that they contained words written in Arabic. A staunch Protestant, Barbot compared the gris-gris to the "supposed saints" worshipped by "Italian and Spanish bigots."[34]

If the intellectual limitations and religious prejudices of European observers make it difficult to understand indigenous African ideas about witchcraft, so, too, does the specific context within which most Africans and Europeans encountered each other: through the slave trade. The historian James Sweet has explored this puzzle for the coasts of West-Central Africa (Kongo and Angola), where evidence of malevolence *increased* with the slave trade. West-Central Africans, for example, believed that when Europeans took Africans away on slave vessels, never to be seen again, they did so in order to eat them. These were not simply metaphorical concerns about being eaten, but a literal belief. Witches were cannibals. They sated themselves on enslaved bodies. If remedies against witchcraft conventionally kept evil in balance, the slave trade introduced a new form of evil, one that could not be combated through customary means. In that respect, the slave trade might have created witchcraft (as Europeans understood and used the term) in Africa and among Africans who lived within its orbit. Africans associated witchcraft with selfishness and greed, and thus linked it not only to harm inflicted on individuals (out of revenge or dislike) but also to political and social institutions, to rulers or traders who sought to enhance their own wealth, power, or prestige at the expense of other members of society. One Kongolese woman, an nganga named Dona Beatriz who was trained in rituals to reach the other world, started a movement in 1703 in which she sought to use her own special powers to combat the malevolence of rulers who permitted decades of civil war and whose wars fed the slave trade. The slave trade fit neatly into this conceptualization of greed as a sign of witchcraft, producing a world of enhanced evil, one in which European merchants and shippers acquired reputations as cannibals.[35]

Africans believed witches could be people with power—men of greed seeking to aggrandize their authority or wealth. Even a king might be feared as a witch. Europeans, in contrast, were far more likely to associate witches with the weak and marginal, people such as Indians, slaves, and elderly women who sought power through diabolical ends precisely because they were people *without* other avenues to power within their communities. Not until the witch hunts among the Shawnees in North America in the early nineteenth century do we see a similar association between witches and men with political power.

Beliefs: Native Americans

Among those who already lived in North America, there was a wide array of belief systems. Historians know most about the people who lived in areas where Europeans colonized, traveled, traded, and proselytized, along coasts and waterways and near other resources valued by Europeans. Our knowledge of Indian religious beliefs comes mostly from the recorded accounts of men who had their own religious agenda and their own demonology. Historians work hard to read these sources sensitively and creatively—and readers of these documents will have the same challenge—to try to recover and comprehend beliefs and cultures of non-Europeans. It is a difficult enterprise in which our understanding will only ever be partial, as if what we are seeing is a shadow cast on the ground, a clouded and imprecise image of something real and tangible but only that, an image. Spanish chroniclers ready to condemn all indigenous healing practices as witchcraft, for example, make it very difficult for historians to understand the cultural context in which these healing traditions existed.[36]

Europeans saw the Devil everywhere in North America.[37] When Fray Alonso de Benavides described indigenous religious practices on his journey to New Mexico in 1625–1626 he labeled all spiritual leaders as wizards or sorcerers guided by demons (see document 1). Thomas Mayhew, a Puritan minister fluent in Wampanoag, derided the Indians he met on Martha's Vineyard in 1652 as "zealous and earnest in the Worship of False gods and Devils."[38] The English also likened Indian shamans to witches. They were disturbed by Indian ideas of direct and personal connections to Indian deities, usually achieved through rituals that required fasting, trances, and the consumption of potent narcotics. The Englishman George Percy put the centrality of Satan succinctly: "They worship the Devill for their God, and have no other beliefe."[39]

It was not just that the Devil was pervasive; Europeans believed that America was in fact his home. As the Jesuit José de Acosta explained in his *Natural and Moral History of the Indies* (1590), directly linking religious reformation in Europe with Catholic endeavors in America, "once idolatry was rooted out of the best and noblest part of the world, the devil retired to the most remote places and reigned in that other part of the world, which, although it is very inferior in nobility, is not so in size and breadth."[40] Because of this certainty that the Americas were the Devil's lair, it is hard to reconstruct with any certainty whether Indians had ideas of "witches" before European contact and what exactly these "witches" did. Europeans believed that evil was concentrated in a single entity (a witch or Satan), but it seems that Indians did not. There was no notion of concentrated evil among Andean people at the time of first contact with Spaniards, but rather a commitment to the idea of complementarity, of good *and* evil existing together. Thus, for example, early Spanish dictionaries reported the Andean word *supay* meaning both "good angel" and "bad angel," but later dictionaries defined this word only as "Devil," thereby erasing the earlier complexity of the concept.[41]

In the northeastern woodlands (where the French and English established themselves) at the moment of contact, Indians' belief systems probably did include ideas about witches and sorcerers. Like Europeans, Indians debated the causes of misfortunes and tried to remedy them with natural cures. But when these cures did not work, they concluded, like Europeans, that witchcraft was present. Early Jesuit accounts—written, of course, by people predisposed to see a world of witches and demons—spoke of sorcerers, people who cast spells and who harmed others in doing so. These witches called on powers to do evil, not good, and were greatly feared by the Senecas (one of the tribes of the powerful Iroquois confederacy) as people distinct from the shamans and other religious practitioners (a distinction that normally eluded Europeans).[42] The Iroquois killed witches if they detected them in their midst. A Jesuit, François-Joseph Le Mercier, told of one such execution in 1637 among the Hurons. A woman accused of witchcraft was sentenced to death and was first tortured with fire before the executioner split her skull with a hatchet and her body was burned to ashes.[43] Other Indians, including the Algonquian-speaking people whom the English encountered at Roanoke (in modern-day North Carolina) in the 1580s, seem not to have believed that witches—at least witches within a tribe—should be executed for witchcraft, and instead reserved that penalty for outsiders.[44]

While Europeans tended to think that most witches were women, a gendered association of women with witchcraft appears not to have been the case among the Iroquois and other woodland people. The evidence, as always, is elusive and indirect. One clue comes from the best-known Iroquois witch, a man named Atotarho, who figures in the Iroquois creation myth and almost destroyed Hiawatha before Hiawatha neutralized him and turned him into a good leader.[45] A second clue comes from the tendency of the Iroquois to accuse the Jesuits (all men) of doing the kinds of malevolent deeds that they associated with witches: spreading disease, for example (see document 2). Some Potawatomis killed a group of priests in the 1680s for precisely this reason.[46] One Jesuit, Isaac Jogues, was killed by the Iroquois in 1646 because they believed him to be a sorcerer (see document 3).[47] The connection between Europeans and disease was common, and because the first Europeans many Indians met were missionaries, they readily linked disease with the new faith and its clergy. Shamans and other leaders sometimes used this connection to thwart the efforts of Catholic missionaries (see document 2).[48] Possibly the association of priests with witchcraft *increased* the gendered association among North American Indians of witchcraft with men, but there is simply not enough evidence to know with any certainty.

The connection of disease to witchcraft—since one thing witches did was to spread sickness—meant that evidence of witches' activities was pervasive in the years during and after European encounters, which brought dreadful epidemic diseases in their wake (see documents 2 and 3). The spread of Eurasian diseases in the Americas accompanied and enabled European military conquest. Historians and epidemiologists talk about "virgin soil populations"—groups unaccustomed to certain diseases and who possess no immunities to them. Indeed, diseases often moved in advance of Europeans, sometimes spread inadvertently by traders. What this meant, for Americans, was sometimes a devastating destruction. Smallpox was perhaps the worst of the new invaders, but almost as deadly were influenza, measles, diphtheria, whooping cough, mumps, and chicken pox. Amid the chaos of an epidemic, crops might not get planted or harvested; thus famine often followed epidemics, and the overall consequences could be catastrophic (see figure 4). The Huron population, for example, plunged from 20,000–35,000 in the early seventeenth century to 10,000 in 1640.[49]

Indians and Europeans sometimes interpreted epidemics differently. Europeans who benefited from these catastrophes might be inclined to attribute them to God. John Winthrop put this view succinctly in a letter in which he described the terrible toll taken by a smallpox epidemic that raged through southern New England in 1633 and 1634, eviscerating Indian communities. "God hathe hereby cleered our title to this place," he explained to a friend in England.[50] Indians, too, could appreciate the supernatural origins of disease, but they had another explanation that was just as logical and consistent with modern ideas about disease transmission: Europeans brought the diseases. Thus the exact same smallpox epidemic had dramatically opposed meanings for those who endured it: for Europeans covetous of land, it was a clear sign of God's favor; for those

Figure 4. An Iroquois healing ritual. Images of ritual life in the northeastern woodlands typically depict Indians in circles, just as European witches formed circles at their Sabbaths. Such healing ceremonies likely increased in frequency in the wake of Indian contact with unfamiliar and deadly Eurasian diseases.

Source: Joseph-François Lafitau, Moeurs des sauvages ameriquains (Paris, 1724). Courtesy of Georgetown University Library Special Collections.

who succumbed to the ravages of the terrible disease, it was just as clear an indication that European witches were at loose in the countryside.

Those launching evangelical missions in North America were optimistic that the Devil could be displaced. William Crashaw conveyed this expectation of Christian triumph in an exhortation to English clerics on their way to Jamestown. "And though Satan visibly and palpably raignes there, more then in any other knowne place of the world: yet be of courage (blessed brethren) *God will treade Satan under your feet shortly*, and the ages to come will eternize your names, as the *Apostles of Virginia*."[51] Moreover, there was strong evidence that the Devil should not hold sway in North America. Europeans believed that the Devil tempted followers with promises of riches, luxury, and goods beyond their economic or social status. Elizabeth Knapp, possessed by the Devil in the English colony of Massachusetts in 1671 (see document 17), reported that the Devil offered her "money, silkes, fine cloaths."[52] When witches testified about gatherings at their Sabbaths, they recounted witches adorned in fabulous garments that were forbidden by sumptuary laws that restricted certain fabrics and colors to people of noble birth. Tituba, an enslaved woman from Barbados but probably of Indian, not African, descent, attested in Salem in 1692 that she saw women wearing silk hoods at a Sabbath she attended.[53] In contrast, French, English, and Dutch observers who recorded their impressions of the people of the northeastern woodlands of North America marveled at their modest economies and at their generosity. In such circumstances, where people had to carry their possessions in their semi-sedentary economies and any gathered surplus could prove a burden, what could the Devil tempt people with? Indeed, as one Jesuit reported in 1634, when people are free of want, "not one of them gives himself to the Devil to acquire wealth."[54]

Colonization, Witchcraft, and Resistance

Europeans regarded the contest for religious dominion in North America as a competition between gods—between the strong Christian God and weaker Indian deities that served Satan and resisted God's rule. If the Devil ruled America, then the colonization efforts that took place there could only be comprehended as an epic struggle between good and evil.[55] The connection between resistance and diabolism is especially important in the colonial context. Europeans believed the Devil was characterized above all by his pride. It was that trait that led him to challenge God's dominion, to prefer (as John Milton put it in *Paradise Lost*) "to reign in Hell than to serve in Heaven."[56] Second to his pride, however, was his obstinacy, and the two were deeply intertwined. Resistance thus confirmed European sus-picions about Indians and witchcraft in two ways, since those who resisted likely used sorcery as one of their weapons, and since Europeans understood other forms of resistance in terms of the diabolical witchcraft they already expected to find.

The growing evidence of the failure of Christian conversion, especially after decades of apparent success in New Spain in the sixteenth century, encouraged despondent priests to look to the Devil as the cause. They blamed him for deceiving the Spanish with false conversions. Some priests worried that converts used their old rituals in a new Christian form, and had been instructed on how to do so by the Devil.[57] Especially insidious, Acosta explained, was the Devil's habit of creating rituals that mimicked Christian practice. Thus Acosta reported monasteries of virgins in Peru and women in Mexico who lived like nuns for the space of a year. The consecration of Indian priests with sweet-smelling oils was another trick of Satan—these oils were made of noxious animal excretions. It was a simple step to conclude, as Acosta did, that the gods of the Americans were identical to the Devil.[58] And the Devil encouraged resistance to the Christian message. When the Jesuits encountered Tepehuan Indians in North America in the early sev-enteenth century who did not want to convert to Christianity, they readily blamed Tepehuan religious leaders whom they identified as witches.[59]

Even a priest who initially had doubts about the presence of the Devil found that his experience among the Indians of New France altered his views. The French Jesuit Paul Le Jeune (1591–1664) originally thought that the Devil was in South America but was not pervasive in New France. There were sorcerers there, he believed, but not the Devil himself. But knowledge, it turns out, can breed distrust as well as understanding. The more Le Jeune learned of the Indians among whom he lived and preached, the more he began to believe that the Devil was in their midst. His view was reinforced by Indian resistance to his Christian message.[60] In the end, the Jesuits in New France came to rely on Satan as a way to explain Indian resistance to Christian conversion.

Europeans associated resistance of all sorts, both to conversion and to secular rule, with diabolism. One case from northern New Spain reveals the connection. In 1599, Spanish officials executed an Indian woman for witch-craft. She was a Guachichil Indian, and she was tried in the region of San Luis Potosí, a part of the northern frontier of New Spain that had only recently come under Spanish control. The Guachichiles were one of several hunter-gatherer tribes that resisted Spanish occupation and conquest between 1548 and 1590 in a protracted series of conflicts called the Chichimeca Wars.

The Spanish, propelled by the discovery of silver in Zacatecas in 1546, were highly motivated to expand commerce and settlement into this region, and the result was regular conflict. The Spanish, and the sedentary Indians who accompanied them in their movement northward, feared the Guachichiles. "So frightening" were they, decorated with animal figures when they fought, "that they even scare mules." But the Spanish moved from fear to irritation, irked by the "audacity" of the Indians who resisted their occupation.[61]

The link between witchcraft and resistance was not subtle in this case. Estimated at approximately sixty years old, the accused woman had endured the ravages of conquest. She lived in a neighborhood occupied by Tlaxcallan and Tarascan Indians who had been moved north with the Spanish. They were Christian converts. The alleged witch went into their churches, removed the sacred images, and broke the crosses. The Indians who reported the case to Spanish authorities were troubled by her powers as a witch. Indians were ready to follow her because she had threatened to destroy them if they did not—and they believed she had the ability to do so. She was alleged to have killed a Tarascan Indian with magic (by grazing his ear with a stick). She turned herself into animals (as Indian witches were believed to do, by both Indians and Spaniards), including a coyote, and transformed others into animals as well.[62] She insisted that she had taken all of the Indian dead and made a pueblo for them—a village of the dead, a fitting symbol of the impact conquest had on Americans.

Witch beliefs were not simply religious; they had a political component, too, tangled as they were with resistance to properly constituted authorities. The Guachichil witch's crime was not only her witchcraft; it was also her ability to persuade the Guachichiles to join her in her rejection of the symbols of Spanish rule. As one Guachichil attested (perhaps self-servingly), before the accused witch rebelled, all of the Indians were "quiet, peaceful, and calm, and because of the said Indian woman they have become stirred up and restless."[63] And so she was put to death. Spanish officials moved quickly, permitting no appeal, because the witch threatened Spanish security. The Spanish justice of the town whisked her to the gallows. There, she was executed in an especially cruel fashion, hanged by her feet until she died, a process that took several hours. A priest in the Andes similarly admitted that he had whipped three women not primarily because they were witches, but rather because their behavior encouraged others in their village to rise up against Spanish rule.[64]

The Spanish inclination to link resistance to their political dominion to witchcraft had the consequence of making witchcraft seem pervasive in the Americas where it had been of minor importance (in terms of executions and

threats to community order) in Spain. In many respects, the same old notions of witchcraft continued in Spanish America, especially those centered
on maleficia and love magic. These ideas played themselves out regularly
in secular and ecclesiastical courts in New Mexico (see below). But a new
element emerged in the context of colonization and resistance, and that was
the association of witchcraft with armed resistance to Spanish authority. In
this respect, witches were not only rebels against godly order (as they were
throughout Europe), but also armed rebels bent on overthrowing established
governments.

The Spanish confronted two major uprisings in North America in the seventeenth century, first between 1616 and 1620 at Tepehuan in the province
of Nueva Vizcaya (established in 1563), and a second, the Pueblo Revolt, in
New Mexico in 1680.[65] Santa Fe de Nuevo México (New Mexico's original
and full name) was established in 1598. Both regions lay within the Viceroyalty of New Spain. The second revolt was so successful that it removed the
Spanish from the region for some ten years. Missionaries, the Jesuits in the
case of the first episode and the Franciscans in the case of the second, blamed
both resistance movements on the Devil.[66] Each revolt had been preceded
by growing doubts of Indian converts, who were questioning both the Christian message and the entire colonial project. In both resistance movements,
the indigenous leaders whom the Spanish defined as demons and witches
organized millenarian movements, predicting a more perfect world and the
restoration of indigenous society once pernicious outside influences were
removed (see documents 4 and 5).

In the Tepehuan revolt, at least 200 Spaniards and their allies were killed,
including 10 priests. Some 4,000 Tepehuanes died. The rebels destroyed
numerous symbols of Spanish occupation, including mines, missions, and
settlements, in Sierra Madre Occidental. They staged mock religious pro-
cessions, and then desecrated the objects, flogging statues and shredding
crucifixes. They deliberately humiliated priests, mocking them with Latin
before clubbing them to death.[67] The most elaborate account (see document
4) of the revolt came from the pen of a Jesuit, Andrés Pérez de Ribas, in his
*History of the Triumphs of the Holy Faith among the Most Barbarous and Fierce
People of the New World* (1645). Pérez de Ribas had a simple explanation for
what had transpired in the Tepehuan revolt: the leader of the revolt, a man
named Quautlatas, was the antichrist, and the other leaders were demons.[68]
This explanation was important to Pérez de Ribas—and to the Spaniards—
because, to them, the uprising was otherwise inexplicable, and with no logical
material explanation, they turned to a logical supernatural one: The revolt
was the work of the Devil.[69] One reason the Tepehuan revolt was so hard

for Spaniards to fathom was that it arose after many years of Spanish activity in the region. Missionary activity had commenced with two Franciscans in 1555, and the Jesuits began their own work in 1596.[70] This interpretation of the uprising as diabolically inspired was useful not only in making sense of its unexpected nature and of the Tepehuanes' assault on churches, missionaries, and religious symbols; it also helped to inspire and justify a counterattack, since those who punished the Tepehuanes were striking at Satan himself.[71]

This link between resistance and witchcraft was especially charged during the Pueblo revolt six decades later because of the character of Spanish expansion in New Mexico. The Spanish had started exploring the region in the early sixteenth century, soon after their conquest of the Mexica in the Valley of Mexico. But concerted settlement efforts did not get underway in New Mexico until the early seventeenth century. Even then, the Spanish presence—in numbers—was sparse. Important features distinguished New Mexico's early decades and shaped the context in which the Pueblo Revolt emerged and was understood by priests and secular officials. The Franciscans who traveled to New Mexico experienced some rapid successes in their conversion efforts—at least as they measured success and as they understood the fragile faith of the neophytes. By 1608, ten years after the first mission was established, several thousand Indians had converted to Christianity. As had been the case with the rapid success of evangelical efforts in the Valley of Mexico in the sixteenth century, these new converts to Catholicism were useful weapons in Europeans' religious conflicts, offering living symbols of the vitality and expansion of the Catholic Church at a time when it endured attacks and retrenchment in Europe.

Because of the missionaries' apparent success, the Spanish crown was loath to abandon the territory despite the absence of any obvious sources of wealth. And also because of their missionary accomplishments, the priests gained a powerful sense of their importance to the fate of the colony. They challenged the authority of the state, and there was regular friction between the colony's governors and the priests. The Indians often emerged as pawns in these struggles. Missionaries required access to Indians to justify their presence in New Mexico, but if there were to be any sort of viable and profitable colonial state in the region, colonial officials needed to find ways to benefit from Indian labor and resources. Thus, governors had to ensure the cooperation of Indians and were not always willing to enforce the Church's decrees against concubinage or ceremonial dances. This latitude permitted many indigenous practices to endure, but only if they were tolerated by governors.[72]

The 1670s were a difficult time for the Pueblos, especially during the rule of Governor Juan Francisco Treviño (1675–1677), who prohibited many important religious practices. He even ordered the unprecedented destruction of the kivas, which are sacred ceremonial underground chambers. Famine in 1670 was followed by death and pestilence and by Apache and Navajo raids in 1672. Sandwiched between raids by nomadic tribes, demands on their labor by Spanish officials and settlers, and violent assaults on their rituals by whip-wielding Franciscans, distraught and angry Pueblos turned to their ancient gods in time-honored ceremonies to ask for rain and fertility, while their religious practitioners used their magic to curse Christians and steal their hearts (a traditional form of Pueblo witchcraft).[73] In response, the governor launched a massive witch hunt.[74] In 1675, Treviño brought some forty-seven accused witches to Santa Fe for trial with allegations that they had bewitched a priest and other people and had even killed ten people, including seven friars. Three of the accused were hanged, and all the rest (except one man who hanged himself) were punished in various ways.[75] The testimonies in the wake of the revolt (see document 5) speak directly to the hostility these actions generated among the Pueblos, and they played a crucial role in sparking the revolt. In 1680, some 17,000 Pueblos rose against a Spanish population numbering only several hundred, and in the wake of the revolt, 20 (out of 41) Franciscans were dead, as were 380 Spanish soldiers and colonists.[76]

The Spanish saw the Devil in the Pueblo Revolt. Spanish officials paid close attention to testimony given after the revolt by Indians who claimed that the revolt's leader, Popé, had communicated with the Devil (see document 5). Witchcraft emerged as a crucial explanation for the revolt, not only in explaining its timing and personnel, but also in helping the Spanish make sense of the targets of Pueblo attack. One of the men whipped in the 1675 witch hunt was Popé. It was Popé who emerged to lead the revolt in 1680, and it was Popé who articulated a vision of a new society, one in which all Spanish influences were expunged and the old gods restored. The millenarian visions that were conveyed so fully in the Tepehuan and Pueblo uprisings, the expectation that the Spanish could be dislodged and old gods restored, were classic expressions of revolts that took place within the first two generations of conquest. In these first decades of occupation and invasion, indigenous people still adhered to precontact religious beliefs and worldviews, and these beliefs empowered shamans and soldiers alike to combat the upheavals caused by epidemic disease, forced labor, and disrupted ritual life.[77] To Europeans, these uprisings and their religious goals looked like witchcraft.

One unusual feature of the historical scholarship on witchcraft in the Americas is the extent to which historians often agree with the interpretation of European colonizers that witchcraft was indeed a form of resistance. In this interpretation, Indians, mestizos, Africans, and others practiced witchcraft (as defined by both themselves and Europeans) and used these practices actively to strike at and to thwart Europeans and those who occupied their territory, claimed their labor, displaced them from their homes, assaulted them sexually, and transformed their world.[78] Irene Silverblatt, for example, argues that Andean women who confessed to witchcraft likely believed themselves to be witches and that their pact with the Devil "was a symbol of their alienation from a society which offered them little more than despair. It was their attempt to gain power in a society in which they were powerless."[79] In their study of the Abiquiu outbreak (1756–1763), Malcolm Ebright and Rick Hendricks similarly argue that witchcraft was indeed being practiced in this major New Mexico episode, and that the Indians there "used witchcraft against the Franciscans as a form of resistance to Christianization."[80]

Historians studying witchcraft in Europe or British America tend not to write frequently about witches as people expressing or seeking social or cultural power. Not least because so many European witches were women, people for the most part without equal legal status in their societies, witches tend to evoke historians' sympathy for the terrible plight in which they found themselves. Mary Lee, an elderly woman traveling alone who was murdered as a witch by frightened sailors on their journey to Maryland, is a perfect case in point (see document 9). Other accused witches were entangled in legal systems in which it was sometimes very difficult to prove innocence, especially given the willingness of courts to apply different standards to witch trials and to allow apparitions to be evidence of guilt (see document 24). Many of these accused witches may well have been guilty of witchcraft as it had come to be defined under evolving European statutes—that is, the practice even of white magic was punishable by death.[81] But their ordeals, the sheer number of executed women, the horrifying accounts of their torture, all combined with the conviction of most historians that these women could not have been guilty of the crimes they admitted (copulating with Satan, flying through the air, giving birth to salamanders, turning into werewolves) has tended to result in representations of these women as victims—of new legal cultures, of economic transformations, of state consolidation, of times of famine and drought and war and fear, of unexpected consequences of a fractured religious world. Witchcraft seems less a form of resistance than a terrible fate that befell marginal figures in a changing world.

The preoccupation by colonizers about witchcraft and resistance to European occupation and rule has the inadvertent consequence of turning indigenous witchcraft practices into actions whose main purpose was to *react* to external forces, and makes it harder for us to see how witchcraft functioned *within* indigenous communities to address concerns that were unconnected to European invasions. And of course it continues to be difficult to determine what the "witches" themselves might have thought they were doing. Were they resisting? Or were they simply engaging in customary practices to solve problems? It is hard to tell whether, by ascribing such power to witches, we are adopting their perspective, or that of their accusers, and thus in fact perpetuating their victimization. Readers are urged to draw their own conclusions about these matters in their analysis of the documents in section II.

New Mexico

For all the European conviction that Indians were linked by their very nature to the Devil, only in one part of North America did Indian "witches" appear regularly in colonial courts. This was in Spanish America, and it was an unexpected outcome of colonization, since the lack of Spanish interest in prosecuting witches in Europe hardly predicted the increased numbers of witches in New Spain. Witchcraft was a central feature of life in New Mexico, from the first Spanish forays into the region through the major outbreak in Abiquiu. The last witchcraft case handled by the Inquisition was in 1800. The Inquisition was a long-standing institution devoted to rooting out heresy, and witchcraft cases often fell within its purview. As Spaniards confronted Indians, and devised racial and cultural systems that placed Europeans, Africans, and Indians in relation to each other, they yoked feminine attributes to some of these non-Europeans. And, colonizers believed, just as weak European women attached themselves to Satan, so too did Indians.

Numerous cases found their way to colonial courts, both those operated by the Inquisition and those managed by civil officials. The first witchcraft allegations that caught the notice of Spanish officials in New Mexico were made in 1626 (the same year as the very first case in the English colonies, contained in document 8), when an Indian woman and her mestiza daughter were accused of sorcery and of using their powers on two Indian servants, both of whom sickened and died. Both women were also accused of love magic: the mother took revenge on a lover, who died, and the daughter, who was married, was accused of infidelity with a lover whom she allegedly poisoned and killed. Accusers alleged that the women were able to transport themselves at night, traveling abroad in an egg to spy on their lovers. After accusations in 1626 and 1628, the charges were investigated in 1631. Skeptical of these claims, officials declined to pursue the case.[82]

In the 1626 case, the accused witches targeted other Indians, but numerous cases from New Mexico reveal the intersecting lives of colonists, Indians, and enslaved Africans. Their entangled lives produced entangled practices, along with ample need for the remedies promised by witchcraft. As early as 1629, a Spanish cowboy named Luis de Rivera, who was denounced to the Inquisition for making a pact with the Devil, confessed that he had sought an herb from an Indian that he could use on a fast day to attract the attention of a woman. His consultation with an Indian expert suggests that he had absorbed the Spanish notion that Indians were likely witches. And in that same year, he continued, he met an African who introduced him to demonology. Rivera was born in Seville and went to Mexico when he was thirteen, and it is interesting that it was his journey out of Europe and to the New World that introduced him to not one but two new forms of magical and religious practice. The African sold Rivera a book with demons painted in it. The African's belief (as reported by Rivera) that the Devil was powerful suggests that the man was a Christian (or possibly a skilled salesmen), and it is also possible that Rivera's confession was designed to play into the cultural assumptions that Spanish officials had—that Indians and Africans were likely to be witches and to consort with the Devil.[83] This recourse to indigenous practitioners was in fact commonplace in much of Latin America. Indians, Africans, and people of mixed race found careers as healers—*curanderos*, as they were called. In a witchcraft trial in New Mexico in 1708, two Indians, Juanchillo and Josepha, called as witnesses in the case, reported to the court that they worked as healers and had cured many Spaniards (see document 12). Widely accepted as legitimate and skilled healers, sometimes curanderos were reported to the Inquisition and accused of being witches or sorcerers by their own clients.[84]

A New Mexico case in 1733 hints at the intersection of healing, witchcraft, and the law. In that year, an Isleta Indian named Melchor Trujillo was accused of bewitching two Spaniards, who fell sick. If Trujillo touched them, he could either heal them or make them worse. Trial depositions revealed that the victims seemed to have had a prior relationship with the accused Indian since they testified that they had received peyote from him—perhaps seeking his expertise for cures or magic. Trujillo, who was a cacique (or leader) of the Isleta pueblo, confessed that he had practiced witchcraft with numerous other Indians. In their witchcraft, they used idols and he described other indigenous practices, including rubbing rocks and using the rocks' dust in their magic. The accused gave the officials a variety of objects, including four dolls, rocks, and a string with beads. Trujillo also reported that there were several Spanish victims, although precisely because the victims had also sought the assistance of the alleged witches, and because of some difficulties with interpreters, officials had trouble sorting out who the witches and victims were—a legal morass that resulted in part from Spanish expectations of magical and medical help from Indian curers (and witches).[85]

Europeans linked products unique to the Americas and important to indigenous ritual life, such as peyote and tobacco, to diabolical practice as well. Peyote is a small, spineless cactus; the name comes from the Nahuatl word, *peyotl*. Inquisition records from 1631 and 1632 suggest some of peyote's uses in New Mexico: it could help a person suffering from bewitchment to identify the witch, and once the witch was revealed, the possessed person would be able to recover. Peyote could also enable a person to have visions that would show who was traveling through New Spain en route to Santa Fe, just the type of unnatural knowledge that Europeans associated with witchcraft. Peyote might help one recover lost objects, and it had medicinal powers, too, since one man of mixed Spanish and African descent reported that he had been told it was a good palliative for a broken arm.[86] The Inquisition tended to be hostile to hallucinogenic drugs offered by indigenous healers, especially those drugs that caused users to fall into trances or that helped users to gain contact with the sacred world.[87]

Tobacco proved similarly puzzling to Europeans, who were not sure if the plant was diabolical. Europeans learned how to consume tobacco first from Americans, and then from experienced Europeans who brought new habits of consumption across the Atlantic with them. But tobacco also featured in theological discussions. Was it a suitable food for Christians? Could it be consumed during Lent? If America was the home of the Devil, what about the plants that were unique to the Devil's lair? The first chroniclers of the New World latched on to Native American beliefs that tobacco was a sacred substance and transformed them, ultimately perceiving tobacco as supernatural and demonic.[88] And so it is no surprise that tobacco crops up in Europe in the context of witch accusations and trials. The women of the Labourd grew tobacco plants in their gardens and smoked the substance, according to the Jesuit witch-hunter Pierre de Lancre, both to clear their heads and to stave off hunger. The tobacco made them smell so bad that it inured the women to its terrible stench and made them more accepting of the still more dreadful smells of the Devil.[89] The road to hell, it seems, was strewn with tobacco leaves. And in the same way that Europeans saw the Americas as Satan's bastion, they supposed American people and American plants might be diabolical.

New Mexico witchcraft cases reveal a variety of features of colonial life in New Mexico that did not exist in other colonized areas of North America. For example, they show the physical proximity in which Indians and Europeans lived and the increasingly intertwined beliefs they shared—about power, about magic, about healing, and about witches. These characteristics of New

Mexico society were especially pronounced after the Spanish returned to the colony in 1706. Witchcraft was so much a part of New Mexico in the eighteenth century that Ramón A. Gutiérrez has suggested that it was one of three main issues that affected life there (the other two being Indian attacks and the important economic and governmental reforms of the 1770s).[90] Document 12 contains extensive excerpts from a trial in 1708 concerning a Spanish woman who believed that she had been bewitched by three Indian women. As the trial testimony unfolds, we learn of a tangled web of relationships, a cheating husband, a young and possibly exploited Indian woman, and a betrayed Spaniard.

Nothing comparable exists among the surviving records in British or French North America, at least as far as indigenous people are concerned. (Readers will have the opportunity to decide for themselves if witchcraft played a similar role in interactions between enslaved Africans and their owners in British America.) It was proximity in New Mexico that enabled Europeans to seek out Indian curers—and it was both the exploitation and new kinds of human relationships that prompted people to need solutions available from witches. Many Indians lived in Spanish households, and because the colony was constantly at war, there were always new Indian captives joining households, and so the number of Indians in Spanish settlements increased. These Indians lived in proximity to Spanish men—who often preyed on Indian women—and also had easy access to food, enabling them to poison those who hurt them. It was this proximity, and the fear Spaniards had of Indians in their midst, that produced so many accusations of witchcraft against Indian and mestiza women. Stories of sex and sexual power, of the sexual freedom of Spanish men, the hurt and humiliation of Spanish women, and the exploitation of and sometimes opportunities for Indian and mestiza women, emerge in these trials. It is no surprise that many of these eighteenth-century cases revolved around love magic.[91] And Indians and Spaniards shared ideas about witchcraft, which is most fully illustrated during the big outbreak at Abiquiu in 1756–1763, when 38 percent of 176 accused witches were of European descent, and 62 percent were Indian.[92]

Spanish witch beliefs flourished and expanded in the New World. The "love magic" that Spaniards resorted to in Spain was of greater importance in the demographic and racial configurations of colonial society, as women sought to retain a husband's loyalty, to repel unwanted attention, to retaliate against those who exploited them, or to get revenge. Amid shifting Spanish belief systems in the Americas, which linked Indians with witchcraft, and amid the disruptions Spanish occupation posed to indigenous lives, Spaniards and Indians found plausible witches everywhere.

New France

If witchcraft was everywhere in New Mexico, its presence was more episodic in other parts of North America. For many other Europeans—especially the French and Germans—settlement in North America offered fewer opportunities or venues for bringing charges of witchcraft. New France illustrates this shift. France lay in the heartland of Europe's witch craze, and perhaps 1,000 people were executed there as witches. Canada was settled by the French precisely in the period of prosecutions. There were, for example, major outbreaks of possession in France in 1611 and 1634. In Normandy between 1600 and 1629, 119 people were condemned to death for witchcraft (although given the French system of appeal, only 59 people were executed).[93] In 1608, during this period of intense witch activity, Samuel de Champlain launched a modest French settlement at Quebec, one dependent on Indian allies for its survival and commercial success. Missionaries joined French traders and soldiers in 1626, and the colony limped along, sustained by the fur trade and crucial diplomatic alliances with Hurons and Algonquian-speaking nations, and reaching a population of 356 (240 men and 116 women) in 1640.[94]

The French possessed an array of witch beliefs, but these beliefs found little traction in the altered circumstances in New France. Although those who migrated to New France seem to have carried their witch beliefs with them, there is no surviving evidence of any witch trials in New France. There was a reported case of demonic possession in Quebec around 1661, which allegedly resulted in an execution. Marie Catherine of Saint Augustine, a member of a religious order, was apparently quite preoccupied by demons.[95] Her concern reveals important continuity with French cases of mass possession, which typically took place in convents, most famously at an Ursuline convent in Loudun in 1632–1634. Yet in New France there is no surviving documentary evidence that accusations there led to trials.

Why? There are a number of possible explanations. One centers on the status and position of the clergy. In France, priests played an especially important role in fostering witch beliefs. Parish priests were often poorly educated, and they relied in part on magic to sustain their status within the community. Their emphasis on magic occasionally led to priests themselves being accused of witchcraft. In the Normandy outbreak, for example, priests were accused of possessing books with diabolical incantations. Convicted priests endured especially gruesome torments. One defendant was ordered to make a public apology at Rouen's cathedral, after which his tongue was pierced with a hot iron and he was hanged.[96] If poorly trained priests could stimulate witch beliefs in France, such was not the case in New France, where there were not many priests; those who lived in the colony tended to have excellent educations; and they worked instead to combat beliefs in magic (as they identified it) among Indians, not to foster them. Also, the European inhabitants of New France proved not to be diligent attenders of mass. It was, in fact, Native Americans who were most likely to identify priests as witches (see documents 2 and 3).

Moreover, it is not clear how much the Jesuits of New France (who comprised the majority of priests there) worried about the Devil. Their attitude toward the Devil differed somewhat from that of their missionary counterparts in New Spain, where missionaries sought a spiritual conquest to accompany Spanish occupation. In New France, the church was weak, with priests few in number. Early missionary efforts (to Acadia from 1610 to 1616 and later Quebec) were aborted, and the Jesuits did not return in force until 1632. The total number of French—secular or religious—in the colony was small as well. Canada was not a place that the French could take over and occupy. Instead, the French sought to establish alliances among local populations. The success of such alliances was evident as early as 1609, when Champlain joined with Algonquian-speaking allies to fend off attacking soldiers of the Iroquois confederation. The French relied on harmonious relationships to secure access to furs, which were central to the colony's economic success. Individual trappers became deeply involved in Indian communities, for example. So the priests who journeyed to New France, while eager to convert souls and always ready for the martyrdom that might await, did not have the expectations that shaped the aspirations—and angry disappointments—of priests in Central and South America. And these different aspirations affected their demonology, as, indeed, did the different indigenous groups they encountered, who did not have the complex and hierarchical religious institutions that fascinated and dismayed European observers in New Spain.

The language Jesuits in New France used to describe Satan and his minions was mocking, derisive, contemptuous—not language conveying the specter of a terrifying enemy. François-Joseph Le Mercier (see document 2), for example, referred to a sorcerer's "pranks."[97] Jesuits described indigenous demons as fraudulent and marginal, not powerful and central. Jesuits believed that there was little doubt that Indian shamans worked with the assistance of the Devil, but the Jesuits also thought that they would be able to control these shamans, and perhaps even find ways to expose shamans as frauds.[98] Unlike other places and times (such as Salem in 1692 or Abiquiu in 1756), where ardent religious leaders played crucial roles in sparking witch outbreaks, the Jesuits in New France do not seem to have engendered such events.

Other factors played a role as well in preventing the expression of witch beliefs in trials in New France, at least as far as surviving evidence indicates. As any study of witchcraft trial records suggests, witch accusations often depended on familiarity. Testimonies suggest the intimacy of communal life: witnesses peered through windows, listened over hedges, barged in un-invited, slept in the next room, or shared a bed or a pallet on the floor. For the most part, victims knew their accusers personally, and those accusations lodged against strangers tended to be discounted by investigating officials. So witch beliefs and accusations were embedded in the particular fabric of a given society. The depositions in documents 8, 10, and 12 all hint at just such relationships. Accusers presented a litany of grievances, some stemming from disputes over twenty years in the past. People who lived in dispersed family units, not in clustered villages, tended to have fewer opportunities to develop these relationships.

In New France, the basic residential unit was the family farm, not the village, even though French officials endeavored to get people to settle in villages. Moreover, these New France settlements were, just like the colony, *new*, without the long-standing relationships, family conflicts, and webs of obligation that sustained witch accusations in Europe. New France also had fewer of the marginal, economically impoverished, elderly women who were perceived as burdensome and became targets of accusation in some regions of France. New France, like most newly settled colonies in the Americas, contained more men than women, and those women who survived to old age often had children to care for them.[99] Finally, the inhabitants of New France came from all regions of France. The two most dominant were Normandy (14.5 percent of immigrants) and Ile-de-France (14.3 percent), with every other part of the kingdom represented. Beliefs about magic, sorcery, and witchcraft had pronounced regional peculiarities in France, and so the beliefs immigrants transferred represented this same heterogeneity. The dominance of migrants from Normandy might have predicted that this region's beliefs (about male witches, shepherds, toads, and magical priests) would prevail, but the key ingredients—the poorly trained priests and the shepherds—were missing.[100] Thus the religious, economic, demographic, and geographic con-text that shaped the legal expression of witch beliefs in France did not exist in New France. Witchcraft beliefs, however, were abundant in the region, and the Indians who comprised the majority of the population continued to identify and punish witches, French and Indian alike, according to their own processes (see documents 2 and 3).

British North America

In the English colonies in North America, in contrast, witch beliefs did plant themselves, and very firmly, too, in some regions. Most witchcraft trials took place in New England (the region containing the colonies of Massachusetts, Plymouth, Rhode Island, New Haven, and Connecticut), where approximately 355 people were accused of witchcraft and of those, 103 (29 percent) were brought to trial between 1620 and 1725.[101] In New England, witches were punished more severely than in England; while conviction rates were comparable, punishments were harsher.[102] Bermuda, a colony with as much puritanical zeal as the colonies of Massachusetts, New Haven, and Connecticut, experienced a witch hunt in the 1650s and 6 witches were executed between 1651 and 1655.[103]

Only a handful of cases went to court in other colonies. Just one person, for example, is known to have been executed in Maryland as a witch: Rebecca Fowler, who was put to death in October 1685 for hurting people in Calvert County.[104] Virginia had only one guilty verdict for a witch in the seventeenth century, and that for a man, who was whipped and banished in 1656. Both colonies experienced the same kind of demographic circumstances as New France. The colonies' sex ratios, with their acute shortages of women, may have dissuaded European inhabitants of the Chesapeake from turning on the few who were there with charges of witchcraft.[105]

Yet despite the scarcity of women and the absence of witchcraft executions, there were certainly witch beliefs and accusations in Virginia. Archaeological evidence is suggestive. A "witch bottle" found in Virginia Beach, at the site of a seventeenth-century house, provides evidence of witch beliefs in the area. This bottle contained pins and nails and was buried in an inverted position. In keeping with English beliefs, the burial of such a bottle was intended to lift a curse and to turn the pain back on the witch.[106] The location of the bottle suggests that it might have been deployed against the region's well-known witch, Grace Sherwood, who appeared in court numerous times to face her accusers over the span of eight years from 1698 to 1706 (see document 10).

And although witchcraft trials may have been rare in Virginia, the first known witch accusations in the English colonies to find their way to court appeared there in 1626, after almost twenty years of English settlement in the Chesapeake. Some thirteen neighbors and acquaintances of Goodwife Wright, of Kickotan, accused her of a range of offenses, especially foretelling deaths and hindering hunting (document 8). The accusations against Wright and her response before the Virginia Council illustrate one of the important features of English beliefs—the relative insignificance of the Devil and the Devil's pact. Both elements would emerge as characteristics in outbreaks (see Salem documents 19–24), but for the most part witchcraft accusations in English colonies centered not on diabolism but rather on maleficia.

Wright's case was early in the history of English settlement in North America. New Englanders did not execute a witch until 1647 (Alice Young in Connecticut, followed by the execution of Margaret Jones in Massachusetts in 1648), after almost twenty years of settlement. In this respect, the pattern of accusations and, more critically, of interest by authorities in pursuing these matters emerged with the same timing we see in Virginia, almost twenty years after first settlement in each case, although the regions of the Chesapeake and New England otherwise followed very different patterns. Virginia was characterized by high mortality and male-dominated migration for most of the seventeenth century. New England was settled between 1630 and 1642 in a big wave called the Great Migration, and families predominated. The colonists tended to be Puritans.[107] In New England, moreover, witchcraft emerged as a permanent fixture of colonial life, unlike Virginia. In New England, the accused witch was likely to be a woman (79 percent of accused witches between 1620 and 1725 were female, and women represented 80 percent of all executed witches), but she was no longer certain to be poor, as was still the case in England. Poor and elderly women were still overrepresented among New England's accused witches, but they were joined by wealthier neighbors, in a pattern distinctive to the region.[108] The execution of Ann Hibbens in 1656 was a case in point.

Ann Hibbens lived in Boston and was the widow of a prominent New England merchant named William Hibbens. William had only recently died, and Ann Hibbens found herself called before the magistrates in May to face accusations of witchcraft. She was alleged to have unnatural knowledge, a sure clue that someone was a witch. In Hibbens's case, she had the misfortune to guess—correctly—that two neighbors she spied talking in the street were talking about her. Although a search of her body revealed no telltale witches' marks, and her home yielded no poppets (or dolls) with which she might work her magic, Hibbens went to trial. She was a woman of considerable wealth. She was not the type of woman who often found herself accused of the crime of witchcraft in England—poor, alone, on the margins of society, perhaps with a reputation as a healer. She was, however, like other accused women, perceived as prone to discontent. She had been embroiled in a case before the Boston church in 1640 over disagreements with some carpenters about their charges for some home repairs. Unable to come to a harmonious agreement with the tradesmen or to satisfy church elders who required her to submit to their authority, Hibbens was expelled from the church. Still, her high status should have protected her in 1656. Her husband had been a magistrate of the colony, a position awarded to very few men. The magistrates afforded her the respect due her station, giving her the honorific of "Mrs." Indeed, they recoiled at the first verdict, and sent the case back for retrial, but to no avail. The second verdict came back guilty as well, and Hibbens was hanged in Boston in June.[109]

Why were wealthy, prominent women in New England accused of witchcraft, in stark contrast to the poor, marginal women who were usually the targets of such accusations in England (and Europe generally)? The historian Carol F. Karlsen examined New England inheritance practices and detected an intriguing pattern. Women who were accused of witchcraft were often women who had inherited land from husbands, fathers, or brothers in the absence of male heirs. The normal English pattern was for male heirs to receive and control property. But 61 percent of accused female witches had no brothers or sons to inherit their property, and such women were more likely to be prosecuted (64 percent), found guilty (76 percent) and executed (89 percent).[110] It is an interesting correlation, and Karlsen does not suggest that the accusations were conscious or deliberate, but it is difficult to know what to make of it. Men, after all, wrote wills, and they could leave land to whomever they wished. If women's inheritance was so disruptive, why did so many men leave land to women?

Karlsen links these fears of propertied women to larger issues in seventeenth-century New England about power and control over resources. By the middle of the seventeenth century, the imbalanced sex ratios of the first decades had evened out. New England's large families, a departure from typical English family size, put great pressure on parental resources, and children competed with each other and with fathers who were reluctant to pass on their property as they sought land and dowries for themselves.[111] The conflict was especially intense between fathers and sons, but Karlsen suggests that sons were unable to make direct accusations against their fathers. Nor, indeed, could they accuse their mothers, although in some cases long-lived mothers and the widow's legal claim on one-third of her deceased husband's property delayed a son's access to family resources. These resentments manifested themselves not as actions against the actual source of the problem, but rather as witchcraft accusations expressed against older women—especially those who held property.[112]

These findings of internal family tension echoed conclusions drawn by John Demos, one of the most active proponents of the value of psychology in the study of witchcraft. He focuses on the "innerlife" dimension, those interior emotions, derived from personal—normally familial—experiences, that shaped how individuals interacted with the world beyond the family. Demos's analysis of New England witchcraft statistics persuaded him to examine the issues facing middle-aged women and young men (who together comprised 49 percent of victims of witchcraft).[113] Demos focuses on the sexuality of the women—menopausal, he characterizes them—and he points to the difficult transition women might experience during these years. The young men were wrestling with their own internal demons—in their case, the desire for personal autonomy in an economy in which fathers held on to land often until their death.

Demos also examines the content of trial testimony for what it reveals about New England fantasies about witches. What did witches do? They attacked, making people and animals sick, in some cases causing dramatic physical collapses. They coveted, demanding assistance, food, lodging, and comfort. They intruded, pushing themselves in where they were not wanted, poking about, appearing in bedrooms. Trial testimonies, moreover, demonstrate that witches had a special interest in infants. The search of an accused witch's body for hidden marks—especially teats—points to the centrality of the association between witches and maternity.[114] His psychological approach thus agrees with some of Karlsen's findings about family tensions across generations and sons' concerns about inheritance.

Numerous studies of witchcraft in New England have revealed some of the peculiarities of colonial life and how these affected witchcraft beliefs in this region. But there is one further oddity about English witch beliefs and their connection to overseas migration: the English killed women as witches even on their initial voyages to the colonies. These cases expose the framework migrants and travelers carried with them. They knew who witches were likely to be and the kinds of behavior that witches engaged in, and when they saw people conforming to these images, they launched accusations. These shipboard executions challenge some of the long-standing conventions in the study of witchcraft, such as that accusations emerged out of familiarity and proximity.

When Europeans boarded ships to travel across the Atlantic, they undertook what was always a risky and often a terrifying voyage. Those who owned enough property to want to safeguard its disposition took care to write wills before they traveled; others must have clung to relatives and friends as they prepared for what was almost always a permanent parting. On board ship, people were flung into each other's company. The practices that people pursued to help ensure good fortune came with them. One indentured servant named Judith Catchpole allegedly performed magic on board ship during her crossing to Maryland in the winter of 1655–1656.[115] Although we do not know what prompted the rituals, it is easy enough to imagine the circumstances that would encourage a traveler to seek extra assistance, through magical means, for a safe and healthy passage.

On other voyages, women were identified as witches, and in some cases executed. Three women were hanged on board ships on their way to the English colonies in the Chesapeake, Mary Lee on her way to Maryland in 1654 (see document 9), Elizabeth Richardson, bound for Maryland in 1658 or 1659, and Katherine Grady on her way to Virginia in 1658.[116] And one vessel reached Bermuda in that same troubled decade with two women on board who were soon identified by their fellow travelers as witches. Court records characterized all three of the Chesapeake travelers as old. Possibly there was something about these women's behavior—either physical manifestations, maladies, odd spasms, muttered prayers, superstitious acts, or unpleasant dispositions—that marked them as witches. Certainly their rapid identification by their fellow travelers points to the tenacity of English expectations about witches: that they were likely to be elderly women and that they could be a particular menace at sea.

Another explanation for their murders comes from the dreadful storms that plagued Grady's and Lee's Atlantic journeys. That witches could conjure storms was a long-standing element of English and Scottish witch beliefs. One of the earliest cases from Scotland featured just such a fear. James VI of Scotland and his new wife, Anne of Denmark, were caught in a terrible storm on their return from Denmark to Scotland. At least seventy, and possibly as many as a hundred, accused witches were rounded up at Berwick in 1590. Under torture many confessed to, among other things, conjuring a storm to sink the ship and murder the king and queen, a crime that was considered, because of the alleged targets, to be treason using sorcery. A large—but unfortunately unknown—number of the accused were executed for their crimes (see figure 5).[117]

Two examples from English popular culture in the seventeenth century hint at the pervasiveness of these ideas. William Shakespeare's *Macbeth*, first performed by 1611 and probably written between 1603 and 1607, famously opens with three witches conjuring in the midst of thunder and lightning. The witches in Henry Purcell's *Dido and Aeneas* (1689), an English opera based on Virgil's *Aeneid*, conjure two such storms, one on land to drive Dido away from a grove and another at sea to destroy the Trojan fleet. Virgil's version contained no witches; the addition of the characters in Purcell's opera (probably by the librettist Nahum Tate, who based his libretto on his own witch-laden 1678 play, *Brutus of Alba, or The Enchanted Lovers*) reflects the

Figure 5.   Scottish witches conjure a storm.

Source: James Carmichael, *Newes from Scotland* (1592). This item is reproduced by permission of *The Huntington Library, San Marino, California.*

importance of such figures in English culture and the dramatic value of their actions for the opera.[118]

One other context might explain the concentration of cases in the 1650s. Two historians, Christine Leigh Heyrman and Elaine Forman Crane, have suggested that women accused of witchcraft in this decade about whom we otherwise know little may have been Quakers.[119] The Quakers were part of a new religious movement that emerged in England in the 1640s. They adhered to what was then regarded as a radical doctrine: that the spirit of God (what they referred to as the inner light) lay within each person. They were aggressively egalitarian in an era of hierarchy. They rejected trained clergy, organized churches, and formal, written doctrine. Because the spirit of God lay within all, anyone could preach the word, which shocked observers in an era when women, children, and untrained men were barred from public professions of faith. Quakers dispersed throughout the world to preach their leveling message, and almost everywhere met hostility from orthodox religious structures and governments. The first Quakers sailed to the colonies in 1655, and in the next few years they visited all the mainland colonies in addition to Bermuda, Barbados, and Jamaica. Banished from Massachusetts, four brave Quakers returned and were hanged between 1659 and 1661 for their pains, the only instances in British America of Protestants dying because of their religious beliefs.[120]

In their opposition to the new movement, Puritans and mainstream Anglicans readily linked Quakers and witchcraft, and the association was especially acute for Quaker women. In 1656, the magistrates of Massachusetts suspected two Quaker missionaries of witchcraft and had their bodies searched for the tell-tale witches' marks. The Salem minister John Higginson, dismayed that members of his congregation joined the Friends, compared the Quaker idea of the "inner light" to "the Devil's Sacrifice." Another cleric, the distinguished minister Increase Mather, wrote in a 1684 publication that Quakers practiced black magic and were likely to experience demonic possession. It is possible that Quakers may have been singled out as witches in Salem in 1692.[121] Witchcraft accusations, however, could intersect with Quakerism in another way, encouraging disaffected people, whether those accused of witchcraft or those repelled by the whole enterprise, to join the Friends. Such was the case for Sarah Hood Bassett, who languished in prison for nine months during the Salem outbreak as an accused witch. After her release, her extended family joined the Salem Quaker meeting.[122]

While the oceanic murders of accused witches and depositions at colonial trials reveal the transmission of many elements of English witch beliefs to North America, the English were not the only Europeans to inhabit English colonies. One distinctive feature of English colonial settlements was authorities' willingness to integrate continental Europeans, particularly Protestants from the Holy Roman Empire (mostly from the region we today call Germany), the Netherlands, and France. Many of these continental Europeans came from lands immersed in witch-hunting, especially those from the Holy Roman Empire, where about half of all prosecutions for witchcraft—perhaps as many as 45,000—took place. There was no territory in the Americas claimed or administered by German-speaking people, but many Germans did immigrate to the British colonies of North America. The migration started small—maybe only 300 migrated to Pennsylvania before 1709—but then the numbers picked up, and by 1775, as many as 84,500 German-speaking people had made the trip.[123] The main German migration transpired well after the peak of the European witch hunts (in contrast to the migrations of the English and French to the Americas in the seventeenth century, which occurred *during* ongoing waves of witch hunts), but certainly the memory of the trials endured and so did the belief system and magical practices. Indeed, the tenacity of these beliefs is striking. But we do not find evidence of witch trials in Pennsylvania, where the vast majority of Germans settled (others went to North Carolina and, later, Georgia). A variety of factors explain this relative silence.

The colonial legal culture where continental Europeans settled did not support witch accusations. Although most English people, Puritan, Quaker, or orthodox Anglican, believed in witchcraft, the laws of England against witchcraft did not always make the trip across the Atlantic. Pennsylvania is a good case in point. The detailed laws devised by William Penn and the colony's first settlers said nothing about witchcraft. Not until 1717 was the English witchcraft statute of James I added to the existing laws by the Pennsylvania assembly.[124]

Even when accusations made it to court, juries and judges were skeptical. One case that did end up in court involved English, Dutch, and Swedes, all meeting around maleficia. The colony of New Sweden (south of Pennsylvania, in what is now Delaware) was established by Gustavus Adolphus of Sweden in 1638. Inhabited mostly by Swedes and Finns and a motley assortment of Northern Europeans, the colony endured until 1654. When the English settled in Pennsylvania, there were still many inhabitants of the defunct colony living in the Delaware Valley. Two colonists, Margaret Mattson and Yeshro Hendrickson, were charged with witchcraft and brought before the Provincial Council of Pennsylvania in February 1684. A Swede acted as their interpreter in the trial, during which they were accused by English and Dutch witnesses of maleficia. The testimony revealed some of the long-standing community connections that shaped witch accusations in this period. One witness, for example, asserted that he had been told twenty years earlier that Mattson was a witch. Others spoke of injuries Mattson brought to their cows. The jury determined that Mattson was guilty of having the reputation of a witch, "but not guilty in manner and forme," and released her to her husband and son; Hendrickson was released to her husband.[125]

Whether or not laws existed, however, or whether accusations found their way into a courtroom, people undoubtedly carried a wide range of beliefs with them, and these beliefs manifested themselves in practices that have come down to us as quaint folkloric customs. The hex sign, for example, adorns barns in Pennsylvania (see figure 6). But the first documented use of a hex sign, a pentagram or "witch's foot" whose purpose is to ward off evil, was only in 1850, so we do not know if it was something that was part of the folkloric practices of the first German migrants.[126] There is, however, extensive evidence of folkloric transmission of witch beliefs and practices in the eighteenth century. German migrants, particularly pietists who believed

Figure 6.   A barn adorned with hex signs, located in Montgomery County, Pennsylvania.
Source: Charles H. Dornsbusch, 1941. Library of Congress, Prints and Photographs Division, HABS PA,39-
NESMI, 1A-1.

in an intensely personal and internal spiritual life, brought a range of mystical and magical religious practices with them. One such figure, Johannes
Kelpius, even cast horoscopes for visitors from his cave outside Philadelphia
along the banks of the Wissahickon in the late seventeenth century.[127] In
Pennsylvania, these mystical figures joined British Quakers, who also had
occult beliefs, to the dismay of their leaders. Other Germans brought a host
of curing and healing rituals that required special words and potions. German healers in eighteenth-century Pennsylvania, for example, invoked the
Trinity when healing wounds.[128] Tempel Anneke, too, had healed with the
words of the Trinity to assist her, calling out "in the name of the Father, the
Son and the Holy Spirit" over a potion of brook weed blood and chick blood:
she was executed as a witch in Germany in 1663.[129]

These practices dispersed as Germans made their way west and then south
along the old wagon road, into Appalachia, where their geographic isolation
enabled some of these traditions, including divination, charms, conjuring,
and healing, to thrive.[130] In Pennsylvania, these magical practices were

called "powwow," or *Brauche* (or *Braucherie*) in Pennsylvania Dutch. There is evidence of its practice by the middle of the eighteenth century in Pennsylvania. Charm books, including *Albertus Magnus: Egyptian Secrets*, existed to guide practitioners. Allegedly authored by a Dominican friar and natural philosopher called Albertus Magnus (1200–1280), named a Catholic saint in 1931, this work contains a variety of spells and recipes. The book first appeared in German in Pennsylvania in 1842; an English edition appeared thirty-three years later.[131] Powwowers (who exist to this day, according to folklorists) seem to function as good witches: they can lift hexes, for example, and heal physical maladies with the appropriate use of charms and ritual incantations. In the Holy Roman Empire in the seventeenth century, all of this activity would have been defined as witchcraft. But in Pennsylvania in the eighteenth century, these rituals became folkloric practice.

Africans and Their Descendants in North America

The largest non-British migrant population to travel to North America was Africans. As many as 481,000 Africans were forcibly transported to North America between 1619 and 1807 (the legal end of the slave trade).[132] Most went to the British colonies of South Carolina, North Carolina, Virginia, Maryland, and Georgia, but a small number—about 28,300—went to Louisiana, the French-controlled territory at the mouth of the Mississippi that was claimed by Spain from 1763–1783 and later purchased by the United States in 1803. Only a small number lived in New Mexico.[133]

As seems to have been true for Germans, Africans, too, continued to believe and practice important elements of their old religions, and, like Germans, Africans often arrived in large concentrations of people of the same ethnicity and settled together. These conditions might ordinarily permit the endurance of Old World customs, rituals, and beliefs, but Africans, of course, lived in the violent and adverse conditions imposed by slavery, which hindered the transmission of culture. It is difficult to find good evidence of their witchcraft practices in colonies governed by the British.

The best evidence for African religious beliefs in the Americas comes from those places where Africans settled in sufficient numbers to be able to transmit and practice elements of the cultures they left behind—and where good sources, most notably Inquisition records, with their detailed depositions and close attention to religious beliefs, exist to uncover these practices. Brazil meets both requirements, and evidence from Inquisition records there from the seventeenth and eighteenth centuries suggests what kinds of linkages might have endured. Witchcraft was not prosecuted frequently in Portugal. In Portuguese Brazil, however, it was a crime that Inquisitors pursued, that Portuguese and Africans alike feared, and that seems to have been an important meeting ground for both Africans and Europeans, as Europeans sought remedies from enslaved practitioners and accused slaves of bewitching them. In 1686, one slaveholder who believed his wife had been bewitched by one of his slaves then called on another enslaved woman to lift the curse with an herbal remedy. These beliefs proved to be long-lived. In the 1780s, for example, a Recife slaveholder called on an exorcist to release him from an inexplicable illness that had left him paralyzed for three years. The priest performed the exorcism to drive out the demons. The slaveholder expelled the requisite assortment of objects—a fish skeleton, some pieces of coal, a few cockroaches—and then looked to his human property for the culprits. Two witches were detected. One was sold at auction and the other was turned over to the Inquisition in Lisbon.[134]

For the British colonies, such evidence of witchcraft activity is much harder to come by. In order to discern African ideas about witchcraft in British colonies, for example, we need to have good sources, whether criminal records or other kinds of accounts provided by observers. Such evidence could have been generated by a European, but most areas of British settlement where Africans were abundant were also regions characterized by skepticism of witchcraft accusations. There is no evidence whatsoever, for example, of witchcraft trials in the places that received the majority of Africans (Barbados and Jamaica). Seventeenth-century Virginia and Maryland contained small African populations, both free and enslaved, but the few records of witchcraft activity there center on Europeans. By the eighteenth century, there were virtually no witchcraft trials at all. And those Europeans who bothered to record their observations needed to be familiar with slaves' practices, to live in proximity, to be close observers, and to understand them. We do not, for example, find sources comparable to the Inquisition records available for New Spain or other parts of the Iberian world, with detailed and personal depositions that give us access to what people believed. Indeed, historians used to wonder whether it was even possible for any African practices to survive the ordeal of the Middle Passage. The historian Jon Butler called this shattering of African religious systems a "spiritual holocaust" in 1990. Most historians, however, argue that core features of West and Central African societies were reconstituted—often in new forms—in the Western Atlantic (see figure 7).[135]

Africans, like Europeans, found that the familiar context in which ideas about magic and witchcraft made sense changed across the Atlantic. In some places, Africans lived in such close proximity to Europeans and their

Figure 7.   A healer conjuring on behalf of a sick man in Suriname, a place where en-slaved Africans retained a closer connection to African culture and practices than they did on the North American mainland. Compare this depiction of healing with figure 4.

Source: "La Mama-Snekie," from Pierre Jacques Benoit, *Voyage à Suriname* (Bruxelles, 1839). Courtesy of the John Carter Brown Library at Brown University.

descendants that they ended up absorbing their beliefs, or understanding them sufficiently to echo them back to interrogators during trials. Such was the case in Salem, where a handful of enslaved people of African descent were accused of witchcraft and testified about their witch beliefs. An enslaved woman named Candy did just that, arguing that she was not a witch but that her white mistress was. The court did not indict her (see document 21). In other instances, African beliefs and European beliefs converged. When the ex-slave William Grimes, born in Virginia in 1784, recalled an encounter in 1811 with a witch in Savannah, he gave details of a hag attack—a nocturnal ordeal in which victims feel suffocated by a weight they believe to be a witch. He also suspected that the witch could change her shape. Hag attacks were an element of West-Central African witch beliefs, but these were also beliefs that people of European descent shared: Grace Sherwood's neighbors in Virginia made just such accusations in 1698 (see document 10).[136]

Elsewhere, however, there is suggestive evidence that some African witchcraft beliefs may have survived—altered in their expression, perhaps, by the challenging dynamics of living in slavery, and not as intact belief systems, but present nonetheless. Archaeological evidence points to the endurance of a range of beliefs about magical practices and powers. Objects with possible ritual significance, including glass beads, amulets, and cowrie shells, found in excavations of slave quarters, might have been charms used for magical purposes.[137] The anthropologist Jerome Handler examined an excavated grave in Barbados in one effort to discern the possible tenacity of West African ideas about witchcraft. A lone burial contained in a mound in a cemetery demonstrated anomalies with other burials. She was the only prone burial, for example; all others were supine. Dating from the late seventeenth or early eighteenth century, the burial occurred at a time when most enslaved workers on Barbados were African born and thus likely to adhere to African practices. The features of the burial, Handler argues, are inconsistent with other burials and in fact resemble mortuary practices used by West Africans (where most Barbados slaves came from in this period) to bury witches. Dangerous people were buried apart and sometimes covered with a mound. They were buried prone, like the excavated Barbados skeleton.[138]

Indeed, there is evidence that witch beliefs might even have *increased* in the Americas, which would be entirely consistent both with African notions that equated witches with greed and the abuse of power and with the new circumstances of violence and coercion in which enslaved Africans found themselves. In North America, for example, benevolent African deities receded in favor of the more frequent practice of sorcery. In this respect, we catch a glimpse of a slave's perception that he lived in a world of enhanced evil. The parallel with Native Americans, who found evil to have increased in their world, too, with the onslaught of deadly epidemics, is pronounced. The heightened importance of malevolent practices and powers can be seen in the shifting meanings of words in Gullah, a language that emerged in the eighteenth-century South Carolina lowcountry as Africans from different regions who spoke multiple languages created a common tongue. It was created out of several African languages. The Ewe word *fufu*, meaning "dust," survived in Gullah, but it acquired a more specific connotation of malevolence, transformed from benign dust into "a fine dust used with the intention of bewitching one or causing harm." A Mende word, *gafa*, meaning "spirit" or "soul," denoted an "evil spirit or devil" in Gullah.[139] These shifts in words reveal the many ways in which beliefs mingled in the American context. Africans did not have—in Africa—an idea of the Devil. Europeans certainly did, and the transformed Mende word *gafa* from "spirit" into "evil spirit"—or Devil—suggests the transformations that were underway as slaves absorbed aspects of Christian doctrine and confronted the horrors of enslavement.

Linguistic and archeological evidence, then, points us toward both the possible survival of African witchcraft beliefs in British America and some likely transformations. The extant colonial records are equally opaque, although it is possible that African witchcraft beliefs endured in the form of the crime of poisoning. This crime existed in abundance in British colonies, where slaveholders fretted regularly about the likelihood of being poisoned by their slaves. Like arson, poisoning did not require any special strength. It did, however, require proximity, and the enslaved workers who toiled and lived in closest proximity to masters—domestic slaves, including cooks, attendants, or butlers—had the best opportunity to kill their owners with poison. In Virginia between 1706 and 1784, 179 slaves were charged with poisoning, many with targeting masters or overseers. Of these, 66 percent were found guilty, and 30 percent of the guilty were executed. The same crime appeared in other slaveholding jurisdictions, from South Carolina to the West Indies, and slaves who were found guilty often endured terrible deaths, burned alive or hanged alive in cages to die slowly, punished so harshly because the English common law regarded poison of a master by a slave as petit treason.[140]

If poison in British America was petit treason, victims in other jurisdictions often understood it to be witchcraft. In Louisiana, colonial authorities revealed mixed feelings about what practices lay behind poisoning. Africans forcibly transported to colonial Louisiana were settled in large concentrations in the colony, many among people from the same ethnic group. This practice facilitated the preservation of many religious and ritual practices, including the creation of charms for poisoning enemies.[141] A case of poison in 1773, during the colony's Spanish period, included depositions that revealed the rituals that lay behind the poison. The accused slaves described a charm called a gris-gris, a word that derives from the Mande word *gerregerys*.[142] The gris-gris was concocted from the heart and gallbladder of a crocodile, and the plotters sought the ritual expertise of a slave who had been born in Africa. The court examined the charm and observed that it was made of a mixture of animal and vegetable substances, although experiments on a dog demonstrated that the contents were not lethal (which was good news both for the alleged poisoners and for the dog).[143] The colony's Superior Council assiduously prosecuted the crime of poisoning, but also wondered about the role of witchcraft, concluding in 1729 that although the council "does not admit the existence of sorcerers, it does punish poisoners, and perhaps it is poisons which do all the damage attributed to sorcery."[144]

But in British America, the crime of poisoning was stripped of its connection to religious or ritualistic practices. Sudden sickness or death might prompt a Brazilian planter to accuse a slave of witchcraft or a Louisiana judicial council to speculate about sorcery, but it led the typical British American slaveholder to press charges of poisoning. Intensified fears about increased poisoning led to new laws (see document 14), in the same way that concerns about witchcraft in England generated new and enhanced statutes (see document 6). In 1749, for example, white colonists in South Carolina grew increasingly agitated about what they regarded as a growing number of cases of poisoning. This concern manifested itself in a number of ways. On July 24 of that year, the *South Carolina Gazette* reprinted a letter about poison in the West Indies originally written for the Royal Society in London and read before that distinguished body in January 1742. Dr. Edward Milward's letter specifically concerned itself with poisons used by slaves and how to find antidotes for them.[145] On October 30, the *South Carolina Gazette* published a short notice decrying the frequent nature of the crime (see document 15). In the wake of these anxieties, the South Carolina assembly revised its existing statutes in 1651 to expand punishments for slaves (see document 14). Slaveholders, as Milward's letter suggests, also worried about the technical expertise required to make toxic potions (see documents 14, 15, and 16). For that reason, laws regulated slave doctors.

Is poison, however, witchcraft? It is hard to make the connection with confidence. There are, nonetheless, a number of interesting parallels that make it difficult to dismiss the issue out of hand. Consider the status of witchcraft as *crimen exceptum*—the exceptional crime for which the normal rules of procedure and evidence were altered to allow torture and testimony by people otherwise regarded as unreliable witnesses. In general, laws directed at slaves in North America followed the same trend—slaves were treated before courts in ways that were not tolerated for free subjects. Punishments for malefactors were draconian; slaves could be dismembered and murdered in especially grisly ways by courts of law. English malefactors suffered terrible torments for crimes such as treason or arson, but slaves *routinely* endured these barbaric ends.

Poison is a perfect case in point. Slaves believed to have poisoned whites were routinely burned alive (see document 15); only two people were burned alive in the colony of Massachusetts, for example, and one was an enslaved woman named Phyllis found guilty of poison. Convicted of petit treason, she was burned alive in 1755, while her coconspirator, a man, was hanged, not burned, in accordance with the gender distinctions in the English statutes for petit treason. His body was hanged in chains, and there his corpse remained for some twenty years.[146] Other poisoners were suspended alive in cages to die slowly, their organs shutting down while their bodies were pecked by impatient carrion. John Bartram, a naturalist who traveled through the southern colonies in the late colonial period, marveled at the power of the poison he believed slaves used, and he observed that only slaves knew the cure. No surprise, given his association of slaves with poison, that he also saw "two negroes Jibited alive for poisoning their Master" as he passed through the lowcountry in 1765.[147] In 1767, four decapitated heads of alleged poisoners, found guilty of conspiracy to poison their overseers, were displayed on the courthouse chimneys in Alexandria, Virginia. The *Pennsylvania Gazette* reported that other suspected poisoners were likely to suffer the same fate shortly.[148]

And poison resembles witchcraft in another way, beyond legal practices: that of perception and fear. In the same way that people feared witches and their actions yet could rarely prove the crime with witnesses and evidence, slave owners worried about being poisoned by their enslaved workers. It was easy to confuse sickness or food poisoning—not uncommon in an era with no reliable food preservation—with a criminal and deliberate act, just as people might worry that the deaths of their crops, livestock, or loved ones were signs of a witch's malfeasance. Poison was a crime of proximity and familiarity, just as witchcraft was, and accusations of poison likewise carried the weight of mistrust, animosity, fear, and sometimes even guilt. In this respect, poisoning scares resemble witch outbreaks: those occasions when multiple individuals were rounded up and targeted for prosecution. The four heads posted on the Alexandria courthouse chimneys echo the multiple bodies hanged in major witch outbreaks.

Yet it is difficult to make the link with certainty. Records about slave poisonings for the colonial period are most abundant for the eighteenth-century British colonies, by which time most colonists had rejected a belief in witchcraft. Moreover, British colonists did not have access to the ritual world that gave poisoning a religious meaning in Africa. Did slaves speak special words as they assembled toxic substances? Did they believe that poison only worked when transformed in certain rituals? The records are silent. All we have are criminal cases in courts, the occasional references to charms and the substances used to make them, reports from colonial newspapers, and scattered observations in the diaries and letters of travelers and colonial inhabitants.[149]

Poison, finally, does not appear to have been a sex-linked crime associated with women as witchcraft was in some places; while the English believed witches were likely to be women, poisoners turn out to have been men. Of 175 slaves accused of poisoning in Virginia through 1780 in twenty-two counties, 143 (82 percent) were men and 32 (18 percent) were women.[150] To be sure, enslaved men outnumbered enslaved women in eighteenth-century Virginia, but by 1775 the sex ratio approached parity.[151] Where witchcraft was an extraordinary crime, poisoning was frequent, with stealing the only crime more frequently punished in Virginia.[152] And the English already had laws against the crime of poisoning, and these seem to have been easily adapted to the new circumstances of slavery. Documents 13–16 invite readers to come to their own conclusions about how well the crime of poisoning fits with the crime of witchcraft. When was poison witchcraft, when was it just poison, when was it a fantasy of frightened slaveholders, and will we ever know for sure?

If African witchcraft practices did not appear in colonial (and later U.S.) courtrooms, in contrast to the witch beliefs and practices of English migrants, there is ample evidence that magical practices intended both to punish and to protect endured. The parallel with German witchcraft practices in the form of powwow is pronounced; in each case magical practices survived as part of folkloric beliefs and coexisted with other religious beliefs and practices. Hoodoo might be considered the African American variant of powwow; it contains a variety of ritual practices derived from African religious systems, but it was also divorced from those contexts and was generally not inconsistent with beliefs in Christianity. Hoodoo centers on specific procedures intended to alter one's immediate circumstances, by removing a burden or grievance or punishing an enemy. (Voodoo, in contrast, is a full religious system, complete with deities and rituals, and fused together from different African religious practices.[153]) The hoodoo specialist known as the conjurer, for example, created charms and amulets that resembled the minkisi bags of Kongo or the gris-gris of the Louisiana poisoning case. The conjurer (also called a root doctor) drew on knowledge of plant medicines, combined with sacred rituals to give these medicines power; to heal the sick; to resolve conflicts; to punish malefactors, enemies, or rivals; and to appease spirits.[154] One substance that was essential for amulets was "goofer dust," or dirt gathered from a grave. The word derives from the kiKongo word, *kufwa*, which means "dead person." Its use conveyed a belief—shared in Kongo and the U.S. South—that the spirits of the dead continued to dwell in the land of the living, and that conjure could link the two.[155] Conjurers survived through the nineteenth century, and white observers in the nineteenth-century U.S. South thought they were so prevalent that each plantation had someone with such expertise.[156] Belief in conjuring eroded over the course of the nineteenth century among African Americans.[157]

Outbreaks: Putting Salem in Context

North America experienced very few massive witch hunts, unlike Europe, where major outbreaks were all too common. Instead, witch beliefs wove themselves into the fabric of daily life, infrequently manifesting themselves in colonial legal systems as formal accusations and, more infrequently still, trials and executions. Occasionally, however, there were outbreaks, episodes when numerous people were accused of witchcraft and several executed. Some were small-scale events, like the scare at Hartford, Connecticut (1662–1663), in which 13 people were accused and 4 were hanged. Others were larger; in New Mexico in 1675, authorities accused 47 Indians of witchcraft and hanged 3; the outbreak at Salem in 1692 ended with 19 people executed and some 162 accused; at Abiquiu, New Mexico (1756–1763), 176 people were accused and none executed (although 5 died in prison). In comparison to major witch hunts in Europe, such as that in Scotland in 1661–1662, when 664 people were named, or two in Würzburg and Bamberg in the Holy Roman Empire between 1616 and 1630, when 2,100 people were executed, the North American outbreaks were modest affairs, although surely participants did not feel that way about them.[158] Three North American outbreaks are represented in documents 18–29.

Historians seeking to explain witchcraft outbreaks tend to look at local circumstances—unrest, war, violence, drought, famine, epidemics, instability, the absence of secular authorities, or the presence of a charismatic minister or priest. In a colonial setting, many of these features were *endemic* to colonial life. Colonies were by definition distant from central authority. They were often established in perilous places where mortality rates could be high, wars were frequent occurrences, and people lived among those unlike themselves—either people of the same nation who might be from different regions with different habits and manners or people from different parts of the world with vastly different customs. Colonies were defined by the complex hierarchies of race and power within them and by the exploitation of people and of natural resources that justified their existence. Enslaved Africans lived involuntarily in European settlements, as did Indian laborers. These were worlds characterized by violence, by racial, ethnic, national, and religious differences, by conflict and tension, and by tenuously replicated church, family, and state structures.

The best-known North American outbreak is without doubt the witch hunt in Salem, Massachusetts, in 1692. Compared to the large witch hunts in continental Europe, or even in England and Scotland, the outbreak at Salem was relatively small. Unlike other big outbreaks, it did not spark a chain reaction beyond the immediate area, spreading fear of witches from town to town. And yet this small outbreak has attracted the attention of scores of historians. Writers struggled to interpret the event even as it was winding down. It has entered U.S. culture, making a "witch hunt" a metaphor whose meaning we all think we know, and thanks to Arthur Miller's play *The Crucible* (1953), which used the events at Salem as an analogy for the persecutions of the McCarthy years, it has stood in for political investigations and, in the modern day, sexual abuse scandals.

Salem Town was, in the seventeenth century, a major commercial center, oriented toward the sea whose shores it hugged and toward the commercial opportunities afforded by trade relations with other parts of the English Atlantic world—the West Indies, Newfoundland, and Europe. The town's hinterlands stretched for miles, and there farmers wrestled and heaved rocks out of the soil to plant grains and raise livestock. Unincorporated villages existed within the legal borders of Salem Town: one such community was Salem Village, the modern town of Danvers. In the winter months of 1692, when night fell early, bringing with it the raw chill of darkness and cheating New Englanders of precious daylight hours, the daughter and the niece of Salem Village's minister, Samuel Parris, started behaving oddly. They spoke out of turn; they crawled about under furniture. Soon joined by other children and teenagers, the group came to comprise the coterie of possessed accusers who have made Salem a place of such fascination to contemporaries and to historians. Before the afflicted were identified as possessed, their parents consulted medical experts. With no natural cure or diagnosis, the Reverend Parris concluded that the girls had been bewitched. When pressed to name names, the girls obliged. Accusers identified 162 witches, and many of these people were interrogated and tried: some were executed, some exonerated, some died in prison, and others languished in jail until the summer of 1693. The executions commenced on June 10, 1692, and continued until the final busy day over three months later on September 22, when eight people hanged on Gallows Hill in a mass execution characteristic of outbreaks (see figure 8).

Participants were themselves among the first to try to make sense of the outbreak. Since then historians have taken their turn. In recent decades, scholars have focused on a number of important attributes of New England culture in general and Salem in particular in order to understand why Salem, of all English settlements in North America, experienced such a painful episode. These explanations center on a variety of features: religious transformations, economic and social tensions, and the challenges of frontier settlement. One of the most powerful and enduring interpretations appeared in 1974, with Paul Boyer and Stephen Nissenbaum's *Salem Possessed: The Social Origins of Witchcraft*.[159] Boyer and Nissenbaum sought to understand the Salem outbreak in terms of the social and economic transformations of the period. They provided a detailed study of the community of Salem—a close

Figure 8.   A mass hanging during an outbreak in Newcastle, England, 1650. The figure labeled "D" on the far right is a Scottish witch-hunter, hired to come to Newcastle to detect witches. Compare this depiction with that of Matthew Hopkins, the witch-hunter illustrated in figure 1. Figure 8 also offers some interesting comparisons with the portrayal of witches in figures 1–3. What might account for these different interpretations of witches and witch-hunters?

Source: Ralph Gardiner, *Englands Grievance Discovered* (London, 1655). By Permission of the Folger Shakespeare Library.

analysis of residential patterns, wills, land ownership, incomes, occupations, family relationships, and religious participation. Boyer and Nissenbaum wrote in the era of the community study, when historians turned to towns to uncover the fabric of human relations and the totality of human experience in intimate geographic spaces. Boyer and Nissenbaum found, for example, that those who were targets of accusations during the outbreak were people who had benefited from an expanding commercial culture. As Salem Town became ever more enmeshed in commercial networks and opportunities beyond the region, Salem Village languished, becoming a rural backwater. It was the villagers who were most likely to launch accusations of witchcraft. They saw themselves as preservers of older traditions, as opponents of the capitalism that was emerging in the town.

Boyer and Nissenbaum's close study of the town highlights the larger processes of transformation underway in New England as a whole, as many inhabitants of riverine and coastal communities (such as Springfield or Boston) benefited from commercial opportunities far from home.[160]

They broadcast their new prosperity in larger homes filled with imported household goods. Others, like the people of Salem Village, engaged in subsistence farming and were relatively removed from the market economy. These economic practices, historians suggest, accompanied different worldviews, with the farmers connected to past habits and values that prized the community and the market-oriented Salemites looking toward a different kind of future, one which tolerated and even accepted individual ambition. These ingredients, in and of themselves, would tell us little, because these features characterized transitions within New England as a whole, albeit especially pronounced in commercial centers. But Salem endured some particular challenges, most notably because of the town's geographic location and legal status but also because of the incendiary mix of personalities who found their way to the region and who gave voice to the conflicts that had begun to constrain and shape daily interactions.

Certain people and temperaments come clearly into view in Salem. Samuel Parris was one such figure. As Salem Village's minister, he was a critical component of the outbreak's existence. His father, Thomas, had first made and then lost his fortune in Barbados. The family cycle repeated itself with Samuel. Thomas Parris managed to fund Samuel's education at Harvard, the only college in the English colonies at the time and the only place to train for the ministry. In 1670 Samuel journeyed to Massachusetts, where he lasted three years in Cambridge, training for the ministry, before returning to Barbados in the wake of his father's death, his education incomplete. Back in Barbados, Parris tried to establish himself as a merchant in Bridgetown. After a few years, however, he decided to move on, and gathering up his human property—the two slaves, Tituba and John Indian, whom he had probably purchased in Barbados in the 1670s—he sailed to Boston.[161] Samuel's career as a trader unfortunately replicated the trials of his father. He had to fend off suits for unpaid bills, but he managed to achieve some modest success. In the process he found a wife, Elizabeth, with whom he had first a son, John, and then two daughters, Elizabeth and Susannah. His commercial success, however, was neither reliable nor sufficient to support his family, and so Parris decided in the mid-1680s to pursue a new career in the ministry. Without a Harvard degree, Parris was out of the running for New England's more prestigious positions, but he found a job, first at Stow, then in Salem Village.[162] His frustration with the unfulfilled conditions of his employment at Salem Village—he wrangled over his salary and other benefits of his position—contributed to the animosities of the community, and his daughter and niece confirmed his fears and suspicions when they identified witches not only in the village, but even in their own house: the slave Tituba.

If Parris might help us understand how a fractured community gave voice to its anger through witch accusations, the pattern of the trials—why Salem became an outbreak—is harder to understand. For two historians, two individuals—and thus two different turning points, and indeed two different political, social, and racial contexts—offer crucial ways to understand the episode. One such figure was Parris's slave, Tituba. She was probably an Indian from South America, a slave on Barbados, and Parris's human property.[163] When Parris transported her to New England, she joined a society where both Indians and Africans were enslaved. Tituba was one of the first three people accused of witchcraft, and unlike the other two, she confessed. Her confession, then, in contrast to the denials of her fellow victims, Sarah Good and Sarah Osborne (see document 19), persuaded her interrogators—and the inhabitants of Salem Village—that there were indeed witches among them.

After an initial rejection of the charge, Tituba explained that the Devil appeared to her in the form of a man, a hog, a dog, and two rats. The dog threatened to hurt her if she would not serve him, and he tempted her with "pretty things." Although the Devil ordered Tituba to kill the children, she did not. At night, Tituba rode on a stick to the witches' meeting place. She named Sarah Good and Sarah Osborne as witches. She spied Good with her animal familiar, she claimed, and saw Osborne with a two-legged winged monster that turned into her. As she provided more information, Tituba drew her interrogators in with shocking details; she recognized one of the witches she saw clad in silk as someone she had seen before in Boston. In her confessions on March 1 and 2, 1692, Tituba encouraged the fears of the justices who sought witches; she assured them that there were indeed witches—many of them. She linked these witches, moreover, to luxury and to New England's largest commercial center, Boston. The historian Elaine G. Breslaw argues that Tituba's confession gave life to the witch hunt in its earliest days.[164]

Mary Beth Norton also identifies a crucial turning point, and a crucial participant, but she places the emphasis elsewhere.[165] In Norton's careful chronological analysis of what happened at Salem, April 19 emerges as an important date. On that day, Abigail Hobbs confessed. She was a teenager who lived in Topsfield, Massachusetts. Notable for her flippant attitude toward Satan, she had made herself the subject of gossip. Her reckless jokes—that, for example, she was not afraid of anything because she had made a pact with the Devil—reveal the different belief systems at work in late seventeenth-century New England. Hobbs was comfortable joking about a pact with Satan while others in her world had such concrete ideas about Satan that they accused their neighbors of heinous crimes and punished them with death. But Hobbs paid dearly for her professed attachment to the Devil, and on April 13, Ann Putnam accused Hobbs's specter (an apparition that took human form) of tormenting her. Hobbs's specter then turned on other possessed accusers, and within a week, Hobbs faced her accusers in court.[166]

After Tituba's, Hobbs's was the second major confession of the trials. Tituba had legitimized the hunt, but now Hobbs set it in a new direction. In her confession, Hobbs made explicit what had been thus far unexplored in the trials. She explained where she met the Devil, and what he looked like. He was a black man, and she had first encountered him in the woods four years earlier, when she lived in Falmouth on the Maine frontier. Hobbs linked the frontier wars that beset New England to the witchcraft outbreak in Salem. The region's first major conflict between Europeans and Native Americans was King Philip's War, also known as Metacom's War, a conflict that was devastating to all of New England's inhabitants. It began in 1675 and endured in northern New England until 1678, when a treaty was signed at Casco (Maine). After only ten years of an uncertain peace, war broke out again in the northeastern frontier, erupting in Maine in August 1688. French-allied raiders swooped into western Massachusetts, too, and colonists found themselves sandwiched between different fronts of the conflict known among English colonists as King William's War (1689–1697). Settlements in Maine, New Hampshire, and northeastern Massachusetts were special targets of attack.

In the wake of Hobbs's confession, the number of witchcraft accusations soared, and the geographic residence and demographic characteristics of the accused shifted. Previously, accused witches came from the area around Salem, but after Hobbs's confession, the accused lived in Maine, in Boston, and beyond. Many of the newly accused were men, both wealthy and prominent, and most were never tried. Their accusers linked them to the Indian wars. Some were men who were implicated in the failures of the wars. Others were leading merchants who had profited from the Indian trade. To those who suffered most in the wars, losing homes, parents, and future plans in the wake of attacks, all of these men were culpable for the vulnerability of colonists living in fragile frontier communities.[167]

Norton was hardly the first historian to make a connection to the Indian wars. Karlsen's careful study of the group of possessed accusers at Salem had alerted historians to the centrality of these frontier wars in explaining what happened in 1692; she was joined by scholars including James E. Kences, Richard Godbeer, and Peter Charles Hoffer, all of whom focused attention on the intersections between frontier conflicts and the tumult in Salem Village.[168] But Norton cast a wider net still, and by attending to the population of those accused of witchcraft whose accusations were not pursued, she was able to sketch a richer understanding of how these frontier wars shaped the outbreak at Salem.[169]

Thus we already find ourselves with two lines of interpretation, with two key players, one Indian slave and one English colonist, both women who occupied vulnerable positions in New England society but who might have been unlikely to appreciate this shared connection. And there are any number of key figures who emerge when we examine Salem in detail. For example, there is Samuel Parris, the village minister, vexed with the remuneration of his employment, perhaps frustrated by personal and professional failures that had prompted him to leave Barbados for Massachusetts; and then there are the Putnam family members of Salem Village, who seem to have found in witch beliefs one way to express their hostility both toward a changing world and toward the people they identified as its transformers and beneficiaries. Without any one of these personalities, would the situation have unfolded differently? That question, indeed, is just what Norton and Breslaw try to get their readers to appreciate: the single transforming moment of one person, one confession, or one accusation. The Salem outbreak provides a good example of contingency—the coincidental convergence of people and events that together produce unanticipated outcomes.

The vast literature on the witchcraft outbreak in Salem offers an ideal opportunity both to use the events there as a way to think about the historiography of witchcraft (how, that is, historians have analyzed the event) and also as a way to assess how Salem fits within a larger context of North American witchcraft. No episode of witchcraft has attracted as much attention among historians of North American witchcraft as Salem. The events there have become the benchmark by which other outbreaks are measured. Thus we have the "other" witch hunts in New England (in Hartford or Stamford), or the Abiquiu hunt, compared by its historians to Salem.[170] Historians of Salem emphasize the exceptional nature of the outbreak there, but when we step back, Salem starts to look a lot like other instances of witchcraft in North America, at least in respect to those features scholars of New England have privileged: its late date, its size, the frequency of confession, and the role of possession.

Take, for example, chronology. In the context of witch beliefs in New England and the British Isles, Salem seems to have been a final sputter in a period in which "mass scares and even isolated accusations were becoming a thing of the past."[171] It is, in fact, one reason why such unusual explanations as ergot poisoning (see below) find their niche; some scholars believe ergotism can explain the late date, the "strange" timing, of the Salem outbreak, as Mary K. Matossian puts it.[172] Why then, and not earlier? Why there, and not elsewhere?

But in terms of witch outbreaks on the North American continent as a whole, Salem falls quite early in the history. New Mexico experienced a major outbreak in Abiquiu in 1756–1763, some seventy years after the events at Salem. Witch hunts were an important part of Native American revitalization efforts in the early nineteenth century, when the number of witches killed certainly surpassed the numbers for Salem, although an exact count is impossible to come by. So from a North American perspective, the chronology of Salem does not look too peculiar. Nor, indeed, does the size of the outbreak. It was outnumbered by the outbreak at Abiquiu, in which 176 people were accused.[173] Unlike Salem, where the majority of those accused were colonists of English descent and mostly women, the composition of the accused at Abiquiu was varied, and reflects the different nature of witch beliefs and their expression in colonial New Mexico. Of those 176, 67 were of European descent (and of these 31 were women and 36 were men); of the 109 accused Indians, 40 were women and 69 were men.[174]

Confession

So if Salem's chronology is in fact not distinctive, and its size is in line with other major outbreaks, what else might turn out to be a shared feature? One of the characteristics that has seemed, at first glance, to be unique to Salem was the propensity of the accused to confess. Certainly, in the context of witchcraft trials within New England, confession was a remarkable feature of the Salem outbreak, before which only four confessions had taken place. At Salem, some fifty people confessed, and most were women (see documents 19, 21, 23, 24).[175]

Why did women confess? After all, if the confession were not true, then a woman committed the grave sin of lying—and the crime of doing so in court. And yet, especially at Salem, women did confess. The historian Elizabeth Reis argues that women in the strict Puritan religious culture of seventeenth-century New England were likely to think about even the most ordinary sins—envious thoughts, greed, or discontent—as renunciations of God, and thus as an unspoken, implicit, pact with the Devil. Women spoke and thought about their sins—and their sinful nature, which any devout Puritan accepted as an inherent feature—differently from men. In conversion narratives, for example, in which men and women explained why they deserved church membership, women recalled their despicable and sinful nature, while men explored specific peccadilloes—whether gambling or drinking.

Reis proposes that these different ways in which men and women thought about their conduct suggests that men believed their sins could be cast aside, while women thought of their sins as internal to their nature. These beliefs played themselves out in confessions to witchcraft. If, that is, women believed that they were almost by nature sinful, then they could be persuaded by the accumulated testimony of their neighbors that they had, perhaps, made a pact with the Devil. Perhaps their sinful thoughts, their envy, their anger, had turned them into Satan's allies. Perhaps they *were* witches.[176]

It was not enough, however, to confess; judges had to be prepared to accept confessions, and here gender roles and Puritan theology played a role. Justices in New England believed these confessions, in part because the exemplary Puritan woman was one who made a confession, who showed a contrite nature and accepted responsibilities for her deviant and sinful ways. By confessing, she modeled redemption for the whole community. Moreover, who was not tainted by sin? This certainty snared Rebecca Nurse at Salem. She denied being a witch and denied having signed a pact with the Devil. But like everyone else, she believed in witches, and she knew that something was terribly wrong with the possessed victims who writhed in court, fighting off pinches and pricks and stabbing pains and struggling to control their speech. And when Nurse, a church member and prominent resident of Salem Village for decades, wondered how she ended up in the terrible plight of being accused of being a witch, she queried "what sine hath god found out in me unrepented of" that she should be so singled out?[177] Indeed, what sin? The magistrates agreed—even if they doubted her satanic pact. She was hanged on July 19 with four other women.

But even the singularity of confession among Puritan women at Salem falls by the wayside in a North American context. Indeed, the very concept of "confession" loses its salience, since it suggests that someone is aware of committing a transgression. Not all practitioners saw their conduct as a source of sin or shame or wrongdoing. As the "sorcerer" Tonneraouanont reportedly announced, "I am a Demon" (see document 2).[178]

Confession was also affected by different legal processes. The presence of torture surely encouraged confessions. Tedapachsit, tortured with fire by the White River Delawares in 1806, admitted that "he had lied from fear" (see document 29). Another man readily confessed to flying to Kentucky with the aid of his grandmother's medicine bundle; although not tortured himself, the recent torture and execution of his grandmother surely encouraged his quick confession.[179] In jurisdictions governed by the Spanish, official understanding of a gradation of magical activity—with virtually none meriting severe punishment—opened the door for frequent confessions, since confession would not mean execution. El Cojo, the most prominent sorcerer in the Abiquiu outbreak, confessed to his witchcraft, although he had an incentive to do so since he was confined to the stocks at the time.[180]

Confession could be a careful strategy, not only to avoid torture, but also to achieve some other goal. Such seems to have been the case for a slave named Juan de Morga, who lived near Mexico City with a vicious owner and who wrote a letter to a church official in 1650 professing that he had made a pact with the Devil. Were the church not to act, he explained, he would renounce his faith altogether. Morga's letter compelled the Inquisition to intervene and investigate his harsh living conditions, and ultimately to sell him to a different master.[181] Not confessing could also be a prudent strategy. In Sweden, for example, executions for the crime of witchcraft were extremely rare until the 1650s, for two main reasons; maleficia had to be proved, and the guilty party was required to reject God openly. Swedish law, moreover, had one unusual feature; the condemned were taken to the place of execution and urged to confess. Those who did were immediately executed; those who refused returned to prison to live another day. This legal principle, although it was supposed to be a closely guarded secret, became general knowledge and emerged during the big Swedish witch hunts in the 1670s as a crucial survival strategy.[182]

While the motivations for these varied confessions (or refusals to confess) surely differed from the particular context of confessions in seventeenth-century New England, they nonetheless remind us that people were not in fact averse to admitting to witchcraft for a wide variety of reasons. The confessions at Salem were products of a particular legal and religious culture, just as was true for confessions elsewhere.

Possession

No group has attracted more attention from historians and especially from the general public than the possessed accusers at Salem, those young women whose physical gyrations and shrieks and torments and visions propelled the witch hunt.[183] The Salem outbreak was remarkable in that the witch hunt's most important accusers were women and teenage girls and even children, people without autonomous legal identities under English law. In New England as a whole there were sixty-seven possessed accusers between 1620 and 1675, and of those, fifty-nine (86 percent) were female. In this respect, possessed accusers differed markedly from nonpossessed accusers, who included both men and women. They differed in another important characteristic as well; nonpossessed accusers tended to know the people they accused, while possessed accusers generally did not (see document 20). Possessed males, moreover, did not figure during witch trials in any significant way. Possessed women were also distinctive in their age concentration: they fell for the most part between the ages of sixteen and twenty-five. Possessed accusers, then, represent a distinctive segment of the population.[184]

The possessed women at Salem fit this general profile. Salem featured twenty-four possessed accusers who were over the age of sixteen (not including, for example, Parris's daughter and niece and one other young accuser). Of these twenty-four, extant evidence survives about the families for twenty-one, and of these, seventeen had lost one or both parents. This pattern was unusual for the place and the time and set these women apart both from other accusers and from their peers. Moreover, these women had lost their parents in a very particular set of circumstances, one unique to their residence in a colonial settlement. Most of the parental deaths transpired during New England's Indian wars. Without their parents, and with family property mostly destroyed during the same attacks that killed parents, these young women had moved south, away from the frontier, to Salem, Andover, and other towns to stay with relatives or family friends who took them in. But their futures, like their pasts, lay in shambles, as prospects for marriage were tied to family fortune and to the dowries in livestock, household goods, or real property that loving and attentive parents tried to provide.

Scholars in many fields have struggled to explain the Salem possessions. Scientific approaches seek medical causes of the behaviors that manifested themselves as possession. A biologist named Linnda R. Caporael argued in 1976 that the symptoms of possession derived from ergot poisoning.[185] Ergot is a fungus (Claviceps purpurea) that grows on certain cereal grains. One such grain is rye, which the people of Salem cultivated and used to make bread. Ergot flourishes in damp conditions, and such conditions were in place in Salem in the spring and summer of 1691. Caporael suggested that the rye harvested in the fall and then baked—with its ergot fungus—into bread produced the convulsions that match the clinical symptoms of ergot poisoning. In 1982, Mary K. Matossian refined aspects of Caporael's argument, suggesting that it was a cold winter, followed by a cool growing season, which enables ergot to flourish.[186] Like Caporael, she found historical explanations insufficient. Ergot poisoning induces a variety of symptoms. In their mild form, a sufferer might endure giddiness, feelings of pressure in the head, nausea, and pains in the limbs. More severe cases produce acutely uncomfortable sensations: that ants are crawling underneath one's skin (a condition called formication), twitches, and spasms of the tongue and facial muscles. The most acute cases might leave sufferers prostrate as if dead for up to eight hours, and they can experience numbness, delirium, and loss of speech.[187] In the very worst cases, patients die. All of these symptoms sound a lot like the sufferings that were endured by the possessed accusers at Salem. But other medical causes might explain these symptoms. In 1999, Laurie Winn Carlson argued that Salem suffered from an encephalitis lethargica epidemic. Also known as sleeping sickness, encephalitis lethargica attacks the brain, making patients lethargic and, in acute cases, putting them in comas.[188]

Ergot poisoning—and indeed any scientific or medical explanation of possession and witch beliefs—is very appealing to twenty-first-century readers. It is difficult to read descriptions of people who suffered the terrible physical afflictions of possession and not reach for the array of medical and psychological diagnoses that we have at our fingertips. It is easy to see the gratifying appeal of such explanations—indeed, the relief they engender—as, finally, we find a material explanation for inexplicable behaviors.

Yet the ergot theory, like other medical interpretations, falls short from a historical perspective. Scientific explanations might well offer tantalizing suggestions about medical conditions (such as epilepsy or neurological disorders) that produced the physical symptoms of possession, but they do not help us understand the content of the possessed victims' visions or why those around them concluded that sufferers were possessed. While Matossian argued that ergot affected primarily adolescents and children, and thus could explain the possession of Salem's teenage girls, we are still left wondering why only the girls of some Salem families (notably ardent witch-hunting clans) demonstrated such behavior, why no Salem boys seem to have been afflicted, and why everyone surrounding the possessed, after first pursuing and then dismissing medical explanations, explained their symptoms as signs of possession. Why, that is, was possession in this era the special plight of adolescents and young adults, and specifically of women and girls?

Modern psychology might offer some answers to this question, however dangerous such a tool is in the hands of historians who have neither the necessary professional and medical training nor access to the people whom they seek to examine as subjects. Sigmund Freud himself took a crack at understanding possession in 1923, when he published a paper about a seventeenth-century case from Germany involving a painter, Christoph Haizmann, who signed a pact with the Devil when he was despondent about his art. Freud presented the tale as a case history. In Freud's hands, the case was one of neurosis: the subject's bond with the Devil was a "neurotic phantasy," one in which the Devil substituted for the painter's father. The painter's pact for nine years signaled, Freud argued, Haizmann's fantasy to bear his father a child.[189]

Also drawing on the social and behavioral sciences, the historian Peter Charles Hoffer analyzes the behavior of the possessed accusers at Salem in light of what modern sociologists understand about adolescence and about gangs. Hoffer suggests that the group's naming of witches derived not only from a desire to gain attention, but also from a need to keep the group itself intact—the group functioned cohesively, depicting possession in collective rituals of shrieking, twitching, writhing, and moaning.[190] Hoffer also raises the possibility that some of the possessed might have suffered from abuse— not just physical abuse, which was probably not uncommon in Salem in this period, but sexual abuse.

Sexual abuse of children is virtually impossible to find in the court records of the period, although certainly, as in many societies, it existed wherever a predatory and powerful adult found a vulnerable child. Hoffer suggests that one way to read Mercy Lewis's accusation against the minister George Burroughs is in light of this possibility. Lewis was an orphan whose parents had been murdered by Indians in 1689. The Burroughs family took her in when she was fourteen, although she soon ended up in the household of the witch-hunting Putnams. When Lewis launched accusations of witchcraft, she named George Burroughs. His specter had appeared to her, tempting her, trying to trick her to sign the Devil's book, a "fashion book" as she called it. When Burroughs (or his specter) returned two days later, she explained, he "carried me up to an exceeding high mountain and showed me all the kingdoms of the earth and tould me that he would give them all to me if I would writ in his book." This testimony, Hoffer suggests, was unlike that presented by all other witnesses, none of whom intimated that an apparition had transported them to a mountaintop. Although the debt to Matthew 4:8 is clear (the text reads "Again, the devil taketh him up into an exceeding high mountain, and sheweth him all the kingdoms of the world, and the glory of them"), Hoffer argues that Lewis selected this metaphor of the mountaintop, rather than other images commonly circulating about apparitions and what they did, because it had special resonance for her. Did Burroughs make sexual advances to her? Did she refuse? In her testimony, Lewis recalled that Burroughs (or his apparition) threatened her, telling her he would "brake my neck" if she did not sign the book.[191]

The challenge with such psychological interpretations and with the use of modern theories of child development is that while the biological processes that adolescents experienced might be common across cultures, the interpretation of this behavior, of course, varies dramatically, as indeed do the socialization goals that parents and community leaders have for children and young people. New England children in religious families, for example, lived in a world with little privacy, one in which conformity to community norms and obedience to parental and adult authority were prized. Historians are not even sure exactly how parents viewed their children. Debates raged in earlier decades about whether parents loved newborns, given the likelihood of early childhood mortality. Did people view childhood as a separate stage from adulthood? The clothing children wore sends a mixed message, since after the age of six children wore diminutive versions of adult garb and were expected to play an active and helpful role in household economies.[192] But the anguished comments by parents who lost their children attest to the deep affection they harbored for their young. It was just that despair that brought parents into court, accusing their neighbors of bewitching and killing their children (see document 8).

Possession was not unique to Salem. Indeed, by the time of the Salem outbreak, the symptoms of possession had become common across Europe, where by the late sixteenth and early seventeenth centuries it became a "new plague."[193] People who demonstrated a particular set of behaviors were understood by those around them to be possessed. Possessed people spoke out of turn. They profaned the Sabbath, they mocked religious rituals, they could not hear the commands of their elders, they jerked in spasms, they vomited, they lay as if dead. Some possessed people had uncommon knowledge— generally understanding and sometimes speaking languages that they had never learned, knowing how to find lost items, or guessing the contents of a wallet or box. They had unnatural strength.

These were exactly the symptoms shown by the afflicted in North America, at Salem and beyond. When Elizabeth Knapp started to show symptoms of possession in Groton, Massachusetts, in 1671–1672, she acted unnaturally (see document 17). She shrieked and laughed. She made inappropriate utterances. She confessed to improper feelings—an impulse to murder a child, the desire for money and luxurious garments. She alternated between trances and convulsions. She was one of several young people who were possessed in New England during the last quarter of the century. She was followed by the four Goodwin children in Boston in 1688 and Margaret Rule, also in Boston, in 1693. The possessed frequently fell into trances and experienced heaviness in their limbs. These were behaviors that were easily recognized by contemporaries as possession. There may well have been clinical conditions that affected some possessed people, but to their contemporaries, their behavior conformed to cultural expectations for possession, especially when the behaviors were exhibited by young people, and even more by young women, and so that is what contemporaries believed to be at stake.

During their affliction, the possessed challenged people in authority. They insulted ministers: Knapp called Willard a "blacke roague," and in Abiquiu

Francisca Barela called Fray Toledo a "kid goat mulatto" (see documents 17 and 18). Devils spoke through the possessed and argued with clergy. Their performance, Karlsen suggests, was a power struggle in which the possessed asserted female independence, striking out from their discontent and anger, and the clergy struggled to reinforce gender and religious roles.[194] The possessed shrieked invectives and insulted the learned; their contorted limbs and convulsing bodies occupied spaces that the meek and submissive would not claim. Indeed, the case of Elizabeth Knapp offers ample evidence of this discontent, and her ability to command the attention of a minister and other powerful neighbors, especially when Satan spoke through her, suggests the role reversal possession might afford (see document 17).

The possessed even had power over life and death. In the trials at Salem, the possessed erupted at crucial moments. During the trial of Sarah Good, the justice asked the possessed if Sarah Good hurt them, "and so they all did looke upon her and said this was one of the persons that did torment them," and soon they were all writhing in a fit (see document 19). Abigail Faulkner's shift from denying her guilt to confessing to witchcraft may have been affected by the conduct of the possessed (see document 24). Ann Putnam's contrition for causing the death of her neighbors with her accusations in 1692 produced a pained admission of responsibility fourteen years later (see document 26).

But if possession might reveal reversals of power, letting us see Indian women insult and slap a priest, or a Puritan teenager roar at her pastor, possession might also have enabled the possessed to find an opportunity for religious expression that was otherwise denied them.[195] There were limited spheres of religious expression for young women, especially Protestants. In Europe, some ardent Catholics sealed themselves up next to churches as anchoresses, dependent on the community for their maintenance. Catholic women with dowries in New France and New Spain could enter convents. But the possessed, too, could find a niche. In this respect, possession was closely linked to expressions of religious zeal, and indeed the symptoms, especially the bodily afflictions and mortifications, are strikingly similar.

Because evangelical enterprise was so important to French and Spanish colonization efforts in North America, priests targeted indigenous people with ardor, exhorting them to convert to Catholicism. Religious fervor among new converts sometimes manifested itself in excesses that looked like possession. Catholic priests in the Americas were often impressed—and sometimes overwhelmed—by the rituals that new converts embraced. These rituals might be a consequence of converts trying to demonstrate their commitment to a new faith, but they also corresponded in parts of the Americas with indigenous practices. Take, for example, the story of Catherine Tekakwitha (1656?–1680), a Mohawk woman who converted to Christianity and moved to the Jesuit mission at Kahnawake in 1677. Like other women converts in New France, Tekakwitha distinguished herself with her ascetic self-denial and her punitive bodily mortifications. These women engaged in self-flagellation. Having heard of the hair shirts and iron girdles (a belt with sharp points to scour the wearer's skin) sometimes donned by the devout, they emulated the practice. One woman stood naked and exposed during a snowstorm as penance, she explained, for her sins. Others broke the ice to immerse themselves in the heart-stopping cold waters, submerging themselves until they had completed the rosary. Some burned themselves, deliberately grasping hot coals or placing them on their bodies. Tekakwitha excelled at such discipline, enduring 1,000–1,200 blows of a switch from an equally devout companion in a single session of flagellation, and participating in such occasions several times a week for a period of almost eighteen months. She walked barefoot through the snow. She fasted twice a week, and when friends begged her to eat, she denied herself the pleasant taste such nutrition might bring by mixing ashes with her food. One day she burned her body up to her knees with brands from a fire. When a friend and sister penitent proposed leaving a coal between her toes—a familiar torture for Iroquois war captives—for as long as it took to recite an Ave Maria, Tekakwitha was inspired by the challenge and did just that. The Jesuits at the mission worried about what they regarded as excessive rituals; they were both impressed by the women's actions and troubled that they went too far. While the bodily mortifications of these converts were embedded in Iroquois practices, including the ability to withstand pain and the use of pain in sacred quests, and were connected to common practices among European Christian ascetics, they also echo the physical assaults endured by those who experienced possession.[196]

Religious zeal is a critical component of outbreaks of possession, which is most often found among people in highly religious societies. Collective possession in North America, like that at Salem, emerged when this religious zeal (at Salem, embodied in the catalyzing figure of Samuel Parris) combined with other challenges to survival—with assaults on colonial communities being one crucial ingredient. Such was the case in Salem, and seems also to have been true in two other mass possessions in New Spain, in Abiquiu and Querétaro.

Abiquiu, first explored by the Spanish in the 1720s, was formally established in 1754 as a buffer between the aggressive and predatory nomadic tribes and the settled villages.[197] It was a community born in violence. The Indians who lived there, called *genízaros*, were a mixture of plains Indians, Pueblos, and Hopis. They practiced a variety of religious beliefs, both Christian and indigenous. Many had spent their lives as servants in Spanish households, and indeed the name *genizaro* connoted a status as a slave or captive. The presence of genizaros points to one of the important features of New Mexico society in these decades: renewed conflict with the independent tribes who surrounded the Spanish-claimed territory. Genizaros often had special roles in the frontier defense of New Mexico, and were a critical force in the heightened violence during the 1740s–1770s. A 1747 Ute and Comanche attack on Abiquiu was so devastating that the colonists most exposed to violence abandoned their homes, and the area was not resettled until 1750.[198] In the 1750s, Plains Indians and Apaches intensified their attacks on Pueblo and Spanish communities, wreaking havoc on the people, their resources, and their livelihoods.[199]

A new Franciscan priest, Fray Juan José Toledo, reached Abiquiu in 1756, and stepped into this situation of heightened apprehension about violence. He had read the Dominican witch-hunting manual, *Malleus Maleficarum*, in addition to a manual for priests that contained detailed information about idolatry, witchcraft, and the Devil's pact. By 1760, Toledo reported that the region had been beset by witchcraft since he first arrived four years earlier. He told of a sect of Devil worshippers, led by a sorcerer who was trying to hinder Toledo's evangelical efforts. The sorcerer, El Cojo (meaning the Cripple) used sympathetic magic, putting pins in dolls, for example, to inflict pain and suffering in others. He also concocted potions. Toledo accused El Cojo of killing another Indian with poison. When confronted by Toledo, El Cojo acknowledged that he had indeed made a pact with the Devil. Toledo had El Cojo placed in the stocks, and he agreed in this uncomfortable position to renounce Satan.

Toledo, who believed in the power of El Cojo's magic, went to a Ute healer to consult her about what he should do. In doing so, Toledo followed the advice in his manual, which recommended consulting a sorcerer as one countermeasure in cases of witchcraft. But this strategy failed, too, and Toledo sought permission to torture El Cojo. It took some three years for legal proceedings to begin; not until April 1763, when a woman said she had been poisoned by another sorcerer, did authorities intervene. Their attention turned well beyond El Cojo to all of the alleged witches and sorcerers. The accused named others, and the accusations spread. The witches confessed to a variety of practices, including using love magic, turning into other creatures, and flying. Toledo was ready—indeed, eager—to do battle with the Devil, whom he was certain had taken up residence in Abiquiu, and he started to perform exorcisms. The evidence of possession was readily apparent to Toledo. When he performed mass in church, some women started writhing, shrieking, and howling like animals (see document 18). One woman even attacked Toledo, slapping him in the face. When he performed his exorcisms, the possessed replied to him in Latin, showing the unnatural knowledge of languages that was one of the hallmarks of possession. One man sucked a stone from another's body (and Toledo helpfully sent the stone to the governor as evidence). Toledo exorcised places as well as people, carrying out his own magic at ceremonial sites (see figure 9).

When the governor finally intervened, he assembled a committee of priests to determine whether the people had in fact been possessed. The priests concluded that they had, and the governor resolved that the possessed were sorcerers who should be punished and denounced. He advocated several measures to improve evangelical efforts in the region: his investigation had revealed that the Franciscans did not know Indian languages, and so they preached in Spanish or Latin (one clue, perhaps, as to how the possessed could respond in this language), and they relied

Figure 9.   Exterior view, San José de Gracia Church, Las Trampas, Taos County, New Mexico. Built between 1760 and 1776, at the same time as the Abiquiu outbreak, this structure is the best preserved colonial church in New Mexico. Las Trampas is about fifty miles from Abiquiu.

Source: Jack E. Boucher, 1961. Library of Congress, Prints and Photographs Division, HABS NM,28-TRAMP,1-1.

on interpreters who were not always faithful in their translations. The governor condemned rote learning as well, and complained that such practices resulted in new converts who did not understand Christian doctrine. When the governor made his report to the Inquisition in Mexico City, the tribunal was reluctant to act and loath to accept the veracity of the possessions. The governor was left to devise his own punishments of the accused witches who still remained in prison (four had died while incarcerated). All but three witches were released to live with Spanish masters, and these three were punished brutally, including one woman who had been accused of killing Spaniards. Her body was covered with honey and feathers, and she was compelled to stand for four hours in the sun.

Modern readers who study accounts of possession often wonder, as the Mexico City Inquisition did in 1764 as it perused reports from Abiquiu, if possessions were faked. Indeed, that was sometimes the case. An outbreak of possession in the city of Querétaro, located in the Bajío, in northern New Spain, provides an example of one such fraud. Like Salem and its neighboring communities, Querétaro was threatened by Indian revolts to the north. Like Salem Village, Querétaro endured economic setbacks as its mines declined. Like Samuel Parris in Salem, the Franciscans in the city observed the commercial decline and frontier violence of the region and saw Devils all around them.[200]

In 1683, a new group of Franciscans from a branch called Propaganda Fide reached this region where missionary enthusiasm had waned in the wake of epidemics and even idolatry.[201] The Franciscans established a college, and they preached sermons that urged the inhabitants toward a more ascetic and rigorous expression of their belief. The sermons apparently had a powerful impact on auditors, and some women left their husbands. Beginning in 1691, the priests heard reports that these women had been possessed by demons. Like so many demoniacs before them, they recoiled from religious symbols, even spitting on the priests, the crucifix, and the church's collection of relics. When the priests presented the Eucharist, the women resisted. They insulted Mary. In the winter months of 1691–1692, just as Salem, Massachusetts, started to be visited by some demons of its own on the other side of the continent, a Franciscan performed an exorcism on one possessed woman, who during the process discharged a remarkable collection of objects from her body; witnesses reported a snake that slithered out her ear, a toad, and some avocado pits. Soon the signs of possession spread, and so too did the expulsion of objects. One woman expelled a paper bag that contained twenty pins. Through the possessed, the Devil spoke to the Franciscans in Spanish (which gave the Franciscans pause, as the Devil customarily spoke Latin, but he still seemed to understand rudimentary forms of the language).[202] The Franciscans concluded that a sorcerer was at work, and identified a mestiza curer named Josepha Ramos, called La Chuparratones (the mice-sucker), as the culprit. She was coerced into confessing that she had made a pact with the Devil and, in consort with other witches, was behind the entire affair.[203]

Like so many other cases of possession, these sparked debate. A Carmelite priest resisted the Franciscan interpretation and insisted that the possessions were faked. Compelling evidence of fraud presented itself when one possessed woman, Doña Juana de los Reyes, lay as if dead, with 400 Devils inhabiting her body, and expelled needles, only to return to her normal self the next day—accompanied by a newborn who had emerged in the night. The Franciscans believed that the child might be the Devil's (specifically, an African devil named Mozambique), so they were undeterred, but the Inquisition quashed the process, accusing the possessed of fraud and admonishing the Franciscans.

The Inquisition's investigations produced a disturbing confession from Doña Juana, who reported that her brother had impregnated her, and she had gone to La Chuparratones to seek help aborting the fetus. The curer's efforts failed, and Doña Juana asked her to kill her with potions. The medicines produced some of the signs of possession, most notably the objects the curer inserted in Doña Juana's body to end the pregnancy. Instead, these items were expelled from Doña Juana's womb in one of the classic signs of possession. The Inquisition sentenced Doña Juana to a year of seclusion and severely admonished the Franciscans. The curer suffered a greater punishment: she was required to appear at an auto-da-fé wearing the symbol of a witch on her clothes, after which she was paraded half-naked through the streets and whipped with 200 lashes.[204] The Inquisition adhered to a policy of skepticism after this episode, worrying in part that the actions of the possessed were so peculiar that they had the effect of making the Devil look weak and ridiculous.

A similar confession in England in 1606 by a woman named Anne Gunter explained another mystery of possession: how the possessed seemed impervious to pain. In Gunter's case, she was able to withstand the pins people plunged in her breasts without discomfort. Her father, she claimed, had compelled her to consume potions that made her ill and, along with a neighbor, Alice Kirfoote, had forced her to cooperate with his hoax. Kirfoote stuck needles in a drugged Anne and mopped up the blood with handkerchiefs after the ordeal. Kirfoote also trained Gunter to hide pins in her mouth and to vomit them up at the appropriate moment.[205]

Although there were clear behaviors that contemporaries regarded as part of the package of traits associated with possession, not every person who exhibited such traits was immediately believed to be possessed. Concerned family members summoned medical experts to see if there might be a natural cause for the symptoms. When doctors failed, or when they concluded that the causes were unnatural—and thus possession—families then turned to ministers or priests. But people could still be skeptical of possession. Experts debated how to understand what they saw. The possessed might be ill (diagnosed in the terminology of the time as melancholia, hysteria, or epilepsy) or crazy. They might be possessed by the Devil (and thus demoniacs)—or possibly by a good spirit. They might fake their possession. And, sometimes, the possession was voluntary, and if that were true, then the possessed was actually a witch, because one hallmark of a witch was her free choice to ally herself with Satan.[206] Samuel Willard weighed the evidence carefully in Groton in 1671–1672 when Elizabeth Knapp started to behave oddly (document 17), and Fray Toledo did the same at Abiquiu (document 18). At Salem in 1692, some observers—and some accused witches—believed that, like Doña Juana in Querétaro, the possessed were faking their plight. Readers will have ample opportunity in their analysis of documents 17, 18, 19, 20, 23, and 24 to reach their own conclusions about whether they think possessions were real or fake.

Prophets and Witch Hunts in the New United States

In the end, Salem, once removed from an English colonial context, begins to share a lot of features with trials and outbreaks of possession in other parts of North America. As the Abiquiu episode indicates, it was not even distinguished by its late chronology. In fact, witch hunts continued to be an important feature of North American life well into the nineteenth century. The complex patterns of interaction between European colonists and Indians that shaped the outbreaks at Salem and Abiquiu also affected the final episodes featured in this volume among the Shawnees, Delawares, and other tribes in the Ohio River Valley and the Senecas in upstate New York in the early nineteenth century (see documents 27–29). These hunts transpired in an important moment of historical transition for the beleaguered people of these regions. In the wake of the American Revolution (1776–1783), the new United States made peace with Great Britain. Most North American Indians who lived east of the Mississippi had allied themselves with the British during the war. Some paid dearly for their loyalty, as the Senecas did during the vicious campaigns of the war years. During the 1779 campaign through New York, American soldiers plundered graves, and some skinned corpses in order to make leggings with the skin.[207] The Shawnees of the Ohio River Valley, already in a state of war in the wake of the French and Indian War (1754–1756) and the Seven Years' War (1756–1763) and struggling against Virginian incursions into their territory, also suffered greatly in the final years of the Revolution.

Others paid a high price after the war, punished for their choice of sides by diminished land, dismantled autonomy, and humiliating peace conditions. Since the individual nations had not taken part in the 1783 peace nego-tiations that produced the Treaty of Paris, they had not been able to make claims for their own territory. Even those who had strived to remain neutral found themselves harmed by the conflict. Fighting continued long after the peace. Several conflicts and humiliating treaties in the 1790s signaled a permanent shift of power toward the new United States, which remained a minor player on the international stage but a bully within the continent.

These accumulated misfortunes—disease, lost land, and the blight of war—produced prophets who preached new messages of revitalization, a common way for indigenous leaders to articulate resistance to European rule and part of the Tepehuan and Pueblo revolts of the seventeenth century (see documents 4 and 5). Several such figures had emerged in North America in the eighteenth century, all exhorting followers to purge their communities of evil influences to restore their gods' favor. Some, like the Delaware prophet Neolin in 1761–1762, demanded that Indians abstain from alcohol and reli-ance on European goods.[208]

Two men emerged as major prophetic leaders. Handsome Lake was a Seneca Indian who experienced a series of apocalyptic visions starting in the summer of 1799 and continuing until his death in 1816. Like Hand-some Lake, the Shawnee prophet, an Indian named Lalawethika, had led a somewhat dissolute life. And also like Handsome Lake, Lalawethika died and came back to life. By 1808 he was known as Tenskwatawa (see figure 10), which meant "the open door." He proclaimed his revelations to other Shaw-nees and their allies. The prophets' goals were to rescue—to revitalize—their societies. Their codes (documents 27 and 28) suggest some of the strategies they envisioned. The Shawnee prophet sought separation from white Ameri-cans, insisting that Indian women leave white husbands and their children and even part with their cats. He demanded that Indians stop trading with whites, consuming whites' foods, or donning whites' fashions. The prophets deplored the use of alcohol. Their codes also reveal considerable anxiety about sexual practices, including divorce, abortion, and polygamy.[209]

While prophets launched attacks on what they defined as foreign inno-vations, they also turned on some long-standing indigenous practices. Both

Figure 10.   A portrait of the Shawnee Prophet and witch-hunter, Tenskwatawa (Philadelphia: F. W. Greenough, c. 1838).
Source: Library of Congress, Prints and Photographs Division, LC-USZC4-3419.

prophets, for example, tended to oppose traditional practitioners, such as shamans, and rejected aspects of shamanism as witchcraft. Shamans sought solutions to problems by placating supernatural powers through rituals (see documents 1 and 2). Prophets, for their part, spurned this approach, looking not to ritual but to individual behavior as ways to redeem their communities.[210] The Shawnee prophet, for example, condemned medicine bundles, sacred items much like the enslaved conjurer's gris-gris, which gave Indian shamans their power to heal and could confer special strength on warriors. François-Joseph Le Mercier described one in document 2: it contained "some hairs, a tobacco seed, a green leaf, and a little cedar twig."[211] The Indian conjurer pictured in figure 11 wears just such a bag. Tenskwatawa redefined such objects as malevolent. The prophets' view of medicine men as at best foolish and at worst evil and satanic was a long-standing opinion of Christian missionaries, but it had traditionally been rejected by Indians. The prophets also foretold doom and disaster for those who failed to follow their teaching. One Delaware prophet's visions in 1806 predicted a whirlwind that would destroy the people if they did not follow prescribed ceremonies. Handsome Lake promised great sickness for those who neglected his message.[212]

Handsome Lake and Tenskwatawa made witch-hunting a central component of their efforts to revitalize indigenous communities, as it had been in similar movements in the 1750s–1770s.[213] The witch hunts of the early nineteenth century revealed both the efforts of these beleaguered tribes to reconstitute themselves in a turbulent period and also the extent to which the

Figure 11. This image is based on a painting by John White, an English artist who traveled to the English colony of Roanoke in 1585 and produced seventy watercolors during his thirteen-month stay in the settlement. The watercolor was then turned into an engraving and first published in 1590. The accompanying text describes this man as a conjurer or "juggler," a spiritual leader or shaman. The bag around his waist likely contained medicines essential to his cures.

Source: The Conjurer, from Thomas Hariot, *A Briefe and true report of the new found land of Virginia* [Frankfort-am-Main, 1590], plate XI. Used by permission of the Folger Shakespeare Library.

groups had become acculturated during centuries of contact with Europeans and Euro-Americans. The Senecas offer an especially clear view of acculturation in their altered definition of witches, who were almost exclusively female during the period of the nineteenth-century witch hunts.

Handsome Lake's code did not invent witchcraft, which had been a part of Seneca beliefs since before European contact. Just two days before his first vision, an accused witch was murdered, stabbed to death while working in a field in full view of the community, because she had allegedly killed a child.[214] But the idea of who a witch was, or what she or he did, had changed from the centuries before and during European contact. After the American Revolution, Seneca witches became women. The prophet's attack on women echoed the gender norms of white Americans, and especially of the Quaker missionaries who had reached Indian country in 1798 and sought to inculcate these values. Quakers hoped to turn Seneca women into submissive women, confined to the household, which would be organized along the patriarchal order central to white American practice, not in the matrilineal lodges inhabited by the Senecas. They rewarded, for example, crops produced by men (Seneca women customarily raised crops), offering men cash for their rye or wheat. These new values had considerable influence on Handsome Lake. When Handsome Lake woke up from his trance, the first sins he addressed were precisely those that the Quakers had been speaking against: divorce; drinking; and the abuse of women, children, and the elderly.[215] The prophet also rejected polygamy for monogamy. Mary Jemison, who had been captured by the Senecas as a child in 1755 and spent her life among them, reported the strains these transformations caused in her own household, where her son John lived with two wives. A second son, Thomas, opposed the practice, "although polygamy was tolerated" within the tribe, and criticized his polygamist brother, even calling him a witch. Thomas also accused Jemison herself of being a witch, for having a witch for a son.[216]

It is impossible to determine exactly how many people were executed in the Seneca witch hunts. The historian Matthew Dennis suggests that some of the oral histories of the period, including the recollection by Mary Jemison that thousands died in the hunts, are exaggerated. But certainly there were times of intense activity, including a campaign in 1801 following the death of Handsome Lake's niece.[217]

While the Seneca witch hunts targeted women, the Shawnee hunts in the Ohio River valley targeted women and men, especially powerful men and Christian converts. Witchcraft was at the center of the Shawnee prophet's code (see document 28). The prophet insisted that he possessed the power to detect witches, and in a ritual reminiscent of the line-up of villagers at

Andover, when the possessed accusers from Salem went on the road and named witches, the prophet gathered people around him and identified the culprits. The first targets were the Delawares, among whom Tenskwatawa lived in 1805 and 1806. The Delawares already believed in witches and were already sure there were some in their midst; a fever that swept through the villages in the spring of 1805 had killed many, and the Delawares, aided by a Munsee prophet, sought the witches who might be responsible for the sickness. This prophet, an ex-Moravian who was called Beata after her Christian baptism, tired of the proceedings, however, and the White River Delawares of Indiana turned to the Shawnee prophet, who lived nearby. He arrived in March 1806, gathered suspected witches around him, and pointed out the guilty parties, according to Moravian missionaries who lived and preached in the area (near modern-day Muncie) and left an account of the proceedings (see document 29). The Delawares coerced confessions using torture by fire. One woman, a Delaware Christian convert, was tortured over a four-day period before she confessed and named her grandson as the recipient of her medicine bundle. When he willingly confessed that he had used the bundle to fly to Kentucky and back, he was released unharmed.[218]

After this first interrogation, the trials continued, ensnaring chiefs and Christian converts. But when the prophet traveled among other Indians in the region, he found less traction for his accusations. Among the Wyandots on the Sandusky River in May 1806, the prophet identified four women as witches. The women were likely Christian converts who had been accused by Wyandots who were critical of the accommodationist policy of the tribe's leaders. But none of the women was executed, as the leaders balked at the charges, and a chief intervened. This pattern proved the new rule, as skepticism vied with acceptance. As a missionary, Joseph Badger, put it in June 1806, he found the Wyandots "in great confusion about their prophet: part of them will not listen to him, others will." While as many as six accused witches were killed in other Wyandot settlements during a power struggle in 1810, the ability of the Prophet to make accusations of witchcraft stick receded. The witch hunts continued, but were not always accompanied by executions.[219]

Assessing the witch hunts in Indian country in the early nineteenth century through the same kind of social and economic approach that Boyer and Nissenbaum applied to Salem reveals some intriguing parallels. Targets of witch accusations in Salem tended to be those associated with the economic transformations of the region—people absorbed in the new commercial culture of the outwardly oriented port. In Indian country, those who pursued an accommodationist approach, who tried to adapt to the expansion of the

United States, or who converted to Christianity were singled out as people abandoning traditional practices—even if "traditions" had been completely transformed from the long-ago world before Europeans arrived. The first accused witches among the Delawares had close connections with the Americans and with their efforts to transform Indian society. Indeed, two of the first accused witches were chiefs, both of whom had signed the Treaty of Greeneville (1795), which placed all of southern, central, and eastern Ohio, in addition to lands in southern Indiana and Illinois, under U.S. control. They had also participated in an 1804 treaty that had ceded Delaware land to the United States. One of these chiefs, Tedapachsit, even endorsed the work of the Christian missionaries who were active among the Delawares. The accusation and execution of two Indians who had converted to Christianity confirmed the peril of association with Americans and with Christianity.[220]

In this respect, the Shawnee prophet's message was overtly political and worked effectively with the efforts of his brother, Tecumseh, to create a pan-Indian movement to oppose the United States. Tecumseh (1768–1813) led a large Indian confederacy and, like his brother, condemned those Indian leaders who sought accommodation with the United States. He fought against the United States from 1810 until his death in 1813. And many Indians were receptive to this message: among the Delawares, for example, many young men were already enraged at the chiefs for land cessions, and it was young warriors who led the chief Tedapachsit to the execution fire.[221] Ultimately, Tenskwatawa's witch hunts proved divisive and aroused considerable opposition from Indians who questioned his leadership. It was this opposition that ended the witch hunts. In the case of Handsome Lake, anti-witch zeal lasted longer, but ultimately the energy focused against witches lost its prominence in the Code of Handsome Lake.

There is a second point of comparison between the Indian witch hunts and those that came before. In North America in the seventeenth and eighteenth centuries, witchcraft and possession often manifested themselves in those areas experiencing the most ardent religious reformation: New England, Querétaro, or Abiquiu. And this correlation seems to have been at work among the Senecas at the time of Handsome Lake and among the Delawares, Shawnees, and Wyandots during the time of Tenskwatawa. Both prophets, like reforming clerics in other places and times, sought to revitalize their societies through rigorous changes in behavior, enforcing conformity and imparting a new rigid code of behavior. And in this setting, just as had been the case elsewhere, those who opposed the reforms, or who were unable or unwilling to alter their conduct and beliefs to exist peacefully with their reform-minded neighbors, languished at the margins, demonized as witches who undermined the reforming mission.

The connection in the early nineteenth century between revitalization and witch hunts also points to a third link to the earlier period, this one to seventeenth-century New Spain. There, Indians in the northern parts of the viceroyalty pursued their own revitalization efforts and sought to expel the Spanish. Both the Tepehuan and Pueblo revolts can be understood in this context, as movements inspired by messianic leaders who hoped to marshal indigenous gods to force the Spanish to withdraw (see documents 4 and 5). And witchcraft, too, figured in these movements. But in this earlier era, it was the European Christians who brought accusations of witchcraft, and they turned these accusations on Indians. In the nineteenth century, Indian prophets saw witchcraft all around, too, but they found it in their midst, not just among their enemies.

Finally, we can see in the Seneca and Shawnee witch hunts the same complex dynamics that Norton argues shaped the events at Salem and that seem to have played a role at Abiquiu and in Querétaro: the challenges of people with opposing interests living in forced proximity, the pressures each endured on land, lives, and livelihoods, and the fear and anger that provoked each to violent action. New Englanders, Europeans, and Indians alike lived in a world full of peril and greed and uncertain futures in the late seventeenth century; so, too, did the remnant nations of Indian Country in the new United States. In a world where people linked witches to all these dangers, was it any surprise that witchcraft defined how people articulated their anger and their fears?

Skepticism

The Indian witch hunts among the Delawares came to an end because people did not act on accusations. This skepticism was pervasive, and it accompanied belief in witchcraft, not only in the same period, but within the same individuals. When people fell ill, they consulted physicians. When people lodged accusations against their neighbors, they reached deep into the past, sometimes referring to events that transpired twenty years earlier, to provide evidence for their claims. For years, neighbors endured the odd behavior of the "witches" in their midst, only bringing accusations forward to civil authorities at a critical juncture or with an accumulation of offenses. What these patterns suggest is that people were not quick to resort to accusations of witchcraft. They weighed the evidence—as we do today—sifting possible explanations, analyzing behavior (theirs and the witch's), surveying the natural world and its unnatural disturbances, and trying to place behavior in a social, cultural, religious, and intellectual context. Witchcraft, far from being the first recourse of a superstitious people, was often the very last solution of the troubled and desperate.

Several skeptical voices raised their critiques within a Christian worldview that accepted the existence of the Devil, demons, and witches but questioned accounts of their activities. Despite the bad press the Spanish Inquisition has received over the years, skepticism defined its approach to witchcraft. Some Inquisition officials were skeptical of diabolical witchcraft in general, while others wondered whether some of the crimes such as sorcery or astrology contained within witchcraft statutes were really heretical at all, and thus not the Inquisition's responsibility. In a meeting in Granada in 1526, for example, ten members of an Inquisitorial committee voted on whether they believed that witches really went to the Sabbath; six voted yes, while four voted that witches went only in their imaginations. The committee also concluded that whatever homicides witches confessed to were likely illusory, so that witches who made such confessions should not be handed over to civil courts. By 1614, skepticism was entrenched as Inquisition policy, and officials viewed witchcraft as a delusion.[222]

Other European skeptics struggled against legal and religious cultures that were committed to destroying witches. Reginald Scot, the English author of a treatise called *The Discoverie of Witchcraft* (1584), drew on the Old Testament to demonstrate that the witches described and condemned there were unlike the witches of his contemporary world. He was equally dismissive of some core beliefs about witches. He rejected, for example, the notion that witches copulated with the Devil, because, he pointed out, "the divell is a spirit, and hath neither flesh nor bones, which were to be used in the performance of this action."[223] Some skeptics argued that to ascribe so much power to witches and to the Devil was to denigrate the power of God. This was a position advocated by Scot, and shared by a Puritan cleric named George Gifford, who wrote two tracts on witchcraft in 1587 and 1593. Like his contemporaries, Gifford did not dispute the existence of witches, and he believed that witches should be punished severely, but he worried that allowing superstitions to flourish that credited witches with too much power overemphasized the power of the Devil.[224]

Skeptics also drew on contemporary medical and scientific ideas. A Dutch demonologist, Johann Weyer, argued in *On the Illusions of the Demons and on Spells and Poisons* (1563) that the women who were accused of witchcraft in fact suffered from melancholy, a disease that derived from an imbalance of the humors (specifically, an excess of bile) and that manifested itself with some of the symptoms now defined within a diagnosis of clinical depression. But melancholy could present itself in a variety of ways, not just as a depressed or subdued demeanor. Weyer described the odd behaviors and delusions one could find, including women who thought they were animals and imitated their sounds and actions; people whose fear of others made them tremble; and men so consumed by religious enthusiasm that they thought they were the Trinity. Weyer believed that melancholic old women were influenced by the Devil. Their condition made them despondent and prone to show lapses of faith in God, and thus all the more vulnerable to the attractions of the Devil. And then, Weyer argued, these confused and addled women, with their weak minds penetrated by Satan, ended up confessing to things that they could not possibly have done. Weyer condemned those Christians who subjected such troubled women, solely on the basis of their confessions, to terrible imprisonment and tortures.[225] If misogyny encouraged most of Weyer's contemporaries to follow the lead of the *Malleus Maleficarum* and to associate women with witchcraft, Weyer's misogyny persuaded him to exonerate women of these same charges. Old women, he believed, were frail, unstable, and mentally deficient, and thus easily duped. Indeed, he wondered whether women were people of reason or mere animals.[226] Thomas Brattle's skepticism likewise encompassed disbelief in women's confessions at Salem in 1692 (document 25). He believed that those who confessed were "deluded, imposed upon, and under the influence of some evill spirit; and therefore unfitt to be evidences either against themselves, or any one else."[227]

Brattle's critique of Salem was not the first skeptical voice raised in British North America. The absence of trials in many jurisdictions might be evidence of skepticism. Take, for example, the action of the Lower Norfolk (Virginia) County Court in May 1655. The justices declared that there had been many accusations of witchcraft lodged against women and damaging their reputations. Those who made accusations in the future and could not prove them would face substantial fines from the court.[228] Thus we see both the persistence of belief—as the reference to numerous accusations suggests—and the justices' expression of skepticism, putting the burden of proof on accusers.

John Winthrop, Jr. (1606–1676), the governor of the English colony of Connecticut, was one such North American skeptic, and unlike the Virginia justices, he lived in a region replete with witchcraft beliefs and accusations. Winthrop first became involved in witchcraft cases in Connecticut as a medical examiner and later as the colony's governor, and in every instance, he sought to prevent the execution of the accused. He was a trained physician as well as an alchemist. Both skills proved relevant in his skepticism about witchcraft; physicians were often consulted about the illnesses that could be diagnosed as the result of witchcraft, and alchemists were men who specialized in transforming substances through chemical processes. Although most famously associated with transforming dross into gold, alchemists engaged in a wide range of scientific endeavors and counted among their ranks some of the most distinguished scientists of the day, including Isaac Newton (see figure 12). In an era when all forms of magic (whatever the intent of the practitioner) were considered diabolical, it is no surprise that alchemists also sometimes faced accusations of witchcraft. As an alchemist, Winthrop knew full well the difficulties of achieving success in scientific experiments, and he doubted that witches could obtain such consistent results with their own concoctions. He thought that his peers were far too likely to explain natural occurrences as witchcraft. As the colony's governor, Winthrop functioned as the chief magistrate in

Figure 12.   Roger Bacon, a thirteenth-century alchemist, carrying out an experiment. Compare this depiction of magical practices with figures 2 or 7.

Source: Michael Maier, *Symbola avraea mensae duodecim nationum* (Frankfort, 1617). Library of Congress, Prints and Photographs Division, LC-USZ62-110316.

all capital cases. His intervention was especially noteworthy during a major outbreak in Hartford in the 1660s. Although Winthrop was out of the colony in England for the first phase of the outbreak, on his return, he refused to enforce the court's guilty verdict of one accused woman, Elizabeth Seager, and his posture of skepticism spread to other judges.[229]

Because so many people believed in witchcraft, skeptics tended to focus on the legal process. Their concerns about the use of evidence displayed an alliance of the acute concern for legal process and fair judgment that permeated the best judicial practice and an intellectual worldview that contained complex systems of religious belief. In their analysis of the case of Katherine Harrison of Wethersfield in 1669–1670, Connecticut's judges paused to assess a number of sticky legal issues and sought help from a group of ministers led by a cleric and alchemist. The committee rejected the evidentiary deviation that permitted one person to testify that he saw an act of witchcraft, and instead, they made convictions hinge on the presence of *two* witnesses, the standard in other criminal cases. They thereby struck an important blow against the idea of witchcraft as *crimen exceptum*. Second, the ministers' committee grappled with the problem that the Devil might assume the appearance of an innocent person and thus encourage witnesses to provide false evidence. The ministers suggested that God would not permit such deceit by the Devil before *multiple* witnesses—although it was presumably still possible that God might allow such deceit before a single witness. Fortunately, the ministers had provided for this exigency in their first recommendation. Finally, the ministers weighed in on the kinds of practices that were truly diabolical. For example, was fortune telling necessarily proof of a pact with the Devil? Perhaps, the ministers said, but there were human ways of knowing the future, including divine revelation, reason, and news. The skepticism of the Connecticut court, then, was embedded in a very particular culture: one that was concerned about legal practices and the use of evidence but that also based its conclusions on assumptions about what God or Satan would—or could—do.

Similar concerns about evidence brought the trials at Salem to a close (see document 25). By the fall of 1692, after nineteen witches at Salem had been hanged on Gallows Hill, and after one unfortunate man was pressed to death in a cruel procedure designed to extract a plea, Increase Mather and Samuel Willard, both Boston ministers, raised questions about the evidence being used in the courts. These were not men who necessarily disbelieved in witchcraft. Willard, for example, is the same man who provided the account of Elizabeth Knapp's possession (see document 17), and he carefully explained in this account why he believed that Knapp was possessed. But how one *proved* witchcraft—that was a more complicated matter. Willard and Mather objected to two kinds of evidence. First, they worried about the use of spectral evidence—the apparitions of "witches" who appeared to the possessed accusers and led the accusers to name the apparition's embodied self as a witch. Was it not possible, they wondered, just as the Connecticut jurists had thirty years earlier, that the Devil might take the form of innocent people? Massachusetts officials had already sought expert opinion on such matters in mid-June, but at that time their conclusion was that God would not allow an innocent person to be used in such a way. Second, they worried about the touch tests used by the Andover courts in September 1692. "Touch tests" acted on the logic that a witch could alleviate the suffering of her victims (see document 20). "We were blindfolded," remembered six accused women who endured this trial, "and our hands were laid upon the afflicted persons, they being in their fits and falling into their fits at our coming into their presence, as they said. Some led us and laid our hands upon them, and then they said they were well and that we were guilty of afflicting them; whereupon we were all seized, as prisoners, by a warrant from the justice of the peace and forthwith carried to Salem."[230]

These skeptical voices were not the sole cause for the demise of witch trials in North America. Instead, it was shifts in legal practice that ultimately terminated prosecutions. Trials required the cooperation of courts of law; the most significant changes came in the application of conventional rules of evidence and the elimination of witchcraft as *crimen exceptum*. Without special circumstances—relaxed rules of evidence, occasional torture, stress positions such as those endured by the Carrier sons at Salem (document 22), who were "tyed . . . Neck and Heels till the Blood was ready to come out of their Noses," and medieval ordeals like the water trial to determine innocence or guilt—witchcraft could not be proven in court, and prosecutors could not extract confessions.[231] By 1735, in the wake of growing opinion that witchcraft did not exist, the English witchcraft law was revised to punish those who pretended to practice witchcraft (not practitioners of actual witchcraft), and in 1951 the act was finally repealed.[232]

Witch beliefs themselves continued to flourish (as the Indian witch hunts attest), as did extralegal persecution by mobs. As late as 1787, for example, in the city of Philadelphia, as the delegates to the Constitutional Convention gathered and sweltered in the summer heat, an elderly woman named Korbmacher who had previously been accused of witchcraft was attacked by a mob on July 10. She lived in Spring Garden in a German neighborhood, and it is probably no accident that her accusers were Germans, given the extensive evidence that Germans brought a range of witch beliefs with them to Pennsylvania. Her neighbors thought she was a witch, and they cut her forehead in an old practice that was supposed to counteract a witch's spells. She appealed for help to authorities, but they could do little to dispel the beliefs of Korbmacher's accusers. Later that month, the mob attacked again. She was carried through the streets and pelted as she went, while her attackers recited the details of her maleficia to curious onlookers. She had killed a child, one woman claimed, with a charm. The *Pennsylvania Gazette* reported the story with outrage and horror and urged authorities to clamp down on this public attack by the "illiterate and youthful part of society." Without firm condemnation from authorities, the *Gazette* feared people would think the state condoned such actions.[233] A week later, Korbmacher died of her injuries. "It is hoped," the paper urged, "that every step will be taken to bring the offenders to punishment, in justice to the wretched victim, as well as to the violated laws of reason and society."[234] When the case against her murderers came to trial in October, the justice condemned those who attacked this "poor wretch whose sorrows and infirmities have sunk her eyes into her head, and whose features are streaked with the wrinkles of extreme old age." In her old age she became "an object of terror," and a witch.[235]

The *Pennsylvania Gazette*'s invocation of the laws of reason posits what seems to be, in light of the longevity of witch beliefs, a premature aspiration. The interest of courts in charging people with witchcraft may have diminished, but witch beliefs endured. Indeed, in some legal jurisdictions in North America, judicial punishment of witches continued, particularly in sovereign Indian nations within the United States. In fact, the very first case in the United States in which state criminal law intruded on a tribal murder concerned witchcraft: this was the 1821 murder of Caugh-quaw-taugh, who was a Seneca woman who lived on a reservation in New York State. Found guilty of witchcraft, she was executed by a Seneca named Soo-non-gize. New York State then pressed murder charges against the executioner. Red Jacket, a Seneca leader, spoke out in 1821 in defense of Seneca witch hunts and of Seneca sovereignty, and he rebuked white Americans in light of their own history. Why, he queried, should Americans regard the Senecas as superstitious fools because they believe in witches? So, too, had the Americans. He pointed specifically to the example of Salem. What had the Senecas done that was any different from what happened there?[236] The state legislature intervened to resolve the issue, asserting state jurisdiction over Indians, but also pardoning Soo-non-gize.[237]

Conflicts between state law and tribal law surrounding issues of witchcraft and murder (as well as many other issues) continued into the late nineteenth century. Many Indians, like other inhabitants of North America, continued to believe in witchcraft; what distinguished them was their ability to act legally on their beliefs, and to punish—and sometimes kill—alleged witches. These actions put Indians at risk of murder charges, even if these killings were executions duly determined by tribal officials. According to the Bureau of Indian Affairs' statistics, some 12 percent of 147 murder cases in the late nineteenth and early twentieth centuries were witch killings.[238]

Witch beliefs were hardly limited to Indian country. The twentieth century was dotted with cases that indicate the endurance of beliefs in witchcraft and magic. In 1928, Nelson D. Rehmeyer, who lived in York County, Pennsylvania, was murdered by three men who believed he was capable of putting hexes on others. The murderers claimed that they had sought only to make Rehmeyer lift a hex, but in the course of a struggle, Rehmeyer was killed. As was true in the cases involving Native Americans, this killing, too, ended up in court, although without the sovereignty issues that surrounded Native American case law. Instead, the case raised issues of superstition, science, and mental illness: the lawyer of one defendant argued that his client was mentally incompetent—the main evidence being his belief in witchcraft and diagnoses by psychiatrists. The accused man was found guilty of second-degree murder and sentenced to twenty years in prison.[239]

If murders of alleged witches have thankfully tended to decline in number since the early twentieth century, Americans continue to believe in the Devil and in demonic possession. Any search engine will reveal horrifying cases of parents who killed their children because they believe they were possessed by demons; other concerned parents arrange for exorcisms to be performed by church members, and sometimes children have died in these rituals.[240] Belief in witches should not seem especially exotic to modern Americans, 70 percent of whom reported a belief in the Devil in 2007. The Devil has, in fact, enjoyed something of a surge in the past twenty years of Gallup polling; 55 percent of adults professed a belief in the Devil in 1990.[241] Witches continue to accompany the Devil. Indeed, a 2005 Harris poll found that 28 percent of adults believed in witches. As a point of comparison, 34 percent of adults believed in UFOs, and 25 percent believed in astrology. Credulity may be slightly on the rise: two years later, a Harris poll found that 31 percent of Americans believed in witches, 29 percent believed in astrology, and 35 percent believed in UFOs.[242] The Catholic Church continues to endorse the ritual of exorcism, which rids people of the demons that possess them, and so do many Protestant churches.

For many modern Americans, witchcraft is an entertaining and quirky remnant of an earlier time, a self-gratifying reminder that people in the past were a superstitious lot. In this conviction of their difference from past credulous inhabitants of the continent, Americans, who live in the most religious of all Western nations, deceive themselves. Americans are especially attached to this belief system, with its polarities of God and Satan, heaven and hell, demons and angels, miracles and curses. Only 37 percent of Canadians and 29 percent of Britons professed belief in the Devil in 2004.[243] Major public figures in the United States espouse these doctrines. The Christian evangelical leader Pat Robertson announced, in the wake of the calamitous earthquake that devastated Haiti in January 2010, that the earthquake was a result of a pact the people of Haiti had made with the Devil over 200 years earlier. These American beliefs about the presence of Devil's pacts and witches even went mainstream in a recent national election. The Republican Party's nominee for vice president in the 2008 United States presidential election, Alaska governor Sarah Palin, had been prayed over by a contemporary Kenyan witch-hunter, Thomas Muthee, during his visit to her Christian church. Muthee claimed to have driven a witch out of her Kenyan home in 1988–1989. Once he identified this woman as a witch, he organized an around-the-clock prayer session in a grocery store basement called the "prayer cave." The woman apparently left town in the wake of this persistent harassment.[244]

For those who are skeptical about the existence of witches and demons, witchcraft and numerous associated beliefs about charms, shape-shifting, potions, and animal familiars nonetheless intrude in modern American life, saturating television and movie screens. Apart from these forms of popular culture, witchcraft also endures in historical tourism. The most popular witch site is modern Salem (which is, ironically, the original Salem Town, not Salem Village, now Danvers, where most witches and possessed victims lived). The tourist experience in Salem is fun, a well-oiled machine intended to part willing tourists from their money with whimsical treats, fortune telling (the alleged divination that sent many people to the gallows), grim reminders of confinement (a fake copy of Salem's jail), self-proclaimed witches, and multimedia museum experiences (at Salem's dazzling Witch Museum).[245] In rural Pennsylvania magnificent barns adorned with hex signs offer another tourist attraction that exploits a history of witch beliefs, in the same way that New Orleans has shops where curious tourists can buy goofer dust or a gris-gris (see figure 13). The competition for tourist dollars has replaced the old contest of cultures within which these varied North American witch beliefs slowly emerged over the centuries of the long colonial period, when Europeans, Africans, Indians, and their descendants collided in the most daunting and uncertain circumstances. In so doing, they reshaped their ideas about power, magic, and evil in light of the world that changed around them.

Figure 13. Edward Curtis's photograph of Piegan medicine bags, circa 1910, rendered here not as sacred ritual objects but as posed art, is emblematic of the transformation of witchcraft objects, rituals, and beliefs into folkloric curiosities.

Source: Library of Congress, Prints & Photographs Division, Edward S. Curtis Collection, LC-USZ62-111288.

Notes

1. "The Examination of Sarah Good," in Paul Boyer and Stephen Nissenbaum, eds., *The Salem Witchcraft Papers* (New York: Da Capo Press, 1977), 2:357.

2. Kenneth Silverman, *The Life and Times of Cotton Mather* (New York: Harper and Row, 1984), 76, 173, 272, 274.

3. Brian Levack, *The Witch-Hunt in Early Modern Europe*, 3rd ed. (Harlow, UK: Pearson, 2006), 22–23.

4. Laura A. Lewis, *Hall of Mirrors: Power, Witchcraft, and Caste in Colonial Mexico* (Durham, NC: Duke University Press, 2003), 38.

5. Ras Michael Brown, "'Walk in the Feenda';: West-Central Africans and the Forest in the South Carolina-Georgia Lowcountry," in Linda M. Heywood, ed., *Central Africans and Cultural Transformations in the American Diaspora* (New York: Cambridge University Press, 2002), 289–317.

6. Richard Bovet, *Pandaemonium, or the Devil's Cloyster* (London, 1684), 221.

7. Maia Madar, "Estonia I: Werewolves and Poisoners," in Bengt Ankarloo and Gustav Henningsen, eds., *Early Modern European Witchcraft: Centres and Peripheries* (Oxford: Clarendon Press, 1990), 270–72; R. C. Ellison, "The Kirkjubol Case: A Seventeenth-Century Icelandic Witchcraft Case Analyzed," *Seventeenth Century* 8 (1993): 217–43; Levack, *Witch-Hunt*, 52; William Monter, "Toads and Eucharists: The Male Witches of Normandy, 1564–1660," *French Historical Studies* 20, no. 4 (Autumn 1997), 575.

8. This discussion of European witch beliefs draws heavily on Levack, *Witch-Hunt*, 4–8, 11.

9. Pierre de Lancre, *On the Inconstancy of Witches: Pierre de Lancre's Tableau de l'inconstance des mauvais anges et demons (1612)*, ed. Gerhild Scholz Williams; trans. Harriet Stone and Gerhild Scholz Williams (Tempe: Arizona Center for Medieval and Renaissance Studies, 2006), 118–19.

10. Peter Morton, ed., *The Trial of Tempel Anneke: Records of a Witchcraft Trial in Brunswick, Germany, 1663*, trans. Barbara Dähms (Buffalo, NY: Broadview Press, 2006), 60–61, 80–81; 98–105; quotations from 61, 98, 100.

11. On women as witches in the Holy Roman Empire, where Tempel Anneke lived, see Lyndal Roper, *Witch Craze: Terror and Fantasy in Baroque Germany* (New Haven, CT: Yale University Press, 2004).

12. See Levack, *Witch-Hunt*, table 2, 142.

13. Monter, "Toads," 581.

14. Monter, "Toads," 584.

15. Ralph Gardiner, *Englands Grievance Discovered* (London, Printed for R. Ibbitson, and P. Stent, 1655), 108. Italics added.

16. Marianne Hester, "Patriarchal Reconstruction and Witch Hunting," in Jonathan Barry, Marianne Hester, and Gareth Roberts, eds., *Witchcraft in Early Modern Europe: Studies in Culture and Belief* (New York: Cambridge University Press, 1996),

294–95. See also Stuart Clark, *Thinking with Demons: The Idea of Witchcraft in Early Modern Europe* (New York: Oxford University Press, 1997), ch. 8.

17. *The Country Justice*, quoted in Hester, "Patriarchal Reconstruction," 296.

18. Hans Peter Broedel, *The Malleus Maleficarum and the Construction of Witchcraft* (Manchester: Manchester University Press, 2003), 169–71.

19. Broedel, *Malleus Maleficarum*, 176.

20. Bengt Ankarloo, "Sweden: The Mass Burnings (1668–1676)," in Ankarloo and Henningsen, eds., *Early Modern European Witchcraft*, 315.

21. Ankarloo, "Sweden," 303.

22. Reginald Scot, *The Discoverie of Witchcraft* (Arundel, UK: Centaur Press, 1964), 39.

23. Christina Larner, "Crimen Exceptum? The Crime of Witchcraft in Europe," in V. A. C. Gatrell, Bruce Lenman, and Geoffrey Parker, eds., *Crime and the Law: The Social History of Crime in Western Europe since 1500* (London: Europa Publications, 1980), 57.

24. Levack, *Witch-Hunt*, 22, 215–16, 218–19.

25. Levack, *Witch-Hunt*, 98.

26. Richard S. Dunn, James Savage, and Laetitia Yeandle, eds., *The Journal of John Winthrop, 1630–1649* (Cambridge, MA: Harvard University Press, 1996), 715.

27. For an interesting account of God's providences, see "Extracts from John Eliot's Records of the First Church of Roxbury, Massachusetts," in John Demos, ed., *Remarkable Providences: Readings on Early American History*, 2nd ed. (Boston: Northeastern University Press, 1991), 447–49. For more on this world of wonders, see David D. Hall, *Worlds of Wonder, Days of Judgment: Popular Religious Belief in Early New England* (Cambridge, MA: Harvard University Press, 1990).

28. Philip D. Morgan, *Slave Counterpoint: Black Culture in the Eighteenth-Century Chesapeake and Lowcountry* (Chapel Hill: University of North Carolina Press, 1998), 62–63.

29. James H. Sweet, *Recreating Africa: Culture, Kinship, and Religion in the African-Portuguese World, 1441–1770* (Chapel Hill: University of North Carolina Press, 2003), 161; John K. Thornton, *The Kongolese Saint Anthony: Dona Beatriz Kimpa Vita and the Antonian Movement, 1684–1706* (New York: Cambridge University Press, 1998), 42.

30. Jason R. Young, *Rituals of Resistance: African Atlantic Religion in Kongo and the Lowcountry South in the Era of Slavery* (Baton Rouge: Louisiana State University Press, 2007), 105.

31. Robin Law, ed., *The English in West Africa, 1685–1688* (New York: Oxford University Press, 2001), part 2, 252, 334; part 3, 491.

32. Young, *Rituals of Resistance*, 54, 113, quotation from 110.

33. Douglas B. Chambers, *Murder at Montpelier: Igbo Africans in Virginia* (Jackson: University Press of Mississippi, 2005), 23, 52.

34. Jean Barbot, *Barbot on Guinea: The Writings of Jean Barbot on West Africa, 1678–1712*, ed. P. E. H. Hair, Adam Jones, and Robin Law (London: Hakluyt Society, 1992), 1:85–86.

35. Sweet, *Recreating Africa*, 162–63; John K. Thornton, "Cannibals, Witches, and Slave Traders in the Atlantic World," *William and Mary Quarterly*, 3rd Series, 55, no. 2 (April 2003): 273–94. On Dona Beatriz, see Thornton, *Kongolese Saint Anthony*.

36. There were, of course, exceptions among chroniclers, including Bernardino de Sahagún, *General History of New Spain* (Salt Lake City: University of Utah, 1950–1982).

37. Fernando Cervantes, *The Devil in the New World: The Impact of Diabolism in New Spain* (New Haven, CT: Yale University Press, 1994), 3.

38. Quoted in Matthew Dennis, "American Indians, Witchcraft, and Witch-Hunting," *OAH Magazine of History* 17, no. 4 (July 2003): 21.

39. "Observations by Master George Percy, 1607," in Lyon Gardiner Tyler, ed., *Narratives of Early Virginia, 1606–1625* (New York: Charles Scribner's Sons, 1907), 6.

40. José de Acosta, *Natural and Moral History of the Indies*, ed. Jane Mangan (Durham, NC: Duke University Press, 2002), 254.

41. Irene Silverblatt, *Moon, Sun, and Witches: Gender Ideologies and Class in Inca and Colonial Peru* (Princeton, NJ: Princeton University Press, 1987), 173, 177–78. For a sensitive discussion of the challenges of reading Spanish sources to find Andean religious practices, see also Kenneth Mills, *Idolatry and Its Enemies: Colonial Andean Religion and Extirpation, 1640–1750* (Princeton, NJ: Princeton University Press, 1997).

42. Matthew Dennis, "Seneca Possessed: Colonialism, Witchcraft, and Gender in the Time of Handsome Lake," in Elizabeth Reis, ed., *Spellbound: Women and Witchcraft in America* (Wilmington, DE: SR Books, 1998), 129.

43. Reuben Gold Thwaites, ed., *The Jesuit Relations and Allied Documents* (Cleveland: OH: Burrows Bros. Co., 1896–1901), 14:37, 39.

44. Alfred A. Cave, "The Failure of the Shawnee Prophet's Witch-Hunt," *Ethnohistory* 42, no. 3 (Summer 1995): 447.

45. Dennis, "Seneca Possessed," 130; see also Dennis, "American Indians," 22.

46. Richard White, *The Middle Ground: Indians, Empires, and Republics in the Great Lakes Region, 1650–1815* (New York: Cambridge University Press, 1991), 35–36.

47. Daniel K. Richter, *The Ordeal of the Longhouse: The Peoples of the Iroquois League in the Era of European Colonization* (Chapel Hill: University of North Carolina Press, 1992), 112–13.

48. Charlotte M. Gradie, *The Tepehuan Revolt of 1616: Militarism, Evangelism, and Colonialism in Seventeenth-Century Nueva Vizcaya* (Salt Lake City: University of Utah Press, 2000), 26.

49. Noble David Cook, *Born to Die: Disease and New World Conquest, 1492–1650* (New York: Cambridge University Press, 1998), 195.

50. John Winthrop to Sir Simonds D'Ewes, July 21, 1634, *Winthrop Papers* (Boston: Massachusetts Historical Society, 1943), 3:171–72.

51. Alexander Whitaker, *Good Newes from Virginia* (London, 1613), C2r. There was, it turned out, an unexpected risk in driving the Devil out of America. Sometimes these exiled demons found their way on ships to Europe. Travelers to Bordeaux

reported seeing them, disguised as humans, as they journeyed through France (Lancre, *Inconstancy of Witches*, 60).

52.   Samuel Willard, "A briefe account of a strange & unusuall Providence of God befallen to Elizabeth Knap of Groton," transcribed by Samuel A. Green, ed., *Groton in the Witchcraft Times* (Groton, MA, 1883), 8.

53.   "Examination of Tituba, March 1, 1691/2," in Bernard Rosenthal, ed., *Records of the Salem Witch-Hunt* (New York: Cambridge University Press, 2009), 135.

54.   *Jesuit Relations*, 6:231.

55.   Jorge Cañizares-Esquerra, *Puritan Conquistadors: Iberianizing the Atlantic, 1550–1700* (Stanford, CA: Stanford University Press, 2006), 5.

56.   John Milton, *Paradise Lost* (London, 1667), Book 1, line 263.

57.   Cervantes, *Devil in the New World*, 37.

58.   Acosta, *Natural and Moral History*, 306–7, 327,

59.   Gradie, *Tepehuan Revolt*, 24.

60.   Peter A. Goddard, "The Devil in New France: Jesuit Demonology, 1611–1650," *The Canadian Historical Review* 78 (1977): 40–62.

61.   Quoted in Ruth Behar, "The Visions of a Guachichil Witch in 1599: A Window on the Subjugation of Mexico's Hunter-Gatherers," *Ethnohistory* 34, no. 2 (Spring 1987): 117.

62.   On the association of Indians with shape-shifting, see Lewis, *Hall of Mirrors*, 103–4.

63.   Quoted in Behar, "Visions," 126.

64.   Silverblatt, *Moon, Sun, and Witches*, 196.

65.   On the Pueblo Revolt, see Andrew L. Knaut, *The Pueblo Revolt of 1680: Conquest and Resistance in Seventeenth-Century New Mexico* (Norman: University of Oklahoma Press, 1995).

66.   For a good comparison of missionary writings about the two revolts, see Daniel T. Reff, "The 'Predicament of Culture,' and Spanish Missionary Accounts of the Tepehuan and Pueblo Revolts," *Ethnohistory* 42, no. 1 (Winter 1995): 63–90.

67.   Susan M. Deeds, *Defiance and Deference in Mexico's Colonial North: Indians under Spanish Rule in Nueva Vizcaya* (Austin: University of Texas Press, 2003), 31.

68.   Reff, "Predicament," 67.

69.   Gradie, *Tepehuan Revolt*, 2.

70.   Gradie, *Tepehuan Revolt*, 94, 98.

71.   Gradie, *Tepehuan Revolt*, 167.

72.   France Vinton Scholes, *Church and State in New Mexico, 1610–1650* (Albuquerque: University of New Mexico Press, 1937), provides an excellent introduction to these institutional and jurisdictional conflicts between Franciscans and secular officials. Details of the complex tensions of Pueblo, Franciscan, official, and settler politics can be found in Ramón A. Gutiérrez, *When Jesus Came, the Corn Mothers Went Away: Marriage, Sexuality, and Power in New Mexico, 1500–1846* (Stanford, CA: Stanford University Press, 1991), ch. 3.

73.   Gutiérrez, *When Jesus Came*, 130.

74. Knaut, *Pueblo Revolt*, 163–64.

75. John L. Kessell, *Kiva, Cross, and Crown: The Pecos Indians and New Mexico, 1540–1840* (Washington, DC: National Park Service, 1983), 226.

76. Knaut, *Pueblo Revolt*, 14.

77. Deeds, *Defiance*, 34.

78. See Kris Lane's discussion of "herbal resistance" in "Taming the Master: *Brujería*, Slavery, and the *Encomienda* in Barbacoas at the Turn of the Eighteenth Century," *Ethnohistory* 45, no. 3 (Summer 1998): 477–507.

79. Silverblatt, *Moon, Sun, and Witches*, 168, 174–75.

80. Malcolm Ebright and Rick Hendricks, *The Witches of Abiquiu: The Governor, the Priest, the Genízaro Indians, and the Devil* (Albuquerque: University of New Mexico Press, 2006), 149.

81. Chadwick Hansen made this argument about the women at Salem. See *Witchcraft at Salem* (New York: George Braziller, 1969).

82. France V. Scholes, "The First Decade of the Inquisition in New Mexico," *New Mexico Historical Review* 10, no. 3 (July 1935): 220–23. The two women were Beatriz de los Angeles, an Indian, and Juana de la Cruz, her mestiza daughter.

83. Scholes, "First Decade," 208–14.

84. Joan Cameron Bristol, "From Curing to Witchcraft: Afro-Mexicans and the Mediation of Authority," *Journal of Colonialism and Colonial History* 7, no. 1 (Spring 2006).

85. Tibo J. Chávez, "Early Witchcraft in New Mexico," *El Palacio* 76, no. 3 (1969): 7–9.

86. Scholes, "First Decade," 219–20.

87. Noemi Quezada, "The Inquisition's Repression of Curanderos," in Mary Elizabeth Perry and Anne J. Cruz, eds., *Cultural Encounters: The Impact of the Inquisition in Spain and the New World* (Berkeley: University of California Press, 1991), 52.

88. Marcy Norton, *Sacred Gifts, Profane Pleasures: A History of Tobacco and Chocolate in the Atlantic World* (Ithaca, NY: Cornell University Press, 2008), 245.

89. Lancre, *Inconstancy of Witches*, 59.

90. Ramón A. Gutiérrez, "Women on Top: The Love Magic of the Indian Witches of New Mexico," *Journal of the History of Sexuality* 16, no. 3 (September 2007): 373.

91. María Helena Sánchez Ortega, "Sorcery and Eroticism in Love Magic," in Perry and Cruz, eds., *Cultural Encounters*, 58–59.

92. Robert D. Martínez, "Fray Juan José Toledo and the Devil in Spanish New Mexico: A Story of Witchcraft and Cultural Conflict in Eighteenth-Century Abiquiu" (MA Thesis, University of New Mexico, 1997), 91.

93. Monter, "Toads," 573, table 2. On witchcraft in France, see also Robin Briggs, *Communities of Belief: Cultural and Social Tension in Early Modern France* (Oxford: Clarendon Press, 1989), and on demonology, see Jonathan Pearl, *The Crime of Crimes: Demonology and Politics in France, 1560–1620* (Waterloo, ON: Wilfrid Laurier University Press, 1999).

94. Ian K. Steele, *Warpaths: Invasions of North America* (New York: Oxford University Press, 1994), 72.

95. Jonathan Pearl, "Witchcraft in New France in the Seventeenth Century: The Social Aspect," *Historical Reflections* 4, no. 2 (Winter 1977): 193–94.

96. Monter, "Toads," 583.

97. *Jesuit Relations*, 13:129.

98. Goddard, "The Devil in New France," 40–62.

99. This discussion of New France comes from Pearl, "Witchcraft in New France," 191–205.

100. Leslie Choquette, *Frenchmen into Peasants: Modernity and Tradition in the Peopling of French Canada* (Cambridge, MA: Harvard University Press, 1997), Table 1.1, 30.

101. Carol F. Karlsen, *The Devil in the Shape of a Woman: Witchcraft in Colonial New England* (New York: Vintage, 1989), 48–49.

102. Jon Butler, *Awash in a Sea of Faith: Christianizing the American People* (Cambridge, MA: Harvard University Press, 1990), 94.

103. Carla Gardina Pestana, *The English Atlantic in an Age of Revolution, 1640–1661* (Cambridge, MA: Harvard University Press, 2004), 138.

104. Raphael Semmes, *Crime and Punishment in Early Maryland* (Montclair, NJ: Patterson Smith Publishing, 1970, 1938), 169.

105. Virginia Lunsford, "The Witch in Colonial Virginia: A Question of Gender and Family Relations," *Northern Neck of Virginia Historical Magazine* 43, no. 1 (1993): 5007–16.

106. Floyd Painter, "An Early Eighteenth-Century Witch Bottle: A Legacy of the Wicked Witch of Pungo," *Chesopiean* 18, nos. 3–6 (1980): 62.

107. On migration in this period, see Alison Games, *Migration and the Origins of the English Atlantic World* (Cambridge, MA: Harvard University Press, 1999).

108. Karlsen, *Devil*, statistics on sex ratio from tables 1 and 2, 48–49; information on age structure, 64–70.

109. Thomas Hutchinson, *The History of the Colony of Massachusetts-Bay* (Boston, 1764), 1:187–88.

110. Karlsen, *Devil*, 102.

111. On parental control over land, see Philip G. Greven, *Four Generations: Population, Land, and Family in Colonial Andover* (Ithaca, NY: Cornell University Press, 1970).

112. See Karlsen, *Devil*, ch. 6.

113. John P. Demos, *Entertaining Satan: Witchcraft and the Culture of Early New England* (New York: Oxford University Press, 1982), 154.

114. Demos, *Entertaining Satan*, ch. 6.

115. Lou Rose, "A Memorable Trial in Seventeenth-Century Maryland," *Maryland Historical Magazine* 83, no. 4 (1988): 365–68; See the trial record in *Archives of Maryland*, vol. 10, *Judicial and Testamentary Business of the Provincial Court, 1649/50–1657* (Baltimore: Maryland Historical Society, 1883–1925), 456–458.

116. The Maryland cases appear in *Proceedings of the Council of Maryland, 1648–1655*, 3:306–8 (Mary Lee), and *Provincial Court Proceedings, 1659*, 41:327–29 (Elizabeth Richardson). For the Virginia case, see Philip Alexander Bruce, *Institutional History of Virginia in the Seventeenth Century* (New York: G. P. Putnam's Sons, 1910), 243.

117. See Christina Larner, *Enemies of God: The Witch-Hunt in Scotland* (Baltimore: Johns Hopkins University Press, 1981).

118. Nahum Tate, *Brutus of Alba, or, The Enchanted Lovers* (London, 1678).

119. See Elaine Forman Crane, "Bermuda, Witchcraft, and the Quaker Threat," a paper delivered to the Society of Early Americanists Biennial Conference, March 2009, Hamilton, Bermuda. On Quakers and witchcraft in Massachusetts, see Christine Leigh Heyrman, *Commerce and Culture: The Maritime Communities of Colonial Massachusetts, 1690–1750* (New York: Norton, 1984), 108–13.

120. Carla Gardina Pestana, "Martyred by the Saints: Quaker Executions in Seventeenth-Century Massachusetts," in Allan Greer and Jodi Bilinkoff, eds., *Colonial Saints: Discovering the Holy in the Americas, 1500–1800* (New York: Routledge, 2003), 169–92.

121. Quakers figured in the Salem outbreak of 1692; there, many accused witches came from households that contained Quakers. Indeed, Heyrman suggests that the Quaker connection is the best way to make sense of an otherwise anomalous accusation during the outbreak, that of Rebecca Nurse, who was a church member, part of a prosperous family, and a well-known member of the community. Nurse and her husband had taken in an orphan ward whose father was Quaker. That, Heyrman suggests, singled her out as an appropriate target for accusations of witchcraft. Heyrman, *Commerce and Culture*, 108–13.

122. Carla Gardina Pestana, *Quakers and Baptists in Colonial Massachusetts* (New York: Cambridge University Press, 1991), 123.

123. On this migration, see Aaron Spencer Fogleman, *Hopeful Journeys: German Immigration, Settlement, and Political Culture in Colonial America, 1717–1775* (Philadelphia: University of Pennsylvania Press, 1996), 2, 5.

124. George Lincoln Burr, ed., *Narratives of the Witchcraft Cases, 1648–1706* (New York: Charles Scribner's Sons, 1914), 82–83.

125. Burr, ed., *Narratives*, 85–87, quotation from 87.

126. John Costello, "Cultural Vestiges and Cultural Blends among the Pennsylvania Germans," *New York Folklore Society* 3, nos. 1–4 (1977): 108.

127. Elizabeth W. Fisher, "'Prophesies and Revelations': German Cabbalists in Early Pennsylvania," *Pennsylvania Magazine of History and Biography* 109, no. 3 (July 1985): 299–333.

128. A. G. Roeber, "'The Origins of Whatever Is Not English among Us': The Dutch-Speaking and the German-Speaking Peoples of Colonial British America," in Bernard Bailyn and Philip D. Morgan, eds., *Strangers within the Realm: Cultural Margins of the First British Empire* (Chapel Hill: University of North Carolina Press, 1991), 270.

129. Morton, ed., *The Trial of Tempel Anneke*, 61. Brook weed is a plant of the primrose family and has curative powers.

130. Gerald Milnes, *Signs, Cures, and Witchery: German Appalachian Folklore* (Knoxville: University of Tennessee Press, 2007).

131. David W. Kriebel, *Powwowing among the Pennsylvania Dutch: A Traditional Medical Practice in the Modern World* (University Park: Pennsylvania State University Press, 2007), 23–26. There were multiple English versions of a similar text, *The boke of secretes of Albertus Magnus: of the vertues of herbes, stones, and certayne beasts: also, a boke of the same author, of the maruaylous thinges of the world, and of certaine effectes caused of certaine beastes*, with an edition as early as 1560, followed by editions printed in London in 1565, 1569, 1570, 1617, 1626, and 1637. On Albertus Magnus, **see** David J. Collins, "Albertus, *Magnus* or *Magus*? Magic, Natural Philosophy, and Religious Reform in the Late Middle Ages," *Renaissance Quarterly* 63, no. 1 (2010): 1–44.

132. Michael A. Gomez, *Exchanging Our Country Marks: The Transformation of African Identities in the Colonial and Antebellum South* (Chapel Hill: University of North Carolina Press, 1998), 18.

133. For the Louisiana statistic, see Gomez, *Exchanging Our Country Marks*, 301, n4. On Africans in New Mexico, see Gutiérrez, *When Jesus Came*, 198.

134. Sweet, *Recreating Africa*, 165, 167-169.

135. Butler, *Awash in a Sea of Faith*, ch. 5. A pioneer in the effort to look for elements of African cultural retentions was Melville Herskovits. See *The Myth of the Negro Past* (New York: Harper, 1941). For interpretations emphasizing continuities, see Thornton, *Africa and Africans*; Sweet, *Recreating Africa*; Gwendolyn Midlo Hall, *Africans in Colonial Louisiana: The Development of Afro-Creole Culture in the Eighteenth Century* (Baton Rouge: Louisiana State University Press, 1992), or Gomez, *Exchanging Our Country Marks*.

136. William L. Andrews and Regina E. Mason, eds., *Life of William Grimes, the Runaway Slave* (New York: Oxford University Press, 2008), 52–53; Young, *Rituals of Resistance*, 132–33. For a folklorist's study of "hag attacks," see David J. Spufford, *The Terror that Comes in the Night: An Experience-Centered Study of Supernatural Assault Traditions* (Philadelphia: University of Pennsylvania Press, 1989).

137. Morgan, *Slave Counterpoint*, 621.

138. J. S. Handler, "A Prone Burial from a Plantation Slave Cemetery in Barbados," *Historical Archaeology* 30, no. 3 (1996): 76–86.

139. Morgan, *Slave Counterpoint*, 622.

140. Philip J. Schwarz, *Twice Condemned: Slaves and the Criminal Laws of Virginia, 1705–1865* (Baton Rouge: Louisiana State University Press, 1988), 92.

141. Hall, *Africans in Colonial Louisiana*, 161–62.

142. Hall, *Africans in Colonial Louisiana*, 162.

143. Laura L. Porteous, "The Gri-Gri Case," *Louisiana Historical Quarterly* 17, no. 1 (January–October 1934): 48–63.

144. Quoted in Hall, *Africans in Colonial Louisiana*, 163.

145. Letter of Edward Milward, *South Carolina Gazette*, July 24, 1749.

146. The other person who suffered being burned alive was also a slave, a woman who was found guilty of arson in 1681. Alan Rogers, *Murder and the Death Penalty in Massachusetts* (Amherst: University of Massachusetts Press, 2008), 24–26.

147. September 1, 1765, John Bartram, *Diary of a Journey Through the Carolinas, Georgia, and Florida, Transactions of the American Philosophical Society*, New Series, 33, part 1 (1942): 22.

148. *Pennsylvania Gazette*, December 31, 1767.

149. On some of the colonial charms used for poison, see Yvonne P. Chireau, *Black Magic: Religion and the African American Conjuring Tradition* (Berkeley: University of California Press, 2003), 73.

150. Morgan, *Slave Counterpoint*, 613.

151. The sex ratio among adults in Virginia dropped from 150:100 in 1700 to 115:100 in 1775. Morgan, *Slave Counterpoint*, 82.

152. Schwarz, *Twice Condemned*, 95.

153. Gomez, *Exchanging Our Country Marks*, 55–56.

154. Chambers, *Murder at Montpelier*, 69.

155. Young, *Rituals of Resistance*, 163–64.

156. Chireau, *Black Magic*, 13.

157. Gomez, *Exchanging Our Country Marks*, 55, 283–90; Young, *Rituals of Resistance*, 119.

158. Wolfgang Behringer, *Witches and Witch-Hunts: A Global History* (Cambridge, UK: Polity Press, 2004), 130.

159. Paul Boyer and Stephen Nissenbaum, *Salem Possessed: The Social Origins of Witchcraft* (Cambridge, MA: Harvard University Press, 1974). On the remarkable staying power of this interpretation, see the "Forum: Salem Repossessed," in *William and Mary Quarterly*, 3rd Series, 65, no. 3 (July 2008): 391–534.

160. On other commercial communities, see, for example, Heyrman, *Commerce and Culture*, or Stephen Innes, *Labor in a New Land: Economy and Society in Seventeenth-Century Springfield* (Princeton, NJ: Princeton University Press, 1983).

161. Elaine G. Breslaw, *Tituba, Reluctant Witch of Salem Village: Devilish Indians and Puritan Fantasies* (New York: New York University Press, 1996), 26.

162. Peter Charles Hoffer, *The Devil's Disciples: Makers of the Salem Witchcraft Trials* (Baltimore: Johns Hopkins University Press), 17–23.

163. Tituba herself has been the subject of extensive reinterpretation. See Bernard Rosenthal, "Tituba," *OAH Magazine of History* 17, no. 4 (July 2003): 48–50. For a fictional version of Tituba's life, see Maryse Condé, *I, Tituba, Black Witch of Salem* (Charlottesville: University of Virginia Press, 1992).

164. Breslaw, *Tituba*, xx, 106, 132; see ch. 6 on the confession itself.

165. Mary Beth Norton, *In the Devil's Snare: The Salem Witchcraft Crisis of 1692* (New York: Vintage, 2000).

166. Norton, *Devil's Snare*, 79.

167. Norton, *Devil's Snare*, 157, 184–93.

168. James E. Kences, "Some Unexplored Relationships in Essex County Witchcraft to the Indian Wars of 1675 and 1689," *Essex Institute Historical Collections* 120 (1984): 179–212; Karlsen, *Devil*, ch. 7; Richard Godbeer, *The Devil's Dominion: Magic and Religion in Early New England* (Cambridge: Cambridge University Press, 1992), ch. 6; and Hoffer, *Devil's Disciples*.

169. For an interesting critique of the association between war and witch hunts, see Gary Jensen, *The Path of the Devil: Early Modern Witch Hunts* (Lanham, MD: Rowman and Littlefield, 2007), ch. 7. As Jensen notes, the correlation of witch outbreaks with war was hardly precise—or causative—given the fact that the Indian wars continued yet the witch hunts did not (220).

170. Richard Godbeer, *Escaping Salem: The Other Witch Hunt of 1692* (New York: Oxford University Press, 2005); Walter W. Woodward, "New England's *Other* Witch-Hunt: The Hartford Witch-Hunt of the 1660s and Changing Patterns in Witchcraft Prosecution," *OAH Magazine of History* 17, no. 4 (July 2003): 16–20; and Ebright and Hendricks, *Witches of Abiquiu*. Ebright and Hendricks explicitly compare the Abiquiu witch hunt to Salem. See, for example, 8, 183, 185, 233.

171. Carla Gardina Pestana, *Protestant Empire: Religion and the Making of the British Atlantic World* (Philadelphia: University of Pennsylvania Press, 2009), 151.

172. Mary K. Matossian, "Ergot and the Salem Witchcraft Affair," *The American Scientist* 70 (1982): 355.

173. The fullest treatment of this outbreak can be found in Ebright and Hendricks, *Witches of Abiquiu*.

174. Martínez, "Fray Juan José Toledo," 91.

175. Karlsen, *Devil*, 39.

176. Elizabeth Reis, *Damned Women: Sinners and Witches in Puritan New England* (Ithaca, NY: Cornell University Press, 1997), especially ch. 4.

177. *Salem Witchcraft Papers*, 2:594.

178. *Jesuit Relations*, 13:105.

179. Cave, "Failure," 456.

180. Ebright and Hendricks, *Witches of Abiquiu*, 125–26.

181. Solange Alberro, "Juan de Morga and Gertrudis de Escobar: Rebellious Slaves," in David G. Sweet and Gary B. Nash, eds., *Struggle and Survival in Colonial America* (Berkeley: University of California Press, 1981), 165–76.

182. Ankarloo, "Sweden," 296.

183. The best profile of the possessed accusers can be found in Karlsen, *Devil*, ch. 7, and this discussion draws heavily from her statistics.

184. Boys and men, too, were occasionally possessed. See the account of the possession of Thomas Darling, a thirteen-year-old boy in Stafford, England, who was possessed in 1597. See Jesse Bee and others, *The Most Wonderfull and True Storie, of a certaine Witch named Alse Gooderige* (London, 1597).

185. L. R. Caporael, "Ergotism: The Satan Loosed in Salem?" *Science* 192, no. 4234 (1976): 21–26. See the response in N. P. Spanos and J. Gottlieb, "Ergotism and the Salem Village Witch Trials," *Science* 194, no. 4272 (1976): 1390–94.

186. Matossian, "Ergot," 355–57.

187. Matossian, "Ergot," 355.

188. Laurie Winn Carlson, A Fever in Salem: A New Interpretation of the New England Witch Trials (Chicago: Ivan R. Dee, 1999).

189. Sigmund Freud, "A Seventeenth-Century Demonological Neurosis," in The Standard Edition of the Complete Psychological Works of Sigmund Freud (London: The Hogarth Press, 1953), 19:69–105, quotation from 84.

190. Hoffer, Devil's Disciples, 97–99.

191. Hoffer, Devil's Disciples, 94–95.

192. See, for example, the English translation of the 1962 book that launched the field, Philippe Ariès, Centuries of Childhood: A Social History of Family Life (New York: Knopf, 1972). For books on family life in early New England, see Lisa Wilson, Ye Heart of a Man: The Domestic Life of Men in New England (New Haven, CT: Yale University Press, 1999); Gloria Main, Peoples of a Spacious Land: Families and Cultures in Colonial New England (Cambridge: Harvard University Press, 2001); John Demos, A Little Commonwealth: Family Life in Plymouth Colony (New York: Oxford University Press, 1970); and Demos, The Unredeemed Captive: A Family Story from Early America (New York: Knopf, 1994).

193. Benjamin J. Kaplan, "Possessed by the Devil? A Very Public Dispute in Utrecht," Renaissance Quarterly 49, no. 4 (Winter 1996): 738.

194. Karlsen, Devil, 231–48.

195. For an interesting interpretation of this issue for France, see Moshe Sluhovsky, "A Divine Apparition or Demonic Possession? Female Agency and Church Authority in Demonic Possession in Sixteenth-Century France," Sixteenth Century Journal 27, no. 4 (Winter 1996): 1039–55.

196. Allan Greer, Mohawk Saint: Catherine Tekakwitha and the Jesuits (New York: Oxford University Press, 2005), 111–24, 133–34, 142–43.

197. James F. Brooks, Captives and Cousins: Slavery, Kinship, and Community in the Southwest Borderlands (Chapel Hill: University of North Carolina Press, 2002), 130–33.

198. Ebright and Hendricks, Witches of Abiquiu, 90. The account that follows draws heavily on this book.

199. Ross Frank, From Settler to Citizen: New Mexican Economic Development and the Creation of Vecino Society, 1750–1820 (Berkeley: University of California Press, 2000), 13, 34.

200. John Tutino, Making a New World: Founding Capitalism in the Bajío and Spanish North America (Durham, NC: Duke University Press, forthcoming), ch. 3.

201. This discussion draws on Fernando Cervantes, "The Devils of Querétaro: Scepticism and Credulity in Late Seventeenth-Century Mexico," Past and Present 130 (February 1991): 51–69.

202. Ellen Gunnarsdóttir, Mexican Karismata: The Baroque Vocation of Francisca de los Angeles, 1674–1744 (Lincoln: University of Nebraska Press, 2004), 45.

203. Gunnarsdóttir, Mexican Karismata, 46.

204. Gunnarsdóttir, *Mexican Karismata*, 47.

205. On Anne Gunter's possession and confession, see James Sharpe, *The Bewitching of Anne Gunter: A Horrible and True Story of Deception, Witchcraft, Murder, and the King of England* (New York: Routledge, 1999), especially 6–12. On another English deception, see Samuel Harsnet, *A Discovery of the Fraudulent Practices of John Darrell* (London, 1599).

206. Kaplan, "Possessed," 739.

207. Colin G. Calloway, *The American Revolution in Indian Country: Crisis and Diversity in Native American Communities* (New York: Cambridge University Press, 1995), 51. This discussion draws heavily on Calloway's analysis.

208. An excellent study of alcohol in colonial North America is Peter C. Mancall, *Deadly Medicine: Indians and Alcohol in Early America* (Ithaca, NY: Cornell University Press, 1995).

209. On Tenskwatawa's code, see White, *Middle Ground*, 506–10. The classic study of Handsome Lake is Anthony F. C. Wallace, *The Death and Rebirth of the Seneca* (New York: Knopf, 1969).

210. Cave, "Failure," 449.

211. *Jesuit Relations*, 13:157.

212. Gregory Evans Dowd, *A Spirited Resistance: The North American Indian Struggle for Unity, 1745–1815* (Baltimore: Johns Hopkins University Press, 1992), 128.

213. Dowd, *Spirited Resistance*, 136–37.

214. Wallace, *Death and Rebirth of the Seneca*, 236. The child was the daughter of Cornplanter, an important Seneca leader.

215. Merle H. Deardorff and George S. Snyderman, eds., "A Nineteenth-Century Journal of a Visit to the Indians of New York," *Proceedings of the American Philosophical Society* 100, no. 6 (December 1956): 591.

216. James E. Seaver, *A Narrative of the Life of Mrs. Mary Jemison* (Canadaigua: J. D. Bemis and Co., 1824), 106–7, quotation from 106.

217. Seaver, *Narrative*, 183–84; Matthew Dennis, *Seneca Possessed: Indians, Witchcraft, and Power in the Early American Republic* (Philadelphia: University of Pennsylvania Press, 2010), 96.

218. Cave, "Failure," 455–56. See also Jay Miller, "The 1806 Purge among the Indiana Delaware: Sorcery, Gender, Boundaries, and Legitimacy," *Ethnohistory* 41, no. 2 (Spring 1994): 246–66.

219. Cave, "Failure," 461–62. See also the account provided in Joseph Badger, *A Memoir of Rev. Joseph Badger* (Hudson, OH: Sawyer, Ingersoll and Company, 1851), 145, quotation from 147.

220. Dowd, *Spirited Resistance*, 114, 137, 139.

221. White, *Middle Ground*, 499.

222. On the Spanish Inquisition and witchcraft, see Henry Kamen, *The Spanish Inquisition: An Historical Revision* (London: Weidenfeld and Nicholson, 1997), 270–76.

223. Scot, *Discoverie*, 78

224. George Gifford, A *Discourse of the subtill Practices of Devilles by Witches and Sorcerers* (London, 1587), and A *Dialogue concerning Witches and Witchcraftes: in which is laide open how craftily the Divell deceiveth not onely the Witches but many other and so leadeth them awrie into many great Errours* (London, 1593).

225. Excerpts from Johann Weyer, *On the Illusions of the Demons and on Spells and Poisons*, in Brian Levack, ed., *The Witchcraft Sourcebook* (New York: Routledge, 2004), 282–83.

226. Clark, *Thinking with Demons*, 118.

227. Burr, ed., *Narratives*, 173.

228. Norfolk Wills and Deeds C, 1651–1656, fol. 157, Library of Virginia, Richmond, Virginia.

229. This discussion of Winthrop's skepticism and of the Hartford witch hunt draws on Woodward, "New England's *Other* Witch-Hunt," 16–20.

230. *Salem Witchcraft Papers*, 3:971.

231. Robert Calef, *More Wonders of The Invisible World* (London, 1700), 105.

232. Marion Gibson, ed., *Witchcraft and Society in England and America, 1550–1750* (Ithaca, NY: Cornell University Press, 2003), 7.

233. *Pennsylvania Gazette*, July 18, 1787.

234. *Pennsylvania Gazette*, July 25, 1787.

235. Edmund S. Morgan, "The Witch and We, the People," *American Heritage*, August–September 1983, 6–11.

236. Quoted in William L. Stone, *The Life and Times of Red-Jacket* (New York: Wiley and Putnam, 1841), 320–21.

237. Sidney L. Harring, *Crow Dog's Case: American Indian Sovereignty, Tribal Law, and United States Law in the Nineteenth Century* (New York: Cambridge University Press, 1994), 37–38.

238. Harring, *Crow Dog's Case*, 117, 172–73, 233, 268–73.

239. Kriebel, *Powwowing*, 115–21.

240. On the murder of "demonic" children by their parents, see, for example, the starvation of Kimberly McZinc in Florida in 1988; the bludgeoning death of Amora Bain Carson in East Texas in 2008; or the death by punching and kicking of a two-year-old in Turlock, California, in front of appalled witnesses in 2008. Javon Thompson was stomped to death in 2006 by members of his mother's religious group, One Mind Ministries, in an effort to expel his demons because he would not say "Amen." In 2003, an autistic child suffocated during an exorcism at Faith Temple Church of the Apostolic Faith in Milwaukee.

241. Frank Newport, "Americans More Likely to Believe in God Than the Devil, Heaven More Than Hell," Gallup, http://www.gallup.com/poll/27877/Americans-More-Likely-Believe-God-Than-Devil-Heaven-More-Than-Hell.aspx.

242. "The Religious and Other Beliefs of Americans," Harris Poll 119, November 29, 2007, http://www.harrisinteractive.com/vault/Harris-Interactive-Poll-Research-Religious-Beliefs-2007-11.pdf.

243. Heather Mason Kieffer, "Divine Subjects: Canadians Believe, Britons Skeptical," Gallup, http://www.gallup.com/poll/14083/Divine-Subjects-Canadians-Believe-Britons-Skeptical.aspx.

244. Jane Lampman, "Targeting Cities with 'Spiritual Mapping' Prayer," *Christian Science Monitor*, http://www.csmonitor.com/1999/0923/p15s1.html.

245. See Robin DeRosa, *The Making of Salem: The Witch Trials in History, Fiction and Tourism* (Jefferson, NC: McFarland and Company, 2009).

SECTION II

PRIMARY DOCUMENTS

First Impressions

Generated in the first years of contact between Europeans and Native Americans, the documents in this section reveal how both parties saw the other through the lens of witchcraft. All of the sources were written by religious European men. How clearly do Indian ideas about witchcraft and about Christianity come through in these selections? How might the authors' Christian beliefs about the Devil have shaped their understanding of Indian notions of witches?

1. Fray Benavides Sees Wizards, Sorcerers, and the Demon in New Mexico, 1625–1627

Born in the Azores near the end of the sixteenth century, Alonso de Benavides was a Franciscan who served as the New Mexican Inquisition's first official in 1626–1629. By the time he set out on his voyage to Santa Fe in 1625, the Spanish had been in New Mexico for almost three decades, and Franciscans had already converted thousands of Indians and established several missions in the region. Benavides spent a year en route, and wrote an account of his journey after he returned to Spain in 1630. What role, according to Benavides, did sorcerers play in New Mexico society? How did wizards and the Devil fit in to Benavides's account of evangelical efforts in the region?

Leaving the Rio del Norte, and departing toward the east ten leagues from the [Queres] nation, the Tompiras nation begins with its first pueblo of Chililí,[1] and extends in that direction more than fifteen leagues, with fourteen or fifteen pueblos, in which there must be more than ten thousand souls; with six monasteries and very good churches; all [are] converted, and for the most part baptized, and others are being catechized and taught, and with their [training] schools of all trades, as in the other [pueblos]. . . . I cannot refrain from telling here a saying of the Demon, by the mouth of an Indian wizard [who was] convinced of the word of God. . . . And it befell that seeing himself convinced, and that under my reasoning all the pueblo had determined to be Christian, the wizard was much angered and said at the top of his voice: "You Spaniards and Christians, how crazy you are! And you live like crazy folks! You want to teach us that we be [crazy] also!" I asked him wherein we were crazy. And he must have seen some procession of penance during Holy Week in some pueblo of Christians, and so he said: "You Christians are so crazy that you go all together, flogging yourselves like crazy people in the streets, shedding [your] blood. And thus you must wish that this pueblo be also crazy!" And with this, greatly angered and yelling, he went forth from the pueblo, saying that *he* did not wish to be crazy. Over which matter all were left laughing, and I much more, since I recognized and was persuaded that it was the Demon, who [thus] went fleeing, confounded by the virtue of the divine word.

Moqui Nation

It is a general custom among all the infidel Indians to receive the Religious in their pueblos very well in the beginning, and submit themselves soon to Baptism; but seeing, when they are catechized, that they have to give up their idolatries and sorceries, the sorcerers so resent it that they disquiet all, and turn them aside that they be not Christians. Not only this, but they drive the Religious out of the pueblo, and if not, they kill him. Thus it befell in the principal pueblo of this Province of Moqui; that they received very well the Father who went to convert them, and his companions, and a few soldiers who were there for escort with them. And seeing that the Religious, with an original Cross of [which had belonged to] the Mother Luisa de Carrión,[2] constrained them with lively and efficacious reasoning, to the adoration of one God and Lord, Creator of all things, and who for our Redemption had died upon a cross like that [one] which they were under obligation to adore likewise, and not their idols with which the Demon had them so deceived— at this the sorcerers were irritated; and seeing that they were being deprived of the jurisdiction which as infernal ministers they had over those souls, they persuaded all the people that the Religious and all those who accompanied him were so many liars who were going to fool them, and that therefore they should kill them. And when they wished to carry this into effect, on sundry occasions, they dared not, on account of the vigilance of the soldiers, but chiefly on account of heaven's aid. . . .

These are the populations which we have, in this region, converted and baptized, in what we call New Mexico. . . . All of which [together] must have close to eighty thousand souls. All these folk and nations were in their gentilism divided into two factions, warriors and sorcerers. The warriors tried, in opposition to the sorcerers, to bring all the people under their [own] dominion and authority; and the sorcerers, with the same opposition, persuaded all that *they* made the rain fall and the earth yield good crops, and other things at which the warriors sneered. Wherefore there were between them continuous civil wars, so great that they killed each other [off] and laid waste whole pueblos, wherein the Demon had his usual crop. Their religion, though it was not formal idolatry, was nearly so, since they made offerings for whatsoever action. As, at the time when they were going out to fight their enemies, they offered up flour and other things to the scalps of those they had slain of the hostile nation. If they were going to hunt, they offered up flour to heads of deer, jackrabbits, cottontail rabbits, and other dead animals. If to fish, they made offerings to the river. The women who wished that the men should desire them, went out into the country fat and well, and set up a stone or some small pole on some hill, and there offered flour to it; and for eight days, or as many as they could [endure], did not eat, except something to disturb their stomachs and provoke vomiting; and they flogged themselves cruelly. And when they could endure no more, and from fat had made themselves lean and of the mien of the Demon, they returned [to the pueblo] very confident that the first man that they might see them would desire them, and would give them *mantas* [cotton]—which is their chief end. But this adoration of these poles and stones is in nowise reverential; for it makes no odds to them [the Indians] that [people] trample upon them nor spit upon them, but as a ceremonial they put them thus. . . . And in this manner the Demon kept them deceived with a thousand superstitions. . . .

Notes

1. On the Arroyo de Chililí, located about twenty-five miles southeast of Albuquerque.

2. Luisa de Carrión (1602–1665) was a nun in Spain who experienced miraculous flights to New Mexico during which visits she assisted the priests in their conversion efforts.

Source: Emma Augustus Burbank Ayer, trans., *The Memorial of Fray Alonso de Benavides 1630* (Chicago: R. R. Donnelley and Sons Company, 1916), 20–21, 28–29, 30–32.

~ ~ ~

2. Making Sense of the Sickness in Huron Country, 1636–1637: Who's a Witch?

This document is culled from a long account by a Jesuit, François-Joseph Le Mercier (1604–1690), published in the massive Jesuit Relations *(1610–1791). Written by Jesuits in Canada whose ambition was to convert Indians to Christianity, these letters give us a rare and remarkable entry into the collision of cultures that transpired when the French first arrived in Canada. Le Mercier reached Canada in 1635, and worked and lived among the Hurons for almost two decades. With Europeans, of course, came terrible sickness, in this particular case, probably measles*

or influenza. Both Indians and French had clear ideas about what caused disease,
even such unfamiliar ones as those the Hurons suffered, and also what steps to
take to cure illness. As the excerpts below make clear, witchcraft and sorcery were
critical elements of these discussions. What (or who) caused illness? Just who was
a witch? How did Jesuit actions increase Indian convictions that they were witches?
Did the Jesuits become witches when they crossed the Atlantic?

On the 1st day of October [1636], I felt some touches of illness; the fever
seized me towards evening, and I had to give up, as well as the others. But I
became free from it too cheaply; I had only three attacks, but the second one
was so violent that I condemned myself to be bled; my blood was obstinate,
however. God reserved for me a more natural remedy, which appeared at the
end of the third attack, and rendered me able to say the holy Mass from the
next day on. However, I was almost unable for six or seven days to render
any service to our Fathers. The Savages wondered at the order we observed in
caring for our sick, and the diet that we made them observe. It was a curious
thing to them, for they had never yet seen French people ill. I have not told
your Reverence that Tonneraouanont, one of the famous Sorcerers of the
country, having heard that we were sick, came to see us. To hear him talk,
he was a personage of merit and influence, although in appearance he was a
very insignificant object. He was a little hunchback, extremely misshapen,
a piece of a robe over his shoulders,—that is, some old beaver skins, greasy
and patched. This is one of the Oracles of the whole country, who has this
Winter made entire villages bend to his decrees. He had come at that time
to blow upon some sick people of our village. . . . Now in order to make our
mouths water, and to sell his Antidote at a better price, "I am not" (said he)
of the common run of men; I am, as it were, a Demon; therefore I have never
been sick. In the three or four times that the country has been afflicted with a
contagion, I did not trouble myself at all about it; I never feared the disease,
for I have remedies to preserve me. Hence, if thou wilt give me something,
I undertake in a few days to set all thy invalids upon their feet." The Father
Superior, in order to get all the amusement he could out of it, asked him what
he wanted. "Thou wilt give me," said he, "ten glass beads, and one extra for
each patient." The Father answered him that, as for the number, he need not
trouble himself about it, that it was a matter of no consequence; that the ef-
ficacy of his remedies did not depend upon that; furthermore, that he would
be always beginning over again, seeing that the number of patients continued to increase from day to day,—so that he firmly believed that we would
satisfy him. Thereupon he told us that he would show us the roots that must
be used; but that, to expedite matters, he would, if we desired it, go to work

himself, that he would pray, and have a special sweat,—in a word, perform all his usual charlatanries,—and that in three days our sick people would be cured. He made a very plausible speech. The Father satisfied him, or rather instructed him thereupon; he gave the sorcerer to understand that we could not approve this sort of remedy, that the prayer he offered availed nothing, and was only a compact with the devil, considering that he had no knowledge of, or belief in, the true God, to whom alone it is permitted to address vows and prayers; that as far as natural remedies were concerned, we would willingly employ them, and that he would oblige us by teaching us some of them. He did not insist further upon his sweat, and named to us two roots,— very efficacious, he said, against fevers,—and instructed us in the method of using them. But we hardly took the trouble to observe their effects,—we are not accustomed to these remedies, and besides, two or three days later, we saw all our patients nearly out of danger. But your Reverence should, at this point, be thoroughly acquainted with the genealogy of this person, according to the version of it that he himself has given. You will hear of his death at the proper time. Here is what he said about it, as it was reported to us by one Tonkhratacouan. "I am a Demon; I formerly lived under the ground in the house of the Demons, when the fancy seized me to become a man; and this is how it happened. Having heard one day, from this subterranean abode, the voices and cries of some children who were guarding the crops, and chasing the animals and birds away, I resolved to go out. I was no sooner upon the earth than I encountered a woman; I craftily entered her womb, and there assumed a little body. I had with me a she-devil, who did the same thing. As soon as we were about the size of an ear of corn, this woman wished to be delivered of her fruit, knowing that she had not conceived by human means, and fearing that this ocki [spirit] might bring her some misfortune. So she found means of hastening her time. Now it seems to me that in the meantime, being ashamed to see myself followed by a girl, and fearing that she might afterwards be taken for my wife, I beat her so hard that I left her for dead; in fact, she came dead into the world. This woman, being delivered, took us both, wrapped us in a beaver skin, carried us into the woods, placed us in the hollow of a tree, and abandoned us. We remained there until, a Savage passing by, I began to weep and cry out, that he might hear me. He did, indeed, perceive me; he carried the news, to the village; my mother came, she took me again, bore me to her cabin, and brought me up such as thou seest me." This charlatan also related about himself that when he was young, as he was very ill-shapen, the children made war upon him and ridiculed him, and that he had caused several of them to die; that, nevertheless, he had finally decided to endure it henceforth, lest he might ruin the country if he should kill all; that was a fine piece of bluster. Your Reverence will hear still more extravagant stories about him, in the course of time. At all events, behold in him one of the great Physicians of the country; nor did he lack practice. As for us, we could well dispense, thank God, with his remedies. . . . It was oftentimes said, during the evil reports that were current about us throughout the country, that if we had not been afflicted as well as the others, they would not have doubted that we were the cause of the disease. Your Reverence knows how they treat poisoners here; we informed you of it last year, and we have lately seen an example of it with our own eyes,—the danger going so far as to enable us to say that we might not have come out of it very cheaply. We all considered ourselves happy to die in this cause; but since it pleased this divine mercy to preserve our lives, it places us under fresh obligations to employ them for his glory, and not to spare ourselves in anything which can advance the conversion of our Savages. . . .

[October]

Meanwhile, the Devil was playing his pranks elsewhere, and speaking through the mouth of the Sorcerer *Tonnerauanont*, was turning aside these peoples from applying to God. Some time before, this little hunchback had declared that the whole country was sick; and he had prescribed a remedy, namely, a game of [la]crosse, for its recovery [see figure 14]. This order had been published throughout all the villages, the Captains had set about having it executed, and the young people had not spared their arms; but in vain. The disease did not cease to spread, and to gain ground all the time; and on the 15th of October we counted in our little village thirteen or 14 sick people. Nor did our Sorcerer engage at this time to undertake the cure of the whole country; yet he ventured one word as rash as it was presuming, for the village of *Onnentisati*, whence he came. He was not satisfied to give some hope that no one there would be sick,—he gave assurances thereof that he made indubitable, by founding them upon the power he claimed to have over the contagion in his character of Demon; he was immediately given something with which to make a feast. This boast spread everywhere, and was accepted as truth; all the people of *Onnentisati* were already considered fortunate and out of danger. This constrained us to exert ourselves with God, and to implore his divine goodness to confound the devil in the person of this wretch, and to obtain glory for himself from this public affliction. And the next day, the 14th, we made a vow to say for this purpose 30 Masses in honor of the glorious Patriarch, saint Joseph. It was not long before we had something with which to close the mouths of those

Figure 14.   An Iroquois lacrosse game.
Source: Joseph-François Lafitau, *Moeurs des sauvages ameriquains* (Paris, 1724). Courtesy of Georgetown
University Library Special Collections.

who boasted to us of their prowess, and this Village was hardly more spared
than the others. There were a great many sick there, several of whom died.
Heaven, as we hope, has gained thereby. . . .

[November]

About this time another old man of our village was sorely troubled; people
talked of nothing else than of going to break his head. For a long time he
had been suspected of being a Sorcerer and a poisoner, and quite recently
one *Oaca* had testified that he believed this Savage was making him die; and
some of them said they had seen him at night roaming around the Cabins,
and casting flames from his mouth. Here was only too much to make a bad
case for him. Indeed, a girl, seeing seven or eight of her relatives carried off
in a few days, had actually had the boldness to go to his Cabin with the de-
termination to accuse him of being the cause of their death; and as he was
not there, she talked to his wife so freely, and with so much passion, that
the son, happening to come in, laid down his robe, and, taking a hatchet,
went off in a transport of rage to the cabin where these evil suspicions had
originated. Sitting down in the middle of the room, he addressed one *Tioncharon*, and said to him with a steadfast countenance and a confident mien:

"If thou thinkest it is we who make thee die, take now this hatchet and split open my head; I will not stir." *Tioncharon* replied to him, "We will not kill thee now at thy word, but the first time we shall take thee in the act." The matter remained thus for that time, but they were always regarded with a great deal of ill will. These peoples are extremely suspicious, especially when life is involved; the experiences that they think they have had in this matter, and a thousand instances of people whom they believe to have died through witchcraft or poison, maintain them in this distrust. On the same day that this incident occurred, the Father Superior having gone to visit a sick man, they showed him a sort of charm he had just been made to throw up by means of an emetic; it consisted of some hairs, a tobacco seed, a green leaf, and a little cedar twig. But as ill luck would have it, in their opinion, one of these little charms was broken, the other part having remained in his body, and that had caused his death. You hear nothing else talked about in this country, there being hardly any sick people who do not think they have been poisoned. Only recently, when the Father Superior was passing through the village of *Andiatae*, he was shown a grasshopper's leg twined about with a few hairs, which a sick person had just vomited. If Sorcerers are as common in the country as they are often upon the lips of the Savages, we can truthfully say that we are preëminently in *medio nationis pravœ* [in the midst of a depraved nation]; and yet, with all this, in the opinion of many of them, we are past masters in this art, and have an understanding with the devils. . . .

For our part, we have now every reason to praise God, who has granted to us all the favor of passing the winter in very good health, although the greater part of the time we have been among the sick and the dead, and although we have seen many fall sick and die, merely through the communication that they had with one another. The Savages were astonished at it, and are still astonished every day, saying in reference to us, "Those people are not men, they are demons." . . . Our poor village continued to be afflicted until spring, and is almost entirely ruined. We are not surprised at this, for the greater part of them showed that their belief consisted only in fine words, and that in their hearts they have no other God than the belly, and the one who will promise them absolutely to restore them to health in their illnesses. . . .

[June, 1637]

They are still saying, almost as much as ever, that we are the cause of the malady. These reports are partly founded upon the fact that it is in this season much more fatal than it was during the severe cold of the winter, and consequently the greater part of those we baptize, die. Besides this, very recently a certain Algonquin captain has given our Hurons to understand that they were mistaken in thinking that the devils caused them to die,—that they should blame only the French for this; and that he had seen, as it were, a French woman who was infecting the whole country with her breath and her exhalations. Our Savages imagine that it is the sister of the late Estienne Bruslé, who is avenging her brother's death. This Sorcerer added that we, even we ourselves, meddle with sorcery; that for this purpose we employ the images of our saints,—that, when we show them, certain tainted influences issue therefrom which steal down into the chests of those who look at them, and therefore they need not be astonished if they afterwards find themselves assailed by the disease. The prominent and chief men of the country show us quite plainly that they do not share this belief, but nevertheless intimate that they fear some heedless fellow will commit some foul deed that will cause them to blush. We are in God's hands, and all these dangers do not make us forfeit a moment of our joy. . . .

It is not only in this country that we have this reputation [as poisoners and sorcerers], for these false reports have been carried even to strange nations, who consider us as the masters and arbiters of life and death. . . . On the day of the baptism of Pierre *Tsiouendaentaha*, we had exhibited an excellent representation of the judgment, where the damned are depicted,—some with serpents and dragons tearing out their entrails, and the greater part with some kind of instrument of their punishment. Many obtained some benefit from this spectacle; but some persuaded themselves that this multitude of men, desperate, and heaped one upon the other, were all those we had caused to die during this Winter; that these flames represented the heats of this pestilential fever, and these dragons and serpents, the venomous beasts that we made use of in order to poison them. This was said in open feast at *Ouenrio*, according to the report of Captain *Enditsacon*. Another one afterward asked us if it were really true that we were raising the malady in our house as if it were a domestic animal, saying that this was quite a common opinion in the country. And very recently, when I was returning from *Ossossané*, a woman who was coming from her field caught a grasshopper and brought it to me, begging me earnestly to teach her some contrivance for killing these little creatures that eat the corn, adding that she had been told that we were past masters in this art.

Source: Reuben Gold Thwaites, ed., *The Jesuit Relations and Allied Documents* (Cleveland, Burrows Bros. Co., 1896–1901), v. 13, 101–7, 111, 131–33, 155–59, 163–65; v. 14, 53–55, 99, 103–5.

~ ~ ~

3. The Execution of Isaac Jogues, 1646

Jerome Lalemant was a Jesuit in Quebec. In his Relation of 1647, he reported the death of Father Isaac Jogues (1607–1646), who had reached Canada in the summer of 1636 and preached to the Hurons. In 1642, Jogues was captured and tortured by the Iroquois. During his captivity and residence in the town of Ossernenon, he tended to the sick, performed Catholic rites, and, it seems, played the part of a shaman. Jogues returned briefly to France, and then went back to Canada in 1646 and was put in charge of a mission to the Mohawks. Twin misfortunes befell the Mohawks: worms infested their corn, and people sickened and died. Was Jogues a witch?

The 24th of September of last year, 1646, Father Isaac Jogues left Three Rivers in order to go to the country of the Agneronon Hiroquois, to the end of maintaining the peace which they had so solemnly concluded, and in order to cultivate and augment the seed of the Gospel which he had begun to cast into that wretched and thankless land. Before he arrived in that country, this people had sent presents to the Hiroquois of the upper countries,— whom we call *Onondageronons, Sountwaronons*, and some others,—in order strongly to confirm their alliances, and to form a conspiracy for the ruin of the French and of their allied tribes. The cause of this treachery proceeds, in my opinion, from their warlike temper, which cannot stay at rest, and from the glory and advantages which they drew from war; and, furthermore, from their superstition, and from the hatred which the captive Hurons have given them for the doctrine of Jesus Christ. Those captives—having seen us the reproach of their whole country, on account of the contagious and general diseases, of which they made us the Authors through our prayers, which they called charms—have cast these notions into the minds of the Hiroquois, that we carried the Demons and that we and our doctrine tended only to their ruin; insomuch that they accused Father Isaac Jogues, on his first journey after the conclusion of peace, of having concealed some spells in a small chest, or little box, that he left with his host as pledge of his return. The Father, seeing them disturbed, took that box, opened it before them, and showed them and left with them everything that was in it. Sickness having fallen upon their bodies after his departure, as we have learned from the Savage prisoners who have escaped, and the worms having perhaps damaged their corn, as the letter of the Dutch testifies,—these poor blind creatures have believed that the Father had left the Demon among them, and that all our discourses and

Figure 15.   The Execution of Isaac Jogues.

Source: Detail from a plate depicting Jesuit martyrdoms in Canada in François Ducreux, *Historiae Canadensis* (Paris, 1664), The Library of Congress, Prints and Photographs Division, LC-USZ62-49877.

all our instructions aimed only to exterminate them. These are the reasons for which they have resumed the war; insomuch that the good Father Jogues, murdered on the eighteenth of October, has had the honor to be a symbol of Jesus Christ,—being regarded as a man who had the Devil with him, and who employed Beelzebub for driving out the Demons from their souls and from all their country. . . .

Source: Thwaites, ed., *Jesuit Relations*, v. 30, 227–29.

Resistance and the Devil

This section contains three documents concerning two major Indian rebellions in North America, one (the Tepehuan revolt of 1616) in the province of Nueva Vizcaya and the other (the Pueblo revolt of 1680) in New Mexico. The second event expelled the Spanish from New Mexico for over a decade. Europeans associated those who worshipped the Devil with obstinacy and connected Indians who resisted evangelization and Spanish occupation with Satan. In document 1, we saw a priest blame sorcerers for Indian resistance to Christian conversion. In documents 4 and 5, the sorcerers resisted the entire Spanish colonial enterprise. Was witchcraft an important aspect of resistance to colonial rule, as the Spanish believed it to be? Were they, in fact, correct in their assessment? Why was it important to the Spanish that those who resisted their enterprise be described as demons?

4. Andrés Pérez de Ribas Explains the Origins of the Tepehuan Revolt, 1616

Andrés Pérez de Ribas (1575–1655) was a Jesuit priest who entered the order in 1602 and sailed immediately for Mexico, where he spent fifteen years working as a missionary. His massive History of the Triumphs of our Holy Faith Amongst the Most Barbarous and Fierce Peoples of the New World, *which he worked on intermittently for some twenty-five years, offers this account of the origins of the Tepehuan revolt, a major uprising against the Spanish in northern New Spain that lasted from 1616 to 1620. What was Pérez de Ribas's opinion of the Tepehuanes? How did Pérez de Ribas understand the revolt? How might the Tepehuanes have explained their own experience? What role did witchcraft play in this event, both according to Pérez de Ribas's account and in your own assessment of the uprising? Compare Pérez de Ribas's account of witches with that of Benavides in document 1. What important differences do you see in the two descriptions of sorcery in Indian society? How might you account for them?*

Before writing about the fierce, barbarous, and infidel decision made by this nation, I must explain the motive and cause of this—one of the greatest uprisings, disturbances, and ravages of war in Nueva España. We could even say that this was the greatest [rebellion] since the conquest. . . . [W] e must record here that which was well known concerning the Tepehuan nation, namely that they could not allege that the Spaniards, far less their missionary priests, had mistreated or maligned them in such a way that they should have any reason to fail in the Faith that was their duty to God. Nor did they have reason to break the peace that they had established with the Spaniards and their king, under whose protection they had placed themselves. There was only one cause of what happened here—it was a scheme invented by Satan and welcomed by these blind people. [The scheme] enraged their spirits to take up arms against the Faith of Christ and all things Christian. . . . This was demonstrated even more clearly by the principal instigators and authors of the uprising—the diabolical sorcerers who had familiar dealings with the devil. . . .

The case began in the following way. There was an old Indian in this nation who was a great sorcerer and had very intimate dealings with the devil. Although he had been baptized, he only pretended to renounce that diabolical pact. Or perhaps he truly did renounce it and subsequently backslid, just as many other heretics in the world have done. He apostatized, taking along with him an idol, which was like his oracle and the means by which he communicated with the devil. When he entered the pueblos of Santiago, Tunal, and Tenerapa, which were all near Durango, he preached perversely against our Holy Faith, with the harmful intention of inciting those people to abandon their Faith and rebel against God and the king. The governor of Nueva Vizcaya received some news of Indian unrest in Durango. He investigated the case and determined that it was nothing more than one of these people's ancient diabolical superstitions. He ordered the usual punishment for this Indian and his accomplices: that they be flogged for the scandal they had caused in those pueblos. This sorcerer was astute and bedeviled, and in order to disguise his intentions (in which he still persisted, as was later demonstrated), he found an image of our holy crucifix and displayed it to some people. He told them that this was the God whom he and his companions worshiped. Afterwards, however, he went to the aforementioned pueblo of baptized Tepehuan, called Tenerapa. . . . There he ordered that his idol be worshiped, and through his lies and tricks he convinced these Indians that he, through his idol, was God. He also convinced them that both he and the idol were angry and offended because he had assigned the Spaniards a homeland in kingdoms on the other side of the ocean in Spain, and yet they had come to these parts without his permission, settling in his lands and introducing the Christian law. He wished to free them of this, and in order to do so, as well as to placate their true gods, they would have to cut the throats of all long-time Christians, particularly the priests and fathers who instructed them, as well as all the Spaniards in the region. If they did not do so, they would receive a terrible punishment in the form of illnesses, plagues, and famines. But if they obeyed him, he promised them safety for their own lives, their women and children, and victory over the Spaniards. Even if some of them should die in battle, he promised them that within seven days they would be resurrected. He who is the father of deception and was this Indian's own familiar demon heaped one lie on top of another. He added that once they had achieved the promised victory, all the old men and women would be made young again. The devil is aware of how strong this desire is in mankind, who do not want even to appear to be old. On this occasion he used this and other lengthy arguments to pervert [these] ignorant people, just as he has done many other times for similar ends with other people of greater [intellectual] capacity.

This trickster did not desist in his lies and false promises. He assured the Tepehuan that they would wipe out the Spaniards in the region, and that afterwards he, [acting] as God through his idol, would create storms at sea, sinking the Spaniards' ships and thus preventing additional Spaniards from reaching these lands. In confirmation of this diabolical hoax and to further terrorize and frighten these people, he gave them an example [of his power], which some said actually occurred. Even if there was some truth to what was said to have happened, owing to the fact that God, for His reasons, allowed it to happen, the Indian trickster nevertheless misled the people. That notwithstanding, some Indians confessed that an Indian named Sebastián, who was a native of Tenerapa, and a woman named Justina, a native of Papasquiaro, were both swallowed up when the earth opened on the order of the sorcerer, who punished them for disobeying him. The same thing happened to another Indian in another pueblo called Cacaria.

By secretly and repeatedly sowing his diabolical doctrine in various places, the bedeviled Indian kept these people demented and fooled. This was ultimately the true origin and cause of this uprising and revolt and the tragic apostasy of the Tepehuan nation.

Source: Andrés Pérez de Ribas, *History of the Triumphs of our Holy Faith Amongst the Most Barbarous and Fierce Peoples of the New World*, trans. Daniel T. Reff, Maureen Ahern, and Richard K. Danford (Tucson: The University of Arizona Press, 1999), 594–95.

~ ~ ~

5. Witchcraft, Sorcery, and the Pueblo Revolt, 1680–1681

These two documents suggest the complex role that ideas about witchcraft played in the Pueblo Revolt in New Mexico in 1680. This revolt, which drove the Spanish out of the territory for over a decade, was unprecedented among North American indigenous resistance movements in its success, and the Spanish struggled to make sense of its origins and its organization. The first document contains the testimony of Pedro Naranjo, a Queres Indian captured by the Spanish. It provides a glimpse at the spiritual power of the Pueblo leader Popé and his message of cultural and religious revitalization, much like that of the "sorcerer" in document 4. An elderly man when he testified, Naranjo had lived most of his life under Spanish occupation.

The second document comes from the testimony of Luis de Quintana, a Spanish official. Which do you think was more troubling to the Spanish—the military uprising or the religious rejection? In what ways did ideas about witchcraft shape Spanish and Indian interactions in New Mexico, and whose ideas? Was witchcraft important to the Pueblos?

The Declaration of Pedro Naranjo of the Queres Nation, December 19, 1681, in the Place of the Rio del Norte.

In the said plaza de armas on the said day, month, and year, for the prosecution of the judicial proceedings of this case his lordship caused to appear before him an Indian prisoner named Pedro Naranjo, a native of the pueblo of San Felipe, of the Queres nation, who was captured in the advance and attack upon the pueblo of La Isleta. He makes himself understood very well in the Castilian language and speaks his mother tongue and the Tegua. He took the oath in due legal form in the name of God, our Lord, and a sign of the cross. . . .

Asked whether he knows the reason or motives which the Indians of this kingdom had for rebelling, forsaking the law of God and obedience to his Majesty, and committing such grave and atrocious crimes, and who were the leaders and principal movers, and by whom and how it was ordered; and why they burned the images, temples, crosses, rosaries, and things of divine worship, committing such atrocities as killing priests, Spaniards, women, and children, and the rest that he might know touching the question, he said that since the government of Señor General Hernando Ugarte y la Concha they have planned to rebel on various occasions through conspiracies of the Indian sorcerers, and that although in some pueblos the messages were accepted, in other parts they would not agree to it; and that it is true that during the government of the said señor general seven or eight Indians were hanged for this same cause, whereupon the unrest subsided. . . .

Finally, in the past years, at the summons of an Indian named Popé who is said to have communication with the devil, it happened that in an estufa [sacred underground chamber] of the pueblo of Los Taos there appeared to the said Popé three figures of Indians who never came out of the estufa. They gave the said Popé to understand that they were going underground to the lake of Copala. He saw these figures emit fire from all the extremities of their bodies, and that one of them was called Caudi, another Tilini, and the other Tleume; and these three beings spoke to the said Popé, who was in hiding from the secretary, Francisco Xavier, who wished to punish him as a sorcerer. They told him to make a cord of maguey fiber and tie some knots in it which would signify the number of days that they must wait before the rebellion. . . . [A]s soon as the Spaniards had left the kingdom an order came from the said Indian, Popé, in which he commanded all the Indians to break the lands and enlarge their cultivated fields, saying that now they were as they had been in ancient times, free from the labor they had performed for the religious and the Spaniards, who could not now be alive. He said that this is the legitimate cause and the reason they had for rebelling, because they had always desired to live as they had when they came out of the lake at Copala. Thus he replies to the question.

Asked for what reason they so blindly burned the images, temples, crosses, and other things of divine worship, he stated that the said Indian, Popé, came down in person, and with him El Saca and El Chato from the pueblo of Los Taos, and other captains and leaders and many people who were in his train, and he ordered in all the pueblos through which he passed that they instantly break up and burn the images of the holy Christ, the Virgin Mary and the other saints, the crosses, and everything pertaining to Christianity, and that they burn the temples, break up the bells, and separate from the wives whom God had given them in marriage and take those whom they desired. In order to take away their baptismal names, the water, and the holy oils, they were to plunge into the rivers and wash themselves with amole, which is a root native to the country, washing even their clothing, with the understanding that they would thus be taken from them the character of the holy sacraments. They did this, and also many other things which he does not recall, given to understand that this mandate had come from the Caydi and the other two who emitted fire from their extremities in the said estufa of Taos, and that they thereby returned to the state of their antiquity, as when they came from the lake of Copala; that this was the better life and the one they desired, because the God of the Spaniards was worth nothing and theirs was very strong, the Spaniard's God being rotten wood. These things were observed and obeyed by all except some who, moved by the zeal of Christians, opposed it, and such persons the said Popé caused to be killed immediately. He saw to it that they at once erected and rebuilt their houses of idolatry which they call estufas, and made very ugly masks in imitation of the devil in order to dance the dance of the cacina; and he said likewise that the devil had given them to understand that living thus in accordance with the law of their ancestors, they would harvest a great deal of maize, many beans, a great abundance of cotton, calabashes, and very large watermelons and cantaloupes; and that they could erect their houses and enjoy abundant health and leisure. As he has said, the people were very much pleased, living at their ease in this life of their antiquity, which was the chief cause of their falling into such laxity. Following what has already been stated, in order to terrorize them further and cause them to observe the diabolical commands, there came to them a pronouncement from the three demons already described, and from El Popé, to the effect that he who might still keep in his heart a regard for the priests, the governor, and the Spaniards would be known from his unclean face and clothes, and would be punished. And he stated that the four persons stopped at nothing to have their commands obeyed. Thus he replies to the question.

Asked what arrangements and plans they had made for the contingency of the Spaniards' return, he said that what he knows concerning the question is that they were always saying they would have to fight to the death, for they do not wish to live in any other way than they are living at present; and the demons in the estufa of Taos had given them to understand that as soon as the Spaniards began to move toward this kingdom they would warn them so that they might unite, and none of them would be caught. . . . What he has said is the truth, and what happened, on the word of a Christian who confesses his guilt. He said that he has come to the pueblos through fear to lead in idolatrous dances, in which he greatly fears in his heart that he may have offended God, and that now having been absolved and returned to the fold of the church, he has spoken the truth in everything he has been asked. . . . He declared himself to be eighty years of age, and he signed [the declaration] with his lordship and the interpreters and assisting witnesses, before me. . . .

The Declaration of Sergeant Major Luis de Quintana, at the Hacienda of
Luis de Carbajal, December 22, 1681

. . . [H]e . . . heard some rumors among the Spaniards to the effect that the
Indians had complained of the present secretary, of Sargento Major Diego
López, of this declarant, and of other persons, letting it be understood that
they had rebelled because of them. This was because the said secretary, this
declarant, and Sargento Mayor Diego López had been justices during the
government of the señor general, Don Juan Francisco Treviño, in the case of
a punishment which he ordered administered to forty-seven Indian sorcerers
and idolaters for having killed seven religious and three Spaniards by witchcraft. Actually, when the iniquity was uncovered, it was found that they had
bewitched the reverend father preacher, Fray Andrés Durán, minister of the
district of San Ildefonso, who is living today very infirm from the spell which
they brought upon him; and a brother of his; the wife of his said brother; and
the Indian interpreter of the pueblo, who denounced them, and as soon as
they rebelled they killed him, as is well known. The said señor general also
had other notices to the effect that some clerical ministers, among them
those of the districts of Teguas, Taos, Acoma, and Zuñi, being unable to
work and fulfill completely their obligations as ministers in the midst of so
much idolatry, were living very disconsolately because of the said superstitions, and it having come to the notice of the said señor general, he gave a
plenary commission . . . to seize the suspects and investigate and substantiate
the said crimes, which he did. Having arrested the Indians in various pueblos,
he brought them into the presence of the said señor general, who sentenced
four of them to death, and some of the rest to lashings and being sold as
slaves and others to imprisonment. It was discovered also that some Indians
were plotting a conspiracy as they had done during the time of other governors, in which many Indians were hanged on different occasions without the
others being cured of the bad vice of witchcraft and idolatry. As a result of
this occurrence they have borne ill will toward this declarant as secretary and
later as son-in-law of the said maestre de campo, toward Sargento Mayor Diego López as interpreter and as collector of the idols and superstitious herbs
which he took from their houses and from the fields, as well as toward the
said maestre de campo as the chief executor of their punishment, who has
always had a commission to act against them, and toward the rest as persons
occupied in the said business. . . .

Source: Charles Wilson Hackett, ed., *Revolt of the Pueblo Indians of New Mexico and
Otermín's Attempted Reconquest, 1680–1682,* trans. Charmion Clair Shelby (Albuquerque: The University of New Mexico Press, 1942), v. 2, 245–49, 289–90.

English Witch Beliefs Cross the Atlantic

These documents explore the transmission of English witch beliefs across the Atlantic. What did English colonists think that witches did? How did their beliefs compare to those of Indians and Spaniards (see documents 1 through 5)? With the exception of the witchcraft law of Connecticut (document 7), the documents focus on a region that historians have not associated with witchcraft—the Chesapeake colonies of Maryland and Virginia. Yet the very first known case of witchcraft in the English colonies took place in Virginia in 1626, and the last known ducking of an accused witch transpired in Virginia as well, in 1706.

6. The English Act against Conjuration, 1604

Because witchcraft was a crime in England, punished in secular courts, jurisdictions passed laws against it. This section contains two such laws, the English law of 1604 (document 6) and the Connecticut law of 1642 (document 7). In England, witchcraft did not become a felony until 1542, when Henry VIII passed a law singling out a witch's evil intent as the main source of the crime. The statute was repealed by Henry VIII's son Edward, and not until the reign of Elizabeth I was a new law passed in 1563. Three years later, the first women convicted of witchcraft in England were hanged at Chelmsford. James I, the author of a treatise on demonology and the victim of witches during his reign as king of Scotland, repealed Elizabeth's law in 1603, and passed a new and harsher version in 1604. This revised law expanded the offenses punishable by the death penalty and made all second offenses punishable by death. The succinct Connecticut law of 1642 follows this lengthy catalogue of crimes.

What, according to the laws, did witches do? Why do you think these laws are so different? What might the differences tell you about the two societies that created them? Are the laws concerned with different kinds of crimes? And what can laws tell us about practices in any given society? For example, witch prosecutions actually declined in England from the 1580s onward, and there is no evidence of any witchcraft trial in Connecticut until 1647. Should we see laws as reflections of society?

An Acte against Conjuration, Witchcraft, and dealinge with Evill and Wicked Spirits
BE it enacted, by the King our Sovraigne Lorde, the Lordes Spirituall and Temporall and the Comons in this present Parliament assembled, and by the authoritie of the same. That the statute made in the fifth yeere of the

Raigne of our late Sovraigne Ladie of moste famous and happie memorie Queene Elizabeth, intituled an Acte againste Conjurations Inchantments and Witchcrafts, be from the Feaste of St. Michaell the Archangell nexte coming, for and concerninge all Offences to be comitted after the same Feaste, utterlie repealed.

II. And for the better restrayninge the said Offenses and more severe pun-ishinge the same, be it further enacted by the authoritie aforesaide, That if any person or persons, after the saide Feaste of St. Michaell the Archangell next cominge, shall use, practise or exercise any Invocation or Conjuration of any evill and wicked Spirit, or shall consult, covenant with entertaine employe feede or rewarde any evill and wicked Spirit, to or for any intent or purpose; or take up any dead man, woman or child out of his her or theire grave, or any other place where the dead bodie resteth, or the skin bone or any other parte of any dead person, to be imployed or used in any manner of Witchcrafte Sorcerie Charme or Inchantment; or shall use practice or exercise any Witchcrafte Inchantment Charme or Sorcerie, wherebie any person shalbe killed destroyed wasted consumed pined [pained, tormented] or lamed in his or her bodie, or any parte thereof; that then everie such Of-fender or Offendors, their Ayders Abettors and Counsellors, being of any the saide Offences dulie and lawfullie convicted and attainted, shall suffer pains of deathe as a Felon or Felons, and shall loose the privilidge and benefit of Clergie and Sanctuarie.

III. And further, to the intent that all manner of practice use or exercise of witchcrafte Inchantment Charme or Sorcerie should be from henceforth utteilie avoyded abolished and taken away, Be it enacted by the authority of this present Parliament, That if any person or persons shall from and after the saide Feaste of St. Michaell the Archangell next cominge, take upon him or them by Witchcrafte Inchantment Charme or Sorcerie, to tell or declare in what place any treasure of Golde or Silver should or might be founde or had in the earth or other secret places, or where Goods or Things lost or stollen should be founde or become; or to the intent to provoke any person to unlawfull love; or wherebie any Cattell or Goods of any person shall be destroyed wasted or impaired, or to hurte or destroy any person in his or her bodie, although the same be not effected and done; that then all and everie such person and persons so offending, and beinge thereof lawfullie convicted, shall for the said Offence suffer Imprisonment by the space of one whole yeare, without baile or maineprise,[1] and once in everie quarter of the saide yeare, shall in some Markett Towne, upon the Markett Day, or at such tyme as any Faire shalbe kepte there, stande openlie upon the Pillorie by the space of six houres, and there shall openlie confesse his or her error and offence;

and if any person or persons beinge once convicted of the same offences as is aforesaide, doe eftsoones [again] perpetrate and commit the like offence, that then everie such Offender, beinge of any the saide offences the second tyme lawfullie and duelie convicted and attainted as is aforesaide, shall suffer paines of death as a Felon or Felons, and shall loose the benefit and privilidge of Clergie and Sanctuarie: Savinge to the wife of such person as shall offend in any thinge contrarie to this Act, her title of dower; and also to the heire and successour of everie such person his or theire titles of Inheritance succession and other Rights, as though no such Attaindor of the Ancestor or Predecessor had been made; Provided alwaies, That if the Offender in any the Cases aforesaide shall happen to be a Peer of this Realme, then his Triall therein to be had by his Peers, as it is used in cases of Felonie or Treason, and not otherwise.

Note

1. That is, no possibility of getting release by finding sureties.

Source: *The Statutes of the Realm* (London: G. Eyre and A. Strahan, 1810–1818), v. 4, 1028–29.

∼ ∼ ∼

7. The Law of the Colony of Connecticut, 1642

If any man or woman be a witch (that is) hath or consulteth with a familiar spirit, they shall be put to death. Ex: 22.18: Lev: 20.27: Deu: 18.10, 11.

Source: *The Public Records of the Colony of Connecticut, from April 1636 to October 1776* (Hartford: Brown & Parsons, 1850–1890), v. 1, 77.

∼ ∼ ∼

8. The Case of Goodwife Wright, Virginia, 1626

Goodwife Wright lived in the English colony of Virginia, which was almost twenty years old when she was called before the Virginia Council to answer charges of witchcraft in 1626. Only four years earlier, the English colonists had endured a calamitous surprise attack led by the Indian leader, Opechancanough, in which over one-third of the 1,230 colonists were killed. By 1625 the colony's population had barely rebounded, with an estimated 1,300 people living in the colony. Far more colonists died of disease than at the hands of Native Americans. Death, then, was a constant preoccupation, and concerns about mortality feature in the accusations against Wright. Wright was married, as the testimony below indicates, and she lived in Kickotan, which is now within the borders of Hampton, Virginia. In 1625, women comprised some 22 percent of colonial inhabitants.[1]

These council proceedings from two days in September are the only source we have for Wright's status as a witch. How safe is it to draw conclusions about English witch beliefs generally in light of this fragmentary evidence? What can these council records tell you about what people in Virginia thought a witch did? How many people took part in the trial? In what ways did her accusers believe that Wright subverted gender roles? If you find the original spelling hard to understand, try reading the text out loud.

11 September 1626

Liut Gieles Allintone sworen and examined sayeth, That he harde Sargeant Booth saye that he was croste by a woman and for a twelve months space he havinge very fayre game to shute at, yet he could never kill any thinge but this deponent cannot say that it was good wiefe Wright. Fourther this deponent sayeth, that he had spoken to good wiefe Wrighte for to bringe his wiefe to bed, but the saide goodwife beinge left handed, his wiefe desired him to get Mrs Grave to be her midwiefe, which this deponent did, and sayeth that the next daye after his wiefe was delivered, the saide goodwiefe Wright went awaye from his howse very much discontented, in regarde the other midwiefe had brought his wiefe to bedd, shortlie after this, this deponents wiefes brest grew dangerouslie sore of an Imposture and was a moneth or 5 weeks before she was recovered, Att which tyme This deponent him selfe fell sick and continued the space of three weeks, And further sayeth that his childe after it was borne fell sick and soe continued the space of two monethys, and afterwards recovered, And so did Contynue well for the space of a moneth, And afterwards fell into extreme payne the space of five weeks and so departed.

Rebecka Graye sworne and examined sayeth That good wief Wright did tell her this deponent That by one Token which this deponent had in her forehed she should burye her Husbande, and fourther sayeth that good wiefe Wright did tell this deponent that she told Mr ffellgate he should bury his wiefe (which cam to pass) And further this deponent sayeth that goodwiefe Wright did tell this deponent, That she tolde Thomas Harris he should burie his first wiefe being then bethrothed unto him (which cam so to pass) further this deponent sayeth that goodwiefe Wright did tell her that there was a woman said to her (I have a cross man to my husband) To whom good wiefe Wright replide (be content) for thow shalte shortlie burie him (which cam so to pass)

Thomas Jones sworne and examined sayeth, that Sargeant Booth told him that goodwiefe Wright would have had som what of him, which the saide Sargeant Booth either would nott or could nott give her, and as this deponent thinketh it was a peece of fflesh, And after the said Sargeant Booth went foorth with his peece, and cam to good game and very fayre to shoote at, But for a longe tyme after he could never kill any thinge.

Robert Wright sworne and examined sayeth that he hath beene maried to his wiefe sixteene yeers, but knoweth nothinge by her touchinge the crime she is accused of

Daniell Watkins sworne and examined sayeth that about february last past, this deponent beinge at Mr Perryes Plantatione Ther was Robert Thresher who had a cowple of henns pourposinge to send them over to Elzabeth Arundle and good wiefe Wright beinge there in place, saide to Robert Thresher, why do you keepe these henns heere tyed upp, The maide you meane to send them to will be dead before the henns come to her.

Mrs Isabell Perry sworne and examined sayeth that uppon the losinge of a logg of light wood owt of the foorte, good wiefe Wrighte rayled uppon a girle of good wiefe gates for stealing of the same, wheruppon good wiefe gates Charged the said good wiefe Wright with witchcrafte, And said that she had done many bad things at Kickotan, whereuppon this Examinate Chid the saide Good wiefe Wright, And said unto her, if thow knowst thyselfe Cleare of what she Charged thee, why dost thow not complaine And cleare thyselfe of the same, To whom good wiefe Wright replied, god forgive them, and so made light of it, And the said good wiefe Wright Threatened good wiefe Gates girle and told her, that if she did nott bringe the light wood againe she would make her daunce starke naked and the next morninge the lightwood was founde in the forte.

And furhter sayeth that Dorethie Behethlem asked this Examint why she did suffer good wiefe to be at her howse, sayinge she was a very bad woman, and was Accompted a witch amoungst all them at Kickotan

And fourther this deponent [sayeth] that good wiefe did tell her that when she lived at hull [England], beinge one day Chirninge of butter there cam a woman to the howse who was accompted for a witch, whereuppon she by directions from her dame Clapt the Chirne staffe to the bottom of the Chirne and clapt her handes across uppon the top of it by which means the witch was not able to stire owt of the place where she was for the space of six howers after which time good wiefe Wright desired her dame to aske the woman why she did not gett her gone, wheruppon the witche fell downe on her knees and asked her forgivenes and saide her hande was in the Chirne, and could not stire before her maide lifted upp the staffe of the Chirne, which the saide good wiefe Wright did, and the witch went awaye but to her perseverance the witch had both her handes at libertie, and this good wiefe Wright affirmteh to be trewe. Fourther Mrs Pery sayeth that good wiefe Wright told her, that she was at Hull her dame beinge sick suspected her selfe to be bewiched, and told good wiefe Wright of it, whereuppon by directione from her dame, That at the cominge of a woman, which was suspected, to take a horshwe and flinge it into the oven and when it was red hott, To fflinge it into her dames urine, and so long as the horshwe was hott, the witch was sick at the harte, And when the Irone was colde she was well againe, And this good wiefe Wright affirmeth to be trwe alsoe

Alice Baylie sworne and examnd sayeth that she asked good wief Wright whether her husbande should bury her, or she burye him To whom good wiefe Wright answered, I can tell you if I would, but I am exclaimde against for such thinges and Ile tell no more

18 September 1626

Richard Thresher sworne and examined sayeth that good wiefe Wright came to him and requested him to give her some plants, He answered that when he had served his owne tourne, she should have some, so she went away and that night all his plants were drownde.

Fourther he sayeth that he left 2 hennes with good wiefe Wright to be sent over to Elizabeth Arundle either by the provost marshall or some other, and that goodwiefe Wright did tell Daniell Watkins that Elizabeth Arundle would be dead before the henns were sent over

Elizabeth Gates sworne and examined sayeth that goodwiefe Wright came to Mr Moores at Kickotan to buy some chickens, but he would sell her none, shortly after the chickens died, and after that the henn died, and this she affirmeth she had hearde from others.

And further sayeth that when goodwiefe Wright Threatened her maide she said she would make her dance naked and stand before the Tree.

Note

1. For population data, see Edmund S. Morgan, *American Slavery, American Freedom: The Ordeal of Colonial Virginia* (New York: Norton, 1975), 111, 404.

Source: H. R. McIlwaine, ed., *Minutes of the Council and General Court of Colonial Virginia*, 2nd ed. (Richmond: The Colonial Press, 1924), 111–12, 114.

~ ~ ~

9. The Execution of Mary Lee en route to Maryland, 1654

Believed by sailors to be a witch, Mary Lee was killed during her voyage from England to Maryland aboard the Charity of London in 1654. She was one of three women known to have been executed as witches during voyages to the Chesapeake colonies of Virginia and Maryland in the 1650s. The first two items are depositions given before the Maryland Council by men who were on the Charity; the third comes from a Jesuit, Francis Fitzherbert, who traveled in the same fleet but not on Lee's ship. How do the three accounts differ in tone, perspective, explanation, and the details of the event? How does Fitzherbert's view of this witch compare with those of the Jesuit authors of documents 2 and 4? Why do you think sailors and passengers believed Lee to be a witch? Was her death an act of mob violence? Did participants believe they followed legal procedures? What—or who—might have saved Mary Lee from murder?

Two Depositions before the Maryland Council

The Deposition of Mr Henry Corbyn of London Merchant aged about 25th years, Sworne and Examined in the Province of Maryland before the Governour & Councell there (whose Names are hereunto Subscribed) the 23th day of June Anno Domini 1654. Saith That at Sea upon his this Deponents Voyage hither in the Ship called the Charity of London mr John Bosworth being Master and about a fortnight or three weeks before the Said Ships arrival in this Province of Maryland, or before A Rumour amongst the Seamen was very frequent, that one Mary Lee then aboard the Said Ship was a witch, the Said Seamen Confidently affirming the Same upon her own deportment and discourse, and the more Earnestly then before Importuned the Said Master that a tryall might be had of her which he the Said Master, mr Bosworth refused, but resolved (as he Expressed to put her ashore upon the Barmudoes) but Cross winds prevented and the Ship grew daily more Leaky almost to desperation and the Chiefe Seamen often declared their Resolution of Leaving her if an opportunity offered it Self which aforesaid Reasons put the Maste[r] upon a Consultation with mr Chipsham and this Deponent, and it was thought fitt, Considering our Said Condition to Satisfie the Seamen in a way of trying her according to the Usuall Custome in that kind whether She were a witch or Not and Endeavoured by way of delay to have the Commanders of other Ships aboard but Stormy weather prevented, In the Interime two of the Seamen apprehended her without order and Searched her and found

Some Signall or Marke of a witch upon her, and then calling the Master mr Chipsham and this Deponent with others to See it afterwards made her fast to the Capstall betwixt decks, And in the Morning the Signall was Shrunk into her body for the Most part, And an Examination was thereupon importuned by the Seamen which this Deponent was desired to take whereupon She confessed as by her Confession appeareth, And upon that the Seamen Importuned the Said Master to put her to Death (which as it Seemed he was unwilling to doe, and went into his Cabbinn, but being more Vehemently pressed to it, he tould them they might doe what they would and went into his Cabbinn, and Sometime before they were about that Action he desired this deponent to acquaint them that they Should doe no more then what they Should Justifie which they Said they would doe by laying all their hands in generall to the Execution of her, All which herein before Expressed or the Same in Effect this Deponent averreth upon his oath to be true, And further Sayth not
Henry Corbyne
Sworne before us the day and year above written
William Stone
Tho: Hatton
Job. Chandler

The Deposition of Francis Darby Gent Aged about 39 yeares Sworne and Examined in the Province of Maryland before the Governour and Councell there whose Names are hereunto Subscribed the 23 day of June Anno Domini 1654. Saith That at Sea upon the Voyage hither about a fortnight or three weeks before the Arrivall of the Ship called the Charity of London in this Province of Maryland, whereof mr John Bosworth was then Master and upon the Same Day that one Mary Lee was put to Death aboard the Said Ship as a witch he the Said mr Bosworth Seeing him this Deponent backward [sic] to Assist in the Examination of her asked this Deponent why? and tould him that he was perplext about the busieness Seeing he did not know how he might doe it by the Law of England afterwards this deponent being present in the Round house heard the Said mr Bosworth give Order that nothing Should be done concerning the Said Mary Lee without Speaking first with him, and after She was put to Death or Executed to the best of this Deponents remembrance he Said he knew nothing of it, And this Deponent Saith that the Said Bosworth was in the inner room of the Roundhouse, he this deponent being in the next room at the time they treated about the busieness And this Deponent could not perceive any thing either by word or Deed whereby he gave order for her Execution or putting to Death and after this he Commanded they Should doe Nothing without his Order and

Figure 16. The title page of Richard Bovet's *Pandaemonium, or the Devil's Cloyster* depicts a wide variety of activities and characters associated with the occult arts, including an elderly witch with a hooked nose (figure A) and a witch riding the Devil (figure E).

Source: From Richard Bovet, *Pandaemonium, or the Devil's Cloyster* (London, 1684). This item is reproduced by permission of *The Huntington Library, San Marino, California.*

alsoe after the Execucon, expressed he knew not of it for that this Deponent hearing these words (She is dead) ran out and asked who was dead, and it was replyed the witch then this Deponent Entred the next Room and Said they have hanged her and he the Said Bosworth thereupon as it were Speaking with trouble in a high Voyce replyed he knew not of it All which herein before Expressed or the Same in Effect this Deponent averreth upon his oath to be true, And further Sayth not.

Francis Darby

Sworne before us the day and Yare abovewritten

William Stone

Tho: Hatton

Job Chandler

Source: *Proceedings of the Council of Maryland, 1648–1655* (Baltimore: Maryland Historical Society, 1885–1912), v. 3, 306–308.

Father Francis Fitzherbert's account of his journey from England to Maryland

Four ships sailed together from England, but were overtaken by a fearful storm as they were passing the Western Isles, and the ship which carried the Father was so shattered that, springing a leak in battling with the continued violence of the sea, the pump became almost useless. Four men at a time, taken not only from the ship's crew but from among the passengers also, were kept constantly working at the great pump, each one in turn day and night.

Having changed their course their intention was to make sail towards Barbados; but no art or labour could accomplish this, and so they decided on abandoning the ship and commiting themselves with their wares to the long boat. As, however, the swelling sea and huge waves prevented this also, many a form of death presented itself to their minds, and the habit of terror, now grown a familiar thought, had almost excluded the particular fear of death. The tempest lasted in all two months, whence the opinion arose that it did not come from the storm of sea or sky, but was occasioned by the malevolence of demons. Forthwith they seized a little old woman suspected of sorcery, and after examining her with the strictest severity, they killed her, whether guilty or not guilty, as the suspected cause of all the evil. The corpse, and whatever belonged to her, they cast into the sea. However, the winds did not in consequence abate their violence, nor did the raging sea smooth its threatening billows. To the troubles of the storm sickness was added next, which attacked almost every person and carried off not a few. The Father himself escaped untouched by the disease, but in working at the pump somewhat too laboriously he contracted a slight fever of a few days' continuance. Having passed through multiplied dangers, at length, by the favor of God, the ship reached the port of Maryland.

Source: Henry Foley, ed., *Records of the English Province of the Society of Jesus* (London: Burns and Oates, 1878), vol. 3, 388–89.

~ ~ ~

10. The Case of Grace Sherwood, Virginia, 1706

Grace Sherwood lived in Princess Anne (formerly Lower Norfolk) County, Virginia, in the area of what is now Virginia Beach. She first appeared in the county court records in 1698, when she and her husband James sued a variety of people for slander and defamation for calling her a witch. It was, apparently, a time of some witchcraft trouble in the county, for in that same year, another woman was accused of "riding" her neighbors, a customary act of a witch and just what Sherwood herself was accused of by her neighbors.[1] In 1701, James Sherwood died, and in December 1705, Grace Sherwood was back in court, suing Luke Hill and his wife for assault. The Hills then brought a complaint to the county court in January 1706, that Sherwood was a witch, and for the next several months, the case continued in the court, culminating in the ducking trial in July of that year. Sherwood survived her ordeal and little is known of her subsequent life. Her will was proved in court in 1740, showing that she lived long after the trials she endured in 1706, and in it she left property to three sons. The legal records enable us to glimpse many points of view—Sherwood's accusers, her neighbors, the local court officials, and the men of the colony's council, who weighed in on the subject. At one point, the justices could not find a jury of women willing to participate in a search of Sherwood's body for witches' marks. Do you think that Sherwood's neighbors agreed that she was a witch? What made her a witch?

At a Court held the 10th of Sept 1698

James Sherwood and Grace his wife sueing John Gisburne and Jane his wife in a action of Slander setting forth by his petition that the Defendents had wronged Defamed and abused the said Grace in her good name and reputation saying that she is a Witch and bewitched their piggs to Death and bewitched their Cotton & prays Judgment against the said Gisburne for £100 Sterling damage with Cost to which the Defendent pleadeth not guilty the whole matter being put to a Jury who bring in their Verdict as followeth Wee of the Jury find for the Defendant. . . .

James Sherwood and Grace his wife suing Anthony Barnes and Elizabeth his wife in an action of Slander setting forth by their petition that the said Elizabeth had wronged and abused the said Grace in her good name & reputation saying the said Grace came to her one night and rid her and went out of the key hole or crack of the door like a black Catt &c prayes Judgment for 100£ sterling damage with Cost: to which the Defendent pleadeth not guilty. The whole matter being put to a Jury who bring in their Verdict as followeth Wee of the Jury find for the Defendent. . . .

[The Sherwoods had to pay costs for their nine witnesses in the case]

[James Sherwood died intestate in 1701, leaving an estate worth 3000 pounds tobacco]

At a Court the 7th Xber [December] 1705

Grace Sherwood Suing Luke Hill & Uxor [wife] In an action of Trespass of Assault & Battery Setting forth how the Defendents Wife had Assaulted Brused Maimed & Barbarously Beaten the plaintiff to her great damage fifty Pounds Sterr: Damage to which the Defendents by Richard Corbitt their Attorney pleaded not Guilty & of this put themselves on the Country with the plaintiff in Like manner whereupon a Jury was Impanelled and Sworne to try the Case who Bring in their verdict wee of the Jury doe in a Difference depending Between Grace Sherrwood plaintiff & Luke Hill & Elizbth his wife defendent find for the plaintiff twenty Shill: Sterr: Damages with Cost. . . .

At a Court held the 3d of January 1705–6

Whereas Luke Hill & uxor Summoned Grace Sherwood to this Court in Suspition of witchcraft & she fayling to appear it is therefore ordered that attachment to the Sherr do Issue to attach her body to answer the said Summons next Court

ffebry 6th 1705–6

Suite for Suspition of witchcraft brought by Luke Hill against Grace Sherwood is ordered to be referr till to morro

ffebry 7th 1705–6

Whereas a Complaint was brought against Grace Sherrwood on Suspition of witchcraft by Luke Hill &c: & the matter being after a long time debated & ordr that the said Hill pay all fees of this Complaint & that the said Grace be here next Court to be Searched according to the complaint by a Jury of women to decide the said Differr: & the Sherr is Likewise ordr to Summon an able Jury accordingly

At a Court held the 7th March 1705/6

Whereas a Complaint have been to this Court by Luke Hill & his wife that one grace Sherrwood of the County was & Have been a long time Suspected of witchcraft & have been as Such Represented wherefore the Sherr at the last Court was ordered to Som a Jury of women to the Court to Serch her on the said Suspicion She assenting to the Same and after the Jury was impannelled and Sworn & Sent out to make Due inquirery & Inspection into all Circumstances After a Mature Consideracon They bring in the verditt wee of the Jury have Serchtt Grace Sherwood & have found Two things like titts with Severall other Spotts Elizr Barnes forewoman Sarah Norris Margrit Watkins Hannah Dinnis Sarah Goodacre Mary Burgess Sarah Sergeent Winifred Davis Ursula Henley ann Bridgs Ezabh waples Mary Cotle

[The action surrounding this case moved in late March to the Council of Virginia]

At a council held at her Majesties Royall Capitol the 28th day of March, 1706:

Luke Hill by his petition informing this Board that one Grace Sherwood of Princess Anne County being suspected of witchcraft upon his complaint to that county court that she had bewitched the petitioners wife, the court ordered a jury of women to serch the said Grace Sherwood who upon search brought in a verdict against the said Grace, but the court not knowing how to proceed to judgment thereon, the petitioner prays that the attorney Generall may be directed to prosecute the said Grace for the same.

Ordered that the said peticon be referred to Mr Attorney Generall to consider & report his opinion to his Excellcy & the council on the first day of the next Genl court

April the 16th 1706

Mr Attorney Generall haveing in pursuance of an order of this Board reported his opinion of Luke Hill against Grace Sherwood as being suspected of witchcraft in the following words to-wit: viz Upon perusal of the above order of this honorable Board I doe conceive & am of the opinion that the charge or accusation is too general that the county court ought to make a further Examinacon of the matters of fact & to have proceeded therein pursuant to the directions & powers of County Courts given by a late act of Assembly in criminal cases made & provided & if they thought there was sufficient cause to have (according to that Law) committed her to the Generall prison of this Colony whereby it would have come regularly before the Generall Court and whereupon I should have prepared a bill for the Grand jury & if they had found it I should have prosecuted it. I therefore with humble submission offer & conceive it proper that the said County Court do make a further Enquiry into the matter, and if they are of opinion there be cause they act according to the above said Law and I shall be ready to present a Bill and if found proceed thereon

Ordered that a copy of the said Report be sent to the court of Princess Anne County for their direction in the premises.

[After this order, the action shifted back to the Princess Anne County Court]

May 2nd 1706

Whereas a former Complaint was brought against Grace Sherwood for Suspicion of Witchcraft which by the Atturny Genrll Report to his Excellency in Councill was to Generall & not Charging her with any particular Act therefore represented to them that Princess Ann Court might if they thought fitt have her examined De Novo & the Court Being of Oppinion that there is great Cause of Suspicion Doe therefore order that the Sherr take the Said Grace into his Safe Costody until She Shall give bond & Security for her appearance to the next Court to be examined Denovo & that the Constable of that precinktt go with the Sherr & Serch the Said graces House & all Suspicious places Carfully for all Images & Such like things as may any way Strengthen the Suspicion & it is likewise Ordered that the Sherr Som an Able Jury of Women also all Evidences as Cann give in anything against her in Evidence in behalf of our Soveraign Lady the Queen To Attend the next Court Accordingly

June 6th 1706

Whereas Grace Sherwood of this County have been Complained of as a person Suspected of Witchcraft & now being Brought before this Court in order for examinacon this Court have therefore requested mr Maxmll Boush to present Informacon against her as Councill in behalf of our Soveraign Lady the Queen in order to her being brought to a regular Tryall

Whereas an Informacon in Behalf of her Magty was presented by Luke Hill to the Court in pursuance to Mr Generall Attorneys Tomson report on his Excellency order in Councill the 16th Aprill Last About Grace Sherwood being Suspected of Witchcraft have thereupon Sworn Severall Evidences against her by which it Doth very likely appear

June 7th 1706

Whereas at the Last Court an order was past that the Sherr should Sommon an able Jury of Women to Serch Grace Sherwood on Suspicion of witchcraft which although the Same was performed by the Sherr yet they refused And did not appear it is therefore order that the Same persons be again Somd by the Sherr for their contempt To be Dealt with according to the utmost Severity of the Law, & that a new Jury of women be by him Somd To appear next Court to Serch her on the aforesaid Suspicion & that he likewise Som all evidences that he Shall Be informed of as materiall in the Complaint & that She continue in the Sherr Costody unless She give good bond And Security for her Appearance at the next Court & that She be of the Good behaviour towards her Majestie & all her Leidge people in the mean time

At a court held the 5th July anno Dom 1706

Whereas for this Severall Courts the Business between luke hill & Grace Sherwood on Suspicion of witchcraft have Benn for Severall things omitted particularly for want of a Jury to Serch her & the Court being Doubtfull That they Should not get one this Court & being willing to have all means possible tried either to acquit her or to Give more Strength to the Suspicion that She might be Dealt with as Deserved therefore it was Ordered that the Day by her own Consent to be tried in the water by Ducking but the weather being very Rainy & Bad Soe that possibly might endanger her health it is therefore ordered that the Sherr request the Justices precisely to appear on wednessday next by tenn of the clock at the Court house & that he Secure the body of the Said Grace till the time to be forth Coming then to be Dealt with as afore said

July 10th 1706

Whereas Grace Sherwood being Suspected of witchcraft have a long time waited for a ffitt uppertunity ffor a further Examinacon & by her Consent & approbacon of the Court it is ordered that the Sherr take all Such Convenient assistance of boate & men as Shall be by him thought ffit to meet at Jno Harpers plantacon in order to take the said Grace forthwith & put her into above mans Debth & try her how She Swims therein having Care of her life to preserve her from Drowning & as Soon as She Comes Out that he requests as many Ansient & Knowing woman as possible he cann to Serch her Carefully for all teats spots & marks about her body not usuall in Others & that as they ffind the Same to make report on Oath to the truth thereof to the Court & further it is ordered that Som women be requested to Shift & Serch her before She goe into the water that She Carry nothing about her to cause any further Suspicion

Whereas on complaint of Luke Hill on behalf of her Majesty that now is against Grace Sherwood for a person Suspected of witchcraft & having had Sundry Evidences Sworne against her proving Many circumstances to which She could not make any excuse or Little or nothing to say in her own Behalf only Seemed to Rely on what the Court should Doe and there upon consented to be tried in the water & Likewise to be Serched againe which experiants being tryed & She Swimming when therein and bound contrary To custom & the Judgment of all the spectators & afterwards being Serched by ffive antient weomen who have all Declared on Oath that She is not like them nor noe Other woman that they knew of having two things like titts on her private parts of a Black Coller being Blacker than the Rest of her Body all which circumstance the Court weighing in their Consideracon Doe therefore order that the Sherr take the Said Grace Into his Costody & to Commit her body to the Common Goal of this county there to Secure her by irons or otherwise Directed in order for her coming to the Common Goale of the county to bee brought to a futture Tyrall there.

Note

1. George Lincoln Burr, ed., *Narratives of the Witchcraft Cases, 1648–1706* (New York: Charles Scribner's Sons, 1914), 436.

Source: Edward W. James, "Grace Sherwood, the Virginia Witch," *William and Mary Quarterly*, vol. 3, no. 2 (October 1894), 99–100; vol. 3, no. 3 (January 1895), 191–92; vol. 3, no. 4 (April 1895), 242–45; vol. 4, no. 1 (July 1895), 18–19.

~ ~ ~

11. Governor Kaine Pardons Grace Sherwood, 2006

In July 2006, three hundred years after county authorities subjected Grace Sherwood to the ducking test, Governor Timothy Kaine of Virginia issued this pardon. How does Kaine's reading of her story square with your own explanation?

With 300 years of hindsight, we all certainly can agree that trial by water is an injustice. We also can celebrate the fact that a women's equality is constitutionally protected today, and women have the freedom to pursue their hopes and dreams.

The historical records that survive indicate that Ms. Sherwood, a midwife and widowed mother of three, survived her "trial by water" in 1706. Those records also indicate that one of my predecessors, Governor Alexander Spotswood, eventually helped her reclaim her property. The record also indicates Ms. Sherwood led an otherwise quiet and law-abiding life until she died at age 80.

Today, July 10, 2006, as 70th Governor of the Commonwealth of Virginia, I am pleased to officially restore the good name of Grace Sherwood.

Sincerely,
[signed]
Timothy M. Kaine

Source: A plaque located at Witchduck Road, Virginia Beach, Virginia, on the
Grace Sherwood statue.

New Worlds

The documents in this section focus on how Europeans, Indians, and Africans lived together in North America. They allow us to glimpse the power
dynamics of colonial societies and how witch accusations featured in those
relationships. The first document, a witchcraft case from New Mexico in
1708, reveals complex ties between Spanish colonists and Pueblo Indians,
in addition to delineating ideas about witches and witchcraft. The second
set of documents in this section focuses on poisonings carried out by slaves.
A variety of short excerpts from a travel account in West Africa, colonial
law books, colonial newspapers, and the letters of Thomas Jefferson invite
readers to debate whether they think that poisoning should be thought of
as witchcraft.

12. A Case of Witchcraft in New Mexico, 1708

*What starts as an accusation of witchcraft lodged by a Spanish colonist against
three Indian women reveals itself as a complicated web of interactions, in which the
accuser, Doña Leonor Dominguez, believed her husband, Miguel Martin, to be
sexually involved with one of the accused women, Angelina Pumazho. The trial ex-
poses the entangled lives of Spaniards and Indians in colonial New Mexico, only a
few years after the Spanish returned to the province following their expulsion in the
wake of the Pueblo Revolt. Witchcraft featured in these new relationships, providing a way for Doña Leonor to articulate her anger. How might the power dynamics
of colonial society explain these witchcraft accusations—who lodged them, against
whom, and why? The trial also gives us a glimpse of the inquisitorial method, common on the European continent, in which charges were brought forward by judicial
authorities. Compare the process with the trial of Grace Sherwood in document 10.
What important differences do you see? How might the legal process in each case
have affected the outcome?*

Santa Fe, May 13, 1708

Doña Leonor Dominguez, native resident of this Province, wife of Miguel
Martin, appears before your lordship in due form and manner according to
law, and of my own will affirm: that being extremely ill with various troubles
and maladies which seemed to be caused by witchcraft, having been visited

by persons practiced and intelligent in medicine, who gave me various remedies, which experiments were followed not only by very slight improvement but also every day increased my sufferings and supernatural extremity, and although I am a catholic christian, by the goodness of God, I know that there have been many examples in this Province of persons of my sex who have been possessed by witchcraft with devilish art, as is well known and perceptible in Augustina Romero, Ana Maria, wife of Luiz Lopez, and Maria Lujan, my sister-in-law, and other persons, the effect being the same in one case as in the others, which has been seen to ensue in some of them [by means of some small inquiry] upon their health, as they declare: Wherefore, I cite them, and having just suspicions of certain [persons] notorious for this crime [mutilated] some things and claiming the protection of your lordship's zeal, I ask that you may be pleased to [order?] one of your agents [to come] to the house and habitation where I am staying, to take my legal declaration and solemn oath of what passed between me and the three Indian women of the village of San Juan, whom I suspect, promising to declare the occasion, cause and reasons for my suspicion, and in order that likewise it may be seen from the condition in which I find myself, which is also a matter of public knowledge and notoriety. . . .

This declarant, being on Holy Thursday last in the church of the Town of Santa Cruz, praying, saw beside her an Indian woman of San Juan, called Catherina Lujan, and further off [she saw] another, who is the wife of Zhiconqueto, the painter; that she heard this Catherina Lujan say to the wife of the said Indian: "Is this the wife of Miguel Martin?" and she answered: "Yes, it is"; and that at this time this declarant heard the wife of the said Indian painter, and one of her daughters, say to the said Catherina Lujan: "Now"; and that the latter said: "Not yet": and that, then, full of terror, this declarant left that place where she was kneeling, and fell on her knees further off, and this time the wife of the said Indian said to the said Catherina: "It would be better now"; and, being on her knees behind this declarant, the said wife of the Indian came close to her and put her hand on her back beside her heart; and then, as she did so, her entire body began to itch, and this declarant [MS. torn] has not lifted her head since then, except that every day she is [MS. torn] whence she is persuaded that those aforesaid [MS. torn] that she suffers and this declarant never knew that the Indian women had done her harm, but thought that perhaps they wanted secretly to steal the buttons from the mantle which she was wearing, and that she went out afraid and she has a horror of that place to the present day, and that she told what had happened to her to Casilda, the wife of Francisco Martin, the Reaper, and that for this [reason] she has preferred this criminal complaint against the said Indian women; and that this is the truth, under pain of the oath she has taken, which she affirmed and certified; and that she is twenty years of age, and she does not sign because she does not know how. . . .

[The three accused witches, Catherina Lujan, Catherina Rosa, and Angelina Pumazho, were apprehended.]

May 16
Declaration of Angelina Pumazho

In this Town of Santa Fe, the sixteenth day of May, seventeen hundred and eight, I, the Captain Juan Garcia de las Ribas, examining justice, in pursuance of this cause, required to appear before me Angelina Pumazho, an Indian of the village of San Juan, wife of Domingo Pobicoa, and administered the oath through the interpreter, who was Maria Madrid, in due legal form, in the name of our Lord God and the Holy Cross; having taken it, she promised to speak the truth in all that she might be asked; and having been asked if it was true that she had illicit intimacy with Miguel Martin that she should so say and declare it: She said that she had not had improper intimacy with the above mentioned and in order to make it clearer they should confront her with the said Miguel Martin and that she would say to his face that she had not been, and, even if they killed her, she could say nothing else, because she knew nothing else; asked if it were true that she was with her mother on Holy Thursday at the church of Santa Cruz, she should so state and declare it; she said that she was not in said town because a child of hers lay dying and Sebastian Martin can testify to this, as he went the same day to the New Town and saw this declarant at home in her house with her mother; Asked why she denies that she was in the New Town [Santa Cruz] when she was seen with her mother behind her by Leonor Dominguez, the sick woman, who avows and declares this as being about to die, let her state and declare it; and she said that the said Leonor did not speak the truth and has no fear of God nor pity on her soul, since she swears falsely; and that this is the truth that she has spoken and which she certifies and affirms under pain of the oath she has taken; and her declaration having been read to her she said that she has nothing to add nor alter and that she is about twenty years old, more or less; and she does not sign this, not knowing how to write. . . .

Declaration of Catherina Rosa, Wife of Zhiconqueto

Then, immediately, on said day, month and year, I, the said examining justice, required to appear before me Catarina Rosa, married to Diego Zhiconqueto, of the village of San Juan and administered the oath to her in due legal form, before our Lord God and the sign of the Holy Cross, and,

having taken it, she promised to speak the truth in all that might be asked
of her, and being asked: if she knew that her daughter, Angelina, was the
concubine of Miguel Martin, before either of them were married, that she
should speak and declare it; the declarant said and replied in Castillian that
she did not know that they had improper relations and had never seen any;
asked: that she should speak and declare with whom she was at mass on Holy
Thursday in the New Town of Santa Cruz, she said that she was at mass at
the said church only on Palm Sunday in the early morning when she was in
said town and that she was not there Holy Thursday, because her daughter,
Angelina, was sick. Asked why she denied she was in the church of the New
Town on Holy Thursday, let her state and declare, since the sick woman,
Leonor Martin said that she saw her near her. To this declarant replied, with
a threat, that she would raise the devil; that it is true that she was near the
said Leonor Dominguez on Palm Sunday and that it was not Holy Thursday
and on account of her illness she does not remember what day it was; Asked
if it is true that she asked Catharina Lujan, the Indian of her village, versed
in languages, whether that was the wife of Miguel Martin, she said that she
neither said nor asked whether she was the wife of the above, but she did say
to her this is the sister of my godfather, Tomas Giron, and this is her answer;
Asked if it is true that she said to the said Catherina Lujan: Now: she should
speak and declare it; the declarant said that she did not say: Now: nor did
such a thing occur. Asked if it is true that she touched and felt her left side,
let her speak and declare it; she said No, nor had she approached her; that
she only wanted to find out what malady the said Leonor was suffering from
and to try to cure her, and that this is the truth, which she affirms and certifies, and that she has nothing to add or alter in this declaration; that she is
forty years old and does not sign this because she cannot write. I, the said
examining justice, with the notary to the Cabildo deposed as to the threat
she made to raise the devil. . . .

Declaration of Catarina Lujan

On the said day, month and year, I, the said examining justice, required to
appear before me Catarina Lujan, unmarried and a native of the village of
San Juan, to whom I administered the oath in due legal form by our Lord
God and the [sign of] the Holy Cross, and, having taken it, she promised
to speak the truth in all that she might know or that might be asked of her,
and, being asked if she was in the Town of Santa Cruz on Holy Thursday
in company with Catharina Rosa, wife of Zhiconqueto, let her speak and
declare it; she said that it is true that on Holy Wednesday Father Fray
Juan Minguez took this declarant to the said Town to clean his cell and in

testimony thereof, he will say whether she left the cell of the said Father, and that she did not see the said Indian Catherina Rosa nor had they [any] opportunity to speak for the reason that she was engaged in the occupation stated, and another [reason] because the said wife of Zhiconqueto did not come to the New Town and that this declarant was not in the Town on Palm Sunday, because she remained in the Convent at San Juan, and that to all this the said Father Minguez and the Maestre de Campo, Eoque Madrid, are witnesses and will declare the truth thereof; and that she never said: This is the sister of my godfather, Tomas Giron; this is the truth under penalty of the oath she has taken; and having read her declaration to her, she said she had nothing to add or alter and that she does not sign it, because she does not know how to write.

New Affidavit and Declaration of Doña Leonor Dominguez, May 22

1st. Asked if what she had declared happened to her Palm Sunday, Holy Thursday or Resurrection [Easter] Day, let her speak and declare it as asked; the declarant said that it was on Holy Thursday while at mass that what she has declared happened to her and that such is the fact that it was on the said day and no other.

2nd. Asked if she had or has any suspicion of the said Indian women being actuated by any rumors passing among them or if it is only a presumption, let her speak and declare it: the declarant said that her suspicion of the said Catherina, wife of Zhiconqueto, is because when coming from the farm, in company with her husband, Miguel Martin, to the village of San Juan to get a little lime, this declarant said to him that he might leave her at the house of Catherina Lujan, and that her said husband took her to the house of the painter, Zhiconqueto, and seeing that he had deceived her, she quarreled with her husband, who smiled and the said Caterina Rosa, having offered to eat a bit of roast meat and some bean [teguas] cakes, he told her to eat, to which this declarant replied that she was fasting and the said Catherina said to her: What, today, Sunday, you are fasting? and that at this moment she looked at her said husband and at Martin Fernandez, his neighbor, who was there, who said to her: Eat what they give you, it won't hurt you, because this Indian woman (pointing to the girl, the wife of little Domingo) is your husband's mistress, and at this moment her said husband's horse started off, and on that account he did not remain.

3rd. Asked if she has any further proofs of what she declared that her husband, Miguel Martin, had been criminally intimate with the said Indian woman, the daughter of Catherina Rosa and of Zhiconqueto, and the wife of little Domingo, that she should speak and so declare it; the declarant said that she has many other reasons because the wife of Peter de Avila, alias "the louse," told her while this declarant was grinding corn kernels that her said husband had slept with the said Indian woman "por una tobaja" [under the sheet—old word for towel] and that this declarant said to her: No matter, I don't want to know anything, and that likewise, while chatting with Alfonso Rael, the cousin of this declarant from Mosedades, her said husband, said he had had two Indian mistresses in the village of Taos and another in the village of San Juan; and that she said nothing to him then because her brother-in-law, Tomas Giron, and her sister, Antonia, his wife were present, and that afterwards, when they were alone, she asked him who the Indian woman was in the village of San Juan, and he told her the woman aforesaid was the wife of little Domingo and that on this occasion her said husband, having gone to the village of San Juan, returned with his arms and hands so swollen that he could not even eat with his hands, and this declarant fed him and that to this day he is suffering, and this is her answer.

4th. Asked to what other persons besides her sister-in-law, Casilda, wife of Francisco Martin, the reaper, she had spoken and communicated what had happened to her on Holy Thursday with the said two Indian women, the two Catarinas, let her speak and declare it: the declarant said that on leaving the said church her said husband met her by chance and she gave him a slap in the face, saying: "Curse you, it is on your account that your mother-in-law hates me," and that the said Miguel Martin replied, asking "Who is my mother-in-law?" and this declarant told him "The wife of Zhiconqueto"; and he answered her—"Don't be a fool, what was not in your year, was not to your injury" and that afterwards, in narrating just what happened with the two Indian women, as well as with her said husband, the said Casilda, her sister-in-law, having been present through it all, said to her: "You are foolish to stay where you are; you will see they will do you harm"; and that this declarant and her husband, leaving the church, went to the New Town and that he was still scratching his arm, and nevertheless she went that night to church, and at the time of the sermon the agonies seized upon her such as she had begun to feel before, so that it was necessary for two women to hold her by force, who were her sister-in-law, Juana, wife of Arrata and Petrona Supa, wife of Simon Martin, and that since then until the present hour the pains and ailments have not ceased to torment her and which she still suffers, and that prior to this aforesaid day she had enjoyed and was enjoying perfect health, and that the convulsion she had that night of the aforesaid day, Holy Thursday, she knew was not from contrition nor repentance, but the violent pain of the disease newly acquired, and this is her answer.

5th. Asked if only for the foregoing she has the suspicious and evil presumption against the said Indian women, or if she knows them to be public or pretended sorcerers, let her speak and declare it: This declarant said she does not know that these Indians are sorcerers, but only that another evil is to be ascribed to them from that which she has already declared as to the criminal intimacy her husband had, having been accused by her after what had happened, said that it was false that he had the aforesaid intimacy and that he had only said it by way of a joke, and thus from this excuse and having heard it said of her said husband that soon after he was married he denied it in order to appease the said Indian women, her distrust increased and also because she knew that her sister-in-law, Maria Lujan, wife of Sebastian Martin, and Augustina Romero had been bewitched and this was public rumor and knowledge and that an Indian called Juanchillo and his wife Chepa took care of them and cured them, it being said likewise that this spell had been cast upon them in this same village of San Juan and for these reasons and circumstances she founds her suspicion and presumption, and this is her answer; and having read to her the first, second and this third declaration, she said that she understood it all, that it is just as she has declared and she has nothing to add or alter and thus it may be signed and sealed under her oath, she being of age given; she did not sign because she cannot write. . . .

[Other depositions followed that same day from the people named in Leonor Dominguez's declaration.]

Declaration of Miguel Martin

Then, immediately, I had appear before me, Miguel Martin, husband of Leonor Dominguez, to whom I administered the oath, in the name of God, our Lord, and the sign of the Holy Cross, which having taken, he promised to speak the truth in whatever he might know or that might be asked him.

Asked if on Holy Thursday or Palm Sunday he took his wife, Leonor Dominguez, to the church in the New Town of Santa Cruz, he should speak and declare it; the declarant said that Holy Thursday was the day on which he took his wife to the said church and not Palm Sunday.

1st. Asked if it is true that his wife, having come out from the said church on this day, met him by chance and gave him a blow in the face, saying "Curse you, it is your fault that your mother-in-law hates me" and that this declarant replied, saying: "Who is my mother-in-law?" and his wife told him the [daughter] of Zhiconqueto and this declarant replied —"Don't be a fool, what was not in your year was not to your hurt," he should speak and declare it; this declarant said that it is true that coming out of the church his said wife gave him a push and said those words that she declares and that this declarant replied, Don't be jealous or lying and that nothing else occurred beyond this, and this is his answer.

2nd. Asked if it is true that he had criminal intimacy with Angelina, daughter of Zhiconqueto, before or after his marriage, he should speak and declare it; declarant said that he never had such intimacy and that what had been told about him in this respect is false.

3rd. Asked why he denies this when in a conversation he had with Alfonso Bael, the youth who is a cousin of his wife, and before his brother-in-law Tornas Giron and his wife, Antonia Dominguez, he confessed that he had had criminal intimacy with two Indian women of the Village of Taos and with another of the village of San Juan, and that when they were alone he confessed to his said wife, Leonor Dominguez, that it was the Indian who is the daughter of the said Zhiconqueto; why did he say that and why he denied that he was married soon after the wedding, let him speak and declare; declarant said that all this which is asked him is of no use and is malicious and trumped up and that neither the one nor the other happened; and this is his answer. . . .

6th. Asked why, having said that it was true that the said Indian woman was his mistress, he afterwards said that he was joking and now denies it; let him speak and declare; declarant said that it is false and that he never said anything of that sort, and this is his answer.

7th. Asked if he does not know that his sister-in-law, Maria Lujan, wife of his brother, Sebastian Martin, had been bewitched, it is suspected, by the Indian women of the same village of San Juan, let him speak and declare; declarant said that he knew nothing about it having been away at that time and when he came back nothing was told him; and although other questions were put to him again and again concerning things, he said he knew nothing more than he had declared; and his declaration having been read to him, he said he had nothing to add nor to alter; that it was just as he stated, which he affirms and certifies under the oath which he has taken and that he is about twenty- two years old and he does not sign because he does not know how. . . .

May 25

Declaration of Juanchillo and his Wife

In this village of San Juan, on the twenty-fifth day of the month of May of the present year, pursuant to these writs, I, the sargento mayor, Juan de Uribarri, the judge appointed therein, required to appear before me the Indian carpenter, Juanchillo and Josepha, his wife, both versed in the Castilian language, and cited in the declaration of Leonor Dominguez, to whom I administered the oath in the name of our Lord God and the sign of the cross and, having taken it, they promised to speak the truth in whatever they might know or be asked.

Asked, what Spanish persons they had cured in past years, by what means and of what diseases, let them speak and declare; They said that Augustina Romero and Maria Lujan, the latter the wife of Sebastian Martin, and the former of Miguel Thenorio; and that the herbs with which they cured them are very beneficial, and that they did not do it with any spell or diabolic art and that although the said Spanish women said that an Indian of this village, named Micaela, also a linguist, had cast a spell on them, and they would see she would come to punish and beat them, these declarants never knew anything nor saw the said Micaela, nor anything else; and this they answer.

Asked, if they know that Catarina Rosa, wife of Zhiconqueto, Catarina Lujan or any other persons cast any evil spell upon Leonor Dominguez, or if they know that there are in this village, or in others, any sorcerers, or if they have heard it said or known, let them speak and declare; these declarants said they do not know whether the said Indians did any harm to the said Leonor Dominguez, nor do they know any other person who may bewitch or harm people, and, although many other questions were put to them, again and again, on various points, they said they knew nothing more than they had declared; which they affirm and certify under the oath taken; that they are about sixty years and they do not sign, because they do not know how. . . .

May 27
Decree And Writ.

Then, immediately, having seen and certified that Catarina Rosa has crippled legs and could not move herself with the weight of the irons with which she was confined, I ordered her to be freed from them, and thus returned to the house of the Captain Antonio y Sassi, placing her there for convenience, pending further proceedings. . . .

May 31

At the Villa of Santa Fe, on the thirty-first day of the month of May, seventeen hundred and eight, I, the Admiral, Don Joseph Chacón Medina Salazar y Villa, Knight of the Order of Santiago, Marqués de la Peñuela Governor and Captain General of this District and the Provinces of New Mexico, having seen and read the declarations certified in these proceedings, and the complaint lodged by Doña Leonor Dominguez against Catharina Rosa, wife of Zhiconqueto, and Angelina Pumazo, his daughter, and Catharina Lujan, Indians of the Village of San Juan, touching their having done her injury by diabolic art, and having considered the declarations thereupon with the attention that such matters require, and the information submitted by the said

Doña Leonor Dominguez, together with [that of] Martin Fernandez, Casilda de Contreras, and the wife of Pedro de Avila, and the husband of the Complainant, all agreed in the aforesaid, in setting forth that it is false, futile and despicable, by reason of which and of the good effects resulting from the said proceedings, I must declare, as I do by these presents declare, the said three Indian women to be free as regards the [matter] produced in the declarations contained in the preceding pages, and be it known that this decree and sentence [judgment] in favor of the above mentioned is signed together with my secretary of the interior and of war, who is ordered to make it publicly known in their persons and certify to its proclamation, dated as above.

Source: Ralph Emerson Twitchell, ed., *The Spanish Archives of New Mexico; compiled and chronologically arranged with historical, genealogical, geographical, and other annotations, by authority of the state of New Mexico* (Cedar Rapids: The Torch Press, 1914), v. 2, 142–43, 144–45, 146–49, 152–54, 158–60, 162, 163.

~ ~ ~

13. Willem Bosman Explains the Ritual Use of Poison in Guinea, 1704

Willem Bosman was a Dutch trader who worked on the coast of West Africa, at the major slaving entrepot of Elmina, and, after fourteen years there, wrote an account that was published first in Dutch in 1704 and a year later in English. In this excerpt, Bosman describes religious practices for a European audience.

I promised just now to explain the Word *Fetiche*, which is used in various Senses. *Fetiche* or *Bossum* in the *Negro* Language, derives its self from their False God, which they call *Bossum*. Are they enclined to make Offerings to their Idols, or desire to be informed of something by them? they cry out, Let us make *Fetiche*; by which they express as much, as let us perform our Religious Worship, and see or hear what our God saith. In like manner, if they are injured by another they make *Fetiche* to destroy him in the following manner: they cause some Victuals and Drink to be Exorcised by their *Feticheer* or Priest, and scatter it in some place which their Enemy is accustomed to pass; firmly believing, that he who comes to touch this conjured Stuff shall certainly dye soon after. Those who are afraid of this coming to such places, cause themselves to be carried over them; for 'tis the wonderful Nature of this Exorcised Truth, that then it does not in the least affect the Person, nor can it at all affect those who carry him, or any Body else besides him. . . .

If they are robbed they make use of much the same means for the discovery and condign Punishment of the Thief: They are so obstinately bigoted to this Opinion, that if you should produce a hundred Instances of Impotence, 'twou'd be impossible to alter their Sentiments, they having always something ready on which to charge its contrary Success. If any person be caught strowing this Poison, he is very severely punished, nay, sometimes with Death, though it be on the last account of Thieving, which is here freely allowed. Obligatory Swearing they also call, making of Fetiche's; is any Obligation to be confirmed, their Phrase is, *let us as a farther Confirmation make Fetiche's*. When they drink the *Oath-Drought*, 'tis usually accompanied with an Imprecation, that the Fetiche may kill them if they do not perform the Contents of their Obligation. Every Person entering into any Obligation is obliged to drink this Swearing Liquor. When any Nation is hired to the Assistance of another, all the Chief ones are obliged to drink this Liquor, with an Imprecation, that their *Fetiche* may punish them with Death, if they do not assist them with utmost Vigour to Extirpate their Enemy. . . . If you ask what Opinion the *Negroes* have of those who falsify their Obligations confirmed by the Oath-Drink; they believe the perjured Person shall be swelled by that Liquor till he bursts; or if that doth not happen, that he shall shortly dye of a Languishing Sickness; The first Punishment they imagine more peculiar to Women, who take this Draught to acquit themselves of any Accusation of Adultery. . . . Thus in the Description of the Religion of the *Negroes*, I find myself insensibly fallen upon their Oaths; but since even that is a part of Religious Worship, I have some excuse for pursuing that Subject yet a little farther. If any Person is suspected of Thievery and the Indictment is not clearly made out, he is obliged to clear himself by drinking the *Oath-Draught*, and to use the Imprecation, that the *Fetiche* may kill him if he be guilty of Thievery. The several ways of taking Oaths are so numerous, that I should tire you as well as my self with a Repetition of them. . . .

Source: Willem Bosman, *A new and accurate description of the coast of Guinea* (London: James Knapton and Daniel Midwinter, 1705), Letter 10, 147–50.

~ ~ ~

14. South Carolina Strengthens Its Laws against Poisoning and Slave Doctors, 1740, 1751

South Carolina, like other colonies, regularly passed and revised laws to regulate enslaved laborers. This excerpt contains a 1740 law and an updated and elaborated

1751 law that detailed the punishments deemed suitable for slaves who poisoned others. The 1749 item from the South Carolina Gazette *(document 15) provides some helpful context for the revised 1751 law. The attack on slave doctors can also be explained in part by document 15; see also document 16 for another reference to slave doctors (see figure 17).*

Why did white colonists worry so much about poisoning, and why did they punish enslaved poisoners so viciously? What similarities and differences do you see between these laws and documents 6 and 7?

1740

And *whereas*, some crimes and offences of an enormous nature and of the most pernicious consequence, may be committed by slaves, as well as other persons, which being peculiar to the condition and situation of this Province, could not fall within the provision of the laws of England; *Be it therefore enacted* by the authority aforesaid, That the several crimes and offences hereinafter particularly enumerated, are hereby declared to be felony, without the benefit of clergy, that is to say:—if any slave, free negro, mulattoe, Indian or mestizo . . . shall willfully or maliciously poison or administer any poison to any person, free man, woman, servant or slave, every such slave, free negro, mulattoe, Indian, (except as before excepted,) and mustizoe, shall suffer death as a felon.

1751

VII. And *whereas*, the detestable crime of poisoning hath of late been frequently committed by many slaves in this Province, and notwithstanding the execution of several criminals for that offence, yet it has not been sufficient to deter others from being guilty of the same; *Be it therefore enacted* by the authority aforesaid, That not only such negroes, mulattoes and mestizoes, whether free or bond, as shall administer poison to any person or persons, whether free or bond, but also all and every negro, mulatto and mestizo, whether free or bond, who shall furnish, procure or convey any poison to any slave or slaves, to be administered to any person or persons as aforesaid, and also all such negroes, mulattoes and mestizoes, whether free or bond, as shall be privy (and not reveal the same,) to the administering of any poison to any person or persons as aforesaid, or be privy (and not reveal the same,) to the furnishing, procuring or conveying any poison to be administered to any person or persons as aforesaid, shall be deemed and adjudged, and all and every of them are hereby declared to be, felons, and shall suffer death, in such manner as the persons appointed and empowered by the Act for the better

Figure 17. Graman (which means great man) Quacy was highly regarded in the Dutch colony of Suriname because of his healing abilities. Born in Guinea circa 1690 and transported to Suriname when he was a child, he eventually gained his freedom from slavery. He is pictured here in the 1770s in the garb he wore on his return to Suriname from a trip to Europe.

Source: John Stedman, *Narrative of a five years' expedition* (London, 1796). This item is reproduced by permission of *The Huntington Library, San Marino, California.*

ordering and governing negroes and other slaves in this Province, for trial of slaves, shall adjudge and determine.

VIII. And for the encouragement of slaves to make discovery of the designs of others to poison any person, *Be it further enacted* by the authority aforesaid, That every negro, mulatto or mestizo, whether free or bond, who shall hereafter give information of the intention of any other slave to poison any person, or of any slave that had furnished, procured or conveyed any poison to be administered to any person, shall, upon conviction of the offender or offenders, be entitled to and receive a reward of four pounds, proclamation money, out of the public treasury of this Province, to be drawn for by the justices before whom such offender or offenders shall be tried: *Provided always nevertheless*, that no slave shall be convicted upon the bare information of another slave, unless poison shall be found upon the party or parties accused, or some other circumstance or overt act appear by which such information shall be corroborated.

IX. *And provided also, and be it further enacted* by the authority aforesaid, That in case any slave shall be convicted of having given false information, whereby any other slave may have suffered wrongfully, every such false informer shall be liable to and suffer the same punishment as was inflicted upon the party accused; any law, usage, or custom to the contrary notwithstanding.

X. *And be it further enacted* by the authority aforesaid, That in case any slave shall teach or instruct another slave in the knowledge of any poisonous root, plant, herb, or other sort of poison whatever, he or she, so offending, shall, upon conviction thereof, suffer death as a felon; and the slave or slaves so taught or instructed, shall suffer such punishment (not extended to life or limb), as shall be adjudged and determined by the justices and freeholders, or a majority of them, before whom such slave or slaves shall be tried.

XI. And to prevent, as much as may be, all slaves from attaining the knowledge of any mineral or vegetable poison, Be it further enacted by the authority aforesaid, That it shall not be lawful for any physician, apothecary or druggist, at any time hereafter, to employ any slave or slaves in the shops or places where they keep their medicines or drugs, under pain of forfeiting the sum of twenty pounds, proclamation money, for every such offence, to be recovered and applied as is hereinafter directed.

XII. And be it further enacted by the authority aforesaid, That no negroes or other slaves (commonly called doctors), shall hereafter be suffered or permitted to administer any medicine, or pretended medicine, to any other slave, but at the instance or by the direction of some white person; and in case any negro or other slave shall offend herein, he shall, upon complaint and proof thereof made to any justice of the peace for the county, suffer corporal punishment, not exceeding fifty stripes.

Source: *The Statutes at Large of South Carolina* (Columbia, S.C.: Printed by A. S. Johnston, 1836–1841), v. 7, 402, 422–23.

~ ~ ~

15. Items about Poisoning from the *South Carolina Gazette*, 1749, 1769

The South Carolina Gazette *was the colony's main newspaper. In the absence of any surviving criminal records for enslaved workers, the newspaper remains one of the best sources for getting a glimpse of the punishments visited on slaves for the crime of poisoning and for understanding how white colonists responded to the crime.*

October 30, 1749
The horrid Practice of poisoning white People, by the Negroes, has lately become so common, that within a few Days past, several Executions have taken Place in different Parts of the Country, by burning, gibbeting, hanging, &c.

August 1, 1769
On Friday last two Negroes, viz. Dolly belonging to Mr. James Sands, and Liverpoole, belonging to Mr. William Price, were burnt on the Work-house Green, pursuant to the sentence that had been passed on them a fortnight before; the former for poisoning an infant of Mr. Sands's, which died some time since, and attempting to put her master out of the world the same way; and the latter (a Negro Doctor) for furnishing the means. The wench made a free confession, acknowledging the justice of her punishment, and died a penitent; but the fellow did neither. A mulatto named Dick, formerly a slave to Mr. D'Harriette, but afterwards manumitted, who stands as instigator of these horrid crimes, has disappeared.

August 17, 1769
The Mulatto Fellow Dick, mentioned in this Paper of the first Instant, as accused of being the Instigator to the poisoning of the late Mr. Sands and

his Family, was on Friday last tried, upon the Negro Act, and adjudged to receive twenty-five Lashes on Saturday Morning at four different Corners, and the same Number last Tuesday, in all 100 each Day, and to lose his Right Ear; which sentence has been executed. A Bill of Sale of him, from Colonel Laurens, to John Mitchell, a free Negro, being produced at his Trial, the Sentence could not be extended to Transportation.

Source: *The South Carolina Gazette*

~ ~ ~

16. Poison at Monticello, 1800

These three letters, one from Thomas Jefferson's daughter Martha Randolph to her father, the second from Thomas Jefferson to his son-in-law, Thomas Mann Randolph, and the third from Thomas Randolph to Jefferson, reported the death of a valuable family of slaves whom Jefferson owned at Monticello. At the time of these letters, Jefferson was vice president of the United States and the Randolphs were helping to run Monticello. Jupiter grew up alongside Thomas Jefferson and worked as his personal servant. George supervised the nailery; his father, Great George, was an overseer; his mother was Ursula. The men died in June (George Junior) and November (George Senior), 1799. What do you make of Randolph's use of the term "conjurer?" Were they poisoned? What did Jupiter think, and how did he try to cure himself?

Martha Jefferson Randolph to Thomas Jefferson, Edge Hill, January 30, 1800

[T]o your enquiries relative to poor Jupiter he too has paid the debt to nature; finding himself no better at his return home, he unfortunately conceived him self poisoned & went to consult the negro doctor who attended the George's. he went in the house to see uncle Randolph who gave him a dram which he drank & seemed to be as well as he had been for some time past; after which he took a dose from this black doctor who pronounced that it would *kill or cure*. 2 ½ hours after taking the medicine he fell down in a strong convulsion fit which lasted from ten to eleven hours, during which time it took 3 stout men to hold him, he languished nine days but was never heard to speak from the first of his being seized to the moment of his death. Ursula is I fear going in the same manner with her husband & son, a constant puking shortness or [*sic*] breath and swelling first in the legs but now extending itself the doctor I understand had also given her *means* as they term it and upon Jupiter's death has absconded. I should think his murders sufficiently manifest to come under the cognizance of the law. . . .

M. Randolph

Thomas Jefferson to Thomas Mann Randolph, Philadelphia, March 31, 1800

[W]hat is mentioned to me in your letter & Richardson's of the state of Ursula is remarkeable. the symptoms & progress of her disease are well worthy attention. that a whole family should go off in the same & so singular a way is a problem of difficulty. . . .

Thomas Mann Randolph to Thomas Jefferson, [circa 19 April 1800]

Ursula is very near her last: tho' her case some time since has declared itself desperate I got Bache to visit her upon your desire to have some theory of so extraordinary a fact as has occurred in that family. All her symptoms are the same with her husband & son; but the Dropsy is general in her tho' the Hydrothorax is as manifest and as violent as in either of them. I think I have always understood that in robust, bulky, middle aged bodies living in a pure & wholesome air, upon strong & plentiful diet with moderate labor; a complete destruction of the tone of the system produces dropsy, when in opposite situations & habits, pulmonary consumption, or atrophy without it, or the bilious declines so common in the low country of Virginia take place. The poisons of the Buckingham Negroe conjuror appear to have a power of unstringing the whole system beyond recovery in a short time; of destroying the elasticity or rather the Vital Virtue of muscular fibre & nervous thread in a few weeks or days as completely in a healthy African slave as the abuse of natural gratifications for years in the luxurious rich, or quantities of Ardent Spirit in those who are just above labor. The instances of death (with the symptoms of your Negroe family), among the latter, are numerous in this part of the Country within my knowledge. . . . The poisons of the Conjurer have the most astonishing effect in producing melancholy & despair—perhaps greatly operative in the catastrophe. . . .

with most sincere affection
Th. M. Randolph

Source: Barbara Oberg, ed., *The Papers of Thomas Jefferson* (Princeton: Princeton University Press, 2004), v. 31, 347-48, 472–73, 522–23.

Two Cases of Possession

The two documents in this section offer examples of possession in North America. The first comes from the English colony of Massachusetts, where a teenager named Elizabeth Knapp suffered afflictions that were diagnosed as possession by the Puritan minister Samuel Willard. The second document is a letter by a Franciscan priest in Abiquiu, New Mexico, who described the collective possession of women in that community during the large outbreak of 1756–1763. In both cases, we have accounts generated by religious men, and in both cases the possessed were women. What kind of power did the possessed gain during their possession?

17. The Possession of Elizabeth Knapp, Massachusetts, 1671–1672

Elizabeth Knapp lived in Groton, Massachusetts, where she was a servant in the household of a minister named Samuel Willard (1640–1707), who later became the president of Harvard College and who criticized the use of spectral evidence during the Salem witchcraft trials of 1692. In October, 1671, when she was sixteen years old, Elizabeth suffered a series of maladies that were ultimately diagnosed as possession. In his account of Knapp's possession, Willard speculated "Whither her distemper be reale or counterfeit." Why do you think that Willard ultimately concluded that Knapp was possessed? What do you think?

THIS poore & miserable object, about a fortnight before shee was taken, wee observed to carry herselfe in a strange & unwonted manner, sometimes shee would give sudden shriekes, & if wee enquired a Reason, would always put it off with some excuse, & then would burst forth into immoderate & extravagant laughter, in such wise, as some times shee fell onto the ground with it: I my selfe observed oftentimes a strange change in here countenance, but could not suspect the true reason, but conceived shee might bee ill, & therefore divers times enquired how shee did, & shee always answered well; which made mee wonder: but the tragedye began to unfold itselfe upon Munday, Octob. 30. 71, after this manner (as I received by credible information, being that day my selfe gon from home). In the evening, a little before shee went to bed, sitting by the fire, shee cryed out, oh my legs! & clapt her hand on them, immediately oh my breast! & removed her hands thither; & forthwith, oh I am strangled, & put her hands on her throat: those that observed her could not see what to make of it; whither shee was in earnest or dissembled, & in this manner they left her (excepting the person that lay with her) complaining of her breath being stopt: The next day shee was in a strange frame, (as was observed by divers) sometimes weeping, sometimes laughing, & many foolish & apish gestures. In the evening, going into the cellar, shee shrieked suddenly, & being enquired of the cause, shee answered, that shee saw 2 persons in the cellar; whereupon some went downe with her to search, but found none; shee also looking with them; at last shee turned her head, & looking one way stedfastly, used the expression, what cheere old man? which, they that were with her tooke for a fansye, & soe ceased; after-wards (the same evening), the rest of the family being in bed, shee was (as one lying in the roome saw, & shee herselfe also afterwards related) suddenly throwne downe into the midst of the floore with violence, & taken with a violent fit, whereupon the whole family was raised, & with much adoe was shee kept out of the fire from destroying herselfe after which time she was fol-lowed with fits from thence till the sabbath day; in which shee was violent in bodily motions, leapings, strainings & strange agitations, scarce to bee held in bounds by the strength of 3 or 4: violent alsoe in roarings & screamings, representing a dark resemblance of hellish torments, & frequently using in these fits divers words, sometimes crying out money, money, sometimes, sin & misery with other words. . . .

These fits continuing, (though with intermission) divers, (when they had opportunity) pressed upon her to declare what might bee the true & real occasion of these amazing fits. Shee used many tergiversations & excuses, pretending shee would to this & that young person, who coming, she put it off to another, till at the last, on thursday night, shee brake forth into a large confession in the presence of many, the substance whereof amounted to thus much: That the devill had oftentimes appeared to her, presenting the treaty of a Covenant, & preffering largely to her: viz, such things as suted her youthfull fancye, money, silkes, fine cloaths, ease from labor to show her the whole world, &c: that it had bin then 3 yeers since his first appearance, occasioned by her discontent: That at first his apparitions had bin more rare, but lately more frequent; yea those few weekes that shee had dwelt with us almost constant, that shee seldome went out of one roome into another, but hee appeared to her urging of her: & that hee had presented her a booke written with blood of covenants made by others with him, & told her such & such (of some wherof we hope better things) had a name there; that hee urged upon her constant temptations to murder her parents, her neighbors, our children, especially the youngest, tempting her to throw it into the fire, on the hearth, into the oven; & that once hee put a bill hooke into her hand, to murder my selfe, persuading her I was asleep, but coming about it, shee met me on the staires at which shee was affrighted, the time I remember well,

& observd a strange frame in her countenance & saw she endeavered to hide something, but I knew not what, neither did I at all suspect any such matter; & that often he persuaded her to make away with herselfe & once she was going to drowne herself in the well, for, looking into it, shee saw such sights as allured her, & was gotten within the curbe, & was by God's providence prevented, many other like things shee related, too tedious to recollect: but being pressed to declare whither she had not consented to a covenant with the Devill, shee with solemne assertions denyed it, yea asserted that shee had never soe much as consented to discorse with him, nor had ever but once before that night used the expession, What cheere, old man? & this argument shee used, that the providence of God had ordered it soe, that all his apparitions had bin frightfull to her; yet this shee acknowledged, (which seemed contradictorye, viz:) that when shee came to our house to schoole, before such time as shee dwelt with us, shee delayed her going home in the evening, till it was darke, (which wee observed) upon his persuasion to have his company home, & that shee could not, when hee appeared, but goe to him. . . .

On the Sabbath the Physitian came, who judged a maine point of her distemper to be naturall, arising from the foulnesse of her stomacke, & corruptnesse of her blood, occasioning fumes in her braine, & strange fansyes; whereupon (in order to further tryall & administration) shee was removed home, & the succeeding weeke shee tooke physicke, & was not in such violence handled in her fits as before; but enjoyed an intermission, & gave some hopes of recovery; in which intermission shee was altogether sencelesse (as to our discoverye) of her state, held under securitye, & hardnesse of heart, professing shee had no trouble upon her spirits, shee cried satan had left her. . . .

I suspecting the truth of her former storye, pressed, whether shee never verbally promised to covenant with him, which shee stoutly denyed: only acknowledged that shee had had some thoughts soe to doe: but on the forenamed Nov. 26. shee was again with violence & extremity seized by her fits, in such wise that 6 persons could hardly hold her, but shee leaped & skipped about the house proforce roaring, & yelling extreamly, & fetching deadly sighs, as if her heartstrings would have broken, & looking with a frightfull aspect, to the amazement & astonishment of all the beholders, of which I was an eye witnesse: The Physitian being then agen with her consented that the distemper was Diabolicall, refused further to administer, advised to extraordinary fasting; whereupon some of Gods ministers were sent for: shee meane while continued extreamly tormented night & day, till Tuesday about noon; having this added on Munday & Tuesday morning that shee barked like a dog, & bleated like a calfe, in which her organs were visibly made use of:

yea, (as was carefully observed) on Munday night, & Tuesday morning, when ever any came neere the house, though they within heard nothing at all, yet would shee barke till they were come into the house, on Tuesday, about 12 of the clocke, she came out of the fit, which had held her from Sabbath day about the same time, at least 48 howers, with little or no intermission, & then her speech was restored to her, & shee expressed a great seeming sence of her state: many bitter teares, sighings, sobbings, complainings shee uttered, bewailing of many sins fore mentioned, begging prayers, & in the houre of prayer expressing much affection. . . .

[She confessed] That after shee came to dwell with us, one day as shee was alone in a lower roome, all the rest of us being in the chamber, she looked out at the window, & saw the devill in the habit of an old man, coming over a great meadow lying neere the house; & suspecting his designe, shee had thoughts to have gon away; yet at length resolved to tarry it out, & heare what hee had to say to her; when hee came hee demanded of her some of her blood, which shee forthwith consented to, & with a knife cut her finger, hee caught the blood in his hand, & then told her she must write her name in his booke, shee answered, shee could not Write, but hee told her he would direct her hand, & then took a little sharpened sticke, & dipt in the blood, & put it into her hand, & guided it, & shee wrote her name with his helpe: what was the matter shee set her hand to, I could not learne from her; but thus much shee confessed, that the terme of time agreed upon with him was for 7 yeers; one yeere shee was to be faithfull in his service, & then the other six hee would serve her, & make her a witch: shee also related, that the ground of contest between her & the devill which was the occasion of this sad providence, was this, that after her covenant made the devill showed her hell & the damned, & told her if shee were not faithfull to him, shee should goe thither, & bee tormented there; shee desired of him to show her heaven, but hee told her that heaven was an ougly place, & that none went thither but a company of base roagues whom he hated; but if shee would obey him, it should be well with her. . . .

shee then declared thus much, that the Devill had sometimes appeared to her; that the occasion of it was her discontent, that her condition displeased her, her labor was burdensome to her, shee was neither content to bee at home nor abroad; & had oftentime strong persuasions to practice in witchcraft, had often wished the Devill would come to her at such & such times, & resolved that if hee would, shee would give herselfe up to him soule & body: but (though hee had oft times appeared to her, yet) at such times hee had not discovered himselfe, and therfore shee had bin preserved from such a thing. . . .

It had bin a question before, whither shee might properly bee called a Demoniacke, or person possessed of the Devill, but it was then put out of Question: hee began (as the persons with her testifye) by drawing her tongue out of her mouth most frightfully to an extraordinary length & greatnesse, & many amazing postures of her bodye; & then by speaking, vocally in her, whereupon her father, & another neighbor were called from the meeting, on whom, (as soon as they came in,) he railed, calling them roagues, charging them for folly in going to heare a blacke roague, who told them nothing but a parcell of lyes, & deceived them, & many like expressions. after exercise I was called, but understood not the occasion, till I came, & heard the same voice, a grum, low, yet audible voice it was, the first salutation I had was, oh! you are a great roague, I was at the first somthing daunted & amazed, & many reluctances I had upon my spirits, which brought mee to a silence and amazement in my spirits, till at last God heard my groanes & gave me both refreshment in Christ, & courage: I then called for a light, to see whither it might not appeare a counterfiet, and observed not any of her organs to moove, the voice was hollow, as if it issued out of her throat; hee then agen called me great blacke roague, I challenged him to make it appear; but all the Answer was, you tell the people a company of lyes: I reflected on myselfe, & could not but magnifye the goodnesse of God not to suffer Satan to bespatter the names of his people, with those sins which hee himselfe hath pardoned in the blood of Christ. I Answered, Satan, thou art a lyar, and a deceiver, & God will vindicate his owne truth one day: hee Answered nothing directly, but said, I am not Satan, I am a pretty blacke boy; this is my pretty girle; I have bin here a great while, I sat still, and Answered nothing to these expressions; but when hee directed himselfe to mee agen, oh! you blacke roague, I doe not love you: I replyed through God's grace, I hate thee; hee rejoyned, but you had better love mee; these manner of expressions filled some of the company there present with great consternation, others put on boldnesse to speake to him, at which I was displeased, & advised them to see their call cleere, fearing least by his policye, & many apish expressions hee used, hee might insinuate himselfe, & raise in them a fearlessenesse of spirit of him: I no sooner turned my backe to goe to the fire, but he called out agen, where is that blacke roague gon: I seeing little good to bee done by discorse, & questioning many things in my mind concerning it, I desired the company to joyne in prayer unto God; when wee went about that duty & were kneeled downe, with a voice louder then before something, hee cryed out, hold your tongue, hold your tongue, get you gon you blacke roague, what are you going to doe, you have nothing to doe with me, &c: but through Gods goodnesse was silenced, &, shee lay quiet during the time of prayer, but as soone as it was ended, began afresh, using the former expressions, at which some ventured to speake to him: Though I thinke imprudentlye: one told him, God had him in chaines, hee replyed, for all my chaine, I can knocke thee on the head when I please: hee said hee would carry her away that night. Another Answered, but God is stronger than thou, He presently rejoyned, that's a ly, I am stronger than God: at which blasphemy I agen advised them to bee wary of speaking, counselled them to get serious parsons to watch with her, & left her, commending her to God: On Tuesday following shee confessed that the Devill entred into her the 2nd night after her first taking, that when shee was going to bed, hee entred in (as shee conceived) at her mouth, & had bin in her ever since, & professed, that if there were ever a Devill in the world, there was one in her, but in what manner he spake in her she could not tell. . . .

She is observed alwayes to fall into her fits when any strangers goe to visit her, & the more goe the more violent are her fits: as to the frame of her spirits hee hath bin more averse lately to good counsell than heretofore, yet sometime shee signifyes a desire of the companye of ministers. . . .

1. Whither her distemper be reale or counterfiet: I shall say no more to that but this, the great strength appearing in them, & great weaknesse after them, will disclaime the contrary opinion: for tho a person may counterfiet much yet such a strength is beyond the force of dissimulation:

2. Whither her distemper bee naturall or Diabolicall, I suppose the premises will strongly enough conclude the latter, yet I will adde these 2 further arguments:

   1. the actings of convulsion, which these come nearest to, are (as parsons acquainted with them observe) in many, yea the most essentiall parts of them quite contrary to these actings:

   2. Shee hath no wayes wasted in body, or strength by all these fits, though soe dreadfulle, but gathered flesh exceedinglye, & hath her naturall strength when her fits are off, for the most part:

3. Whither the Devill did really speake in her: to that point which some have much doubted of, thus much I will say to countermand this apprehension:

   1. The manner of expression I diligently observed, & could not perceive any organ, any instrument of speech (which the philosopher makes mention of) to have any motion at all, yea her mouth was sometimes shut without opening sometimes open without shutting or moving, & then both I & others saw her tongue (as it used to bee when shee was in some fits, when speechlesse) turned up circularly to the roofe of her mouth.

2. the labial letters, divers of which were used by her, viz. B. M. P. which cannot bee naturally expressed without motion of the lips, which must needs come within our ken, if observed, were uttered without any such motion, shee had used only Lingualls, Gutturalls &c: the matter might have bin more suspicious:

3. the reviling termes then used, were such as shee never used before nor since, in all this time of her being thus taken: yea, hath bin always observed to speake respectively concerning mee;

4. They were expressions which the devill (by her confession) aspersed mee, & others withall, in the houre of temptation, particularly shee had freely acknowledged that the Devill was wont to appear to her in the house of God & divert her mind, & charge her shee should not give eare to what the Blacke coated roage spake:

5. wee observed when the voice spake, her throat was swelled formidably as big at least as ones fist: These arguments I shall leave to the censure of the Judicious:

4. whither shee have covenanted with the Devill or noe: I thinke this is a case unanswerable, her declarations have been soe contradictorye, one to another, that wee know not what to make of them & her condition is such as administers many doubts; charity would hope the best, love would alsoe feare the worst, but thus much is cleare, shee is an object of pitye, & I desire that all that heare of her would compassionate her forlorne state, Shee is (I question not) a subject of hope, & thererfore all meanes ought to bee used for her recoverye, Shee is a monument of divine severitye, & the Lord grant that all that see or heare, may feare & tremble: Amen.
S. W.

Source: Samuel Willard, A briefe account of a strange & unusuall Providence of God befallen to Elizabeth Knap of Groton, transcribed by Samuel A. Green, ed., Groton in the Witchcraft Times (Groton, MA: [s.n.] 1883), 7–9, 10, 11, 14, 16, 17–18, 19, 20–21.

~ ~ ~

18. Possession at Abiquiu, New Mexico, 1763–1764

A major outbreak erupted in Abiquiu, New Mexico, in 1756, when Fray Juan José Toledo reached the mission church. The letter excerpted here was written by the priest in 1764, and it describes an outbreak of possession among women in the church of Abiquiu in December 1763. While many women were involved, two, both Indians, come through clearly in Toledo's account: María Trujillo, who *started to manifest the signs of possession right before she gave birth, and who was the focus of Toledo's attention, and Francisca Barela. The account also introduces us to some important witches: Jacinta and Atole Caliente, and Joaquin, the discoverer, who helped the Spanish identify the witches in Abiquiu and surrounding pueblos. Who was in charge in Abiquiu, the priest or the possessed?*

Fray Juan José Toledo to Carlos Fernández, Abiquiu, 22 January 1764, C.

Lord don Carlos Fernández: retired lieutenant of the royal presidio, alcalde mayor and war captain of the Villa nueva de la Santa Cruz and its pertaining pueblos, commissary judge in the proceedings regarding the discovery of genizaro Indian sorcerers at the Pueblo of Santo Tomás Apóstol de Abiquiu.

My Lordship, . . .

On the seventeenth day of December of the past year, I started to exorcise María Trujillo in the Holy Church, who is the wife of José Valdez, resident of this jurisdiction, who for the love of God pleaded with me to exorcise María, who, since the month of June and for nine consecutive days after mass and inside the church, would faint at the moment of the prayer of exorcism. We have witnessed that she would become covered with purple blemishes on the right shoulder, the elbow, the palm of the hand, and the knee.

She appeared to be free of this illness until the eleventh day of November, when, having arrived at the hour of childbirth close to daybreak, she experienced a great fainting spell and, coming to, she followed through in the delivery with great ease. When the sun arose, she had given birth to a child that was well and healthy.

On the fourteenth day, she felt a great headache, and there appeared a weight in her stomach and a blockage in her intestines. After all this, apparently she was given to great sadness of an extreme nature. On the day of the allegiance to Our Lady, it happened that while in the church, she would get very sleepy during the mass and sermon and could not be amused by the diversions of the fiesta.

She remained in her state of melancholy until the fourteenth day of December, when she fainted after the prayer in her house and, instead of awaking, she went into a fury and began to exhaust herself with unnatural strength. For this reason and because of the continued evil which continued at all hours, I resorted to the spiritual remedy and as such I proceeded exorcising on the eighteenth day of the month of December, which was Sunday.

Francisca Barela, also a resident of this place, a young maiden, poor and cloistered, eighteen years old more or less, left her home about four in the afternoon with an earthen jar to supply the house with water. Upon reaching a small spring which is located between two rocky and rugged hills close to the chapel in order to take some water, she felt a certain motion in her body. With great dread and fear and without knowing from where this originated, she returned to her home. She then heard the sound of a pig, which lived in those places as well as in domestication. She could not see what had scared her. Having got her water, she arrived at her house and, having placed corn in her mill to crush it for supper, she was suddenly stunned by a tingling sensation that she felt over her body. She returned a second time before it got too late to get some more water to finish the task. She filled the earthen jar at the small spring and once again heard the same noise as before. Having seen nothing, she felt a major shudder and fear until she arrived at her home, and her anxiety increased. She was further afflicted and the sensations caused her to fall into a seizure. Her brother noticed the movements she had in her body and, upon seeing her on the floor, attempted to lift her, and when she felt this movement, she began to give furious and frightful shouts which the people heard. When asked what was wrong, she responded that she did not see anything nor was she afflicted by any pain. By common agreement and in view of the astonishing occurrence, they brought the woman to this mission with difficulty, as she was resistant to my presence. As soon as she arrived and saw me, there were imponderable shouts which issued forth from her mouth and the clamor of the members of her body and the movement of her eyes. Her coloring had changed to a faded grey. The fury that she was in at each instant fatigued the people who held her. They held her so that she would not get loose from those hands, which she tried to do, becoming livid in her attempt to break loose, throwing punches and trying to bite and grab the hair of those around her. Given the tumult she made, it took a lot of work to undo the seizure. I tried to observe her for a while and seeing how realistically she mimicked the sound of pigs, cows, horned and spotted owls, and other animals, I got the stole, cross, and holy water and said the gospel of Saint John and other petitions over her head in order to finish discovering if this was the will of our Lord or something else.

At the words of the Holy Gospel, her body made wild movements, she shouted and shrieked, which ceased immediately once I grabbed the book of exorcisms. She began to make insolent remarks to me: that I was a kid goat mulatto, and that she did not fear me nor what I intended to accomplish. When I began the exorcism, she cursed me and tried to interrupt and impeded the exorcism with great shouts, disgraces, and extreme shaking. By the time she appeared to be secured, the four men who held her were exhausted. She wanted to escape from their hands, arching her body upward, then to one side, and at an instant of the men's weakness, she kicked off one of her shoes with such violence that those who had her secured were unable to avoid the shoe. She continued in this manner during the night of the same day until daybreak. As she rested, she was thrown onto the floor, howling in a very loud voice like the Indians of this land are accustomed to do. . . . [On December 19, a twelve-year-old girl named María de Chavez started to show the signs of possession.]

At the start of the Introit, the afflicted women fell to the floor at the same time, beginning to exasperate and exhaust themselves so that people went to their aid to hold them and, upon realizing they had been seized, they let out Indian war howls of the type which the Indians are accustomed to giving when they grind corn. After making motions with their hands of that exercise, and when they finished with the manic behavior, they sang like an owl, a fox, a pig, a cow, etc. They then were raised up high and fell without being assisted by those who held them. The disturbance in the temple was so great that one was unable to hear the chorus of the singers, nor the minister at the altar. The other energumens, having quieted for a while, began the uproar once more. Francisca Barela continued in her insolence and loud shouts when she was seated. It became necessary to order her to be removed from the church, which caused the others who remained in the church to scream and move about as they had done at the start of the mass, though they were tolerable, as this happened every once in a while, and they did not disturb the congregation. When the mass was over, I performed the exorcism of the evil spirit which the devil felt a great deal, as he was inside the bodies of the sick women. This was not only a bewitching, but also the devil who is behind such things. Removed from the church, after the exorcism, the possessed women were more furious, remaining in such a state of suffering that there is not a pen that can adequately explain it.

All of this went on the same night and day in full view of many people, and it became necessary to contain the sick women so they would not injure themselves with the major afflictions of this sickness, I mean sick woman. During the exorcisms, María shouted in an intelligible voice that the Indian Jacinta and her mother, the old woman called Atole Caliente, were suffocating her. This was apparent by the anxieties and demonstrations she made with her body and hands. She also said that they commanded her the other day, which was a Holy Day of Obligation and festival, not to attend Mass. I said she should be taken by force. She responded that I did not govern her, that she was subject to the two Indians referred to, who controlled her. Their motive was that she should not go to the church and report what she talked about, and she declared they would suffocate her more.

At daybreak, María had a short rest. On that same day, the sick women entered the church and, because people were there, I went to the altar and began to examine the missal before putting on the vestments. All the sick women fell to the floor, the first being María de Chávez. I turned my face to see her while some men held her down. The Indian Atole Caliente was above her head, holding the sick woman by the throat with one hand, and with the other, gesturing to suffocate her by inserting the point of a blanket into her mouth in the manner that an executioner does with a gag used for hanging. I heard someone try to quiet her by saying, "Mariquita, Mariquita," which was the reason it was necessary for me to turn around and, leaving the altar, put myself in the middle of the disturbance in order to remove the Indian Atole Caliente, whose insolence caused me great indisposition. I was not so incapacitated that I could not celebrate the Mass. It was the Mass of Our Lady. Nevertheless, I should have done what Our Lord did when he whipped those who profaned the temple, by leaving part of the deserved penalty for this sort of boldness in full view of so much of the congregation. Instead I did it afterward outside the church in the presence of the lieutenant and many people, charging that the punishment was given for such irreverence committed in such a place and questioning Atole about her motives for committing such an act. Atole Caliente did not respond beyond saying she did it charitably to remove the evil. Immediately, she was prepared for the legal proceeding and entrusted to her daughter Jacinta. The Indian Joaquín went to the Lord Governor (whom he was referred to), so that he might participate in [the] situation he started, which was the exposure of the sorcery. This woman did not rest, nor did the others during the day or night until close to daybreak. (See figure 18.)

On the twenty first day of the same month, all these women were in place below the altar steps for the Mass and exorcisms. They were calm until I began to sing the first phrases of the gospel, which is when they let loose, one after the other, with grimaces, shaking, trembling, fainting, violent acts and other controversies. Because they exhibited so much cackling, annoyances, etc., which were horrifying, I had the good sense to perform the exorcism with the exposition of the sacrament and with the recital of "*quomodo caecidisti Lucifer qui mane orievaris.*"[1] One of the possessed women responded "by way of insolence and arrogance," and in the same instance her body fell to the floor and she remained exhausted until the exorcism entered her mind so that she could get up and then the exorcism was finished.

This same day, another young maiden furiously let loose inside the church exhibiting a certain spirit of illness discovered in the month of September of 1763 with such a powerful evil that four to six men were overcome by her.

Figure 18. Interior view, San José de Gracia Church, Las Trampas, Taos County, New Mexico. The church in which the possessed women of Abiquiu disrupted services likely resembled this one.

Source: Jack E. Boucher, 1961. Library of Congress, Prints and Photographs Division, HABS NM,28-TRAMP,1-8.

In this bad state, her tongue let loose and they, the energumens, all began to chatter. By their responses, it was evident they understood Latin, which is a most certain sign of possession, and on the words of the major mysteries, they laughed, giving shouts, and making idle conversation. When I said *in nominee Patri*, etc., they made demonstrations with their heads that the doctrine of the Trinity was not true. When I said "*al verbum caro factum est*,"[2] they did the same. Continuing in this manner, I questioned Francisca Barela in Latin, "Why do the spirits injure this creature?" She responded that what was happening came from above. At this point, she exited the church. On the same day outside of the church, the women spent the whole day talking, wanting to exhaust themselves. One after the other they began to reveal various people. On different days, they identified the people according to their names, signs, homes and places of residence. As is evident in the attached document, the possessed affirmed that all the men and women named were evil sorcerers who murder with their arts. The women gave the reason that the principal foundation of the declaration was so the sorcery would be discovered, along with all of the wickedness, even beyond this particular situation, that was in the land. They also said that the Lord Governor wanted to make an example and leave this land clean. On the same day, they ended their fantastic demonstrations, howls, and extreme chants, opening their eyes. They loudly declared some other imaginings with their eyes closed very tightly. . . .

On the twenty-second day of this illness with the women of the church, a spirit left Francisca Barela, who said through her mouth that it had been there in order to treat her badly and that it was there in order to enter José Valdez, so that he might murder his wife, induced by two of his sisters-in-law. It wanted to enter him and said that their wills should be reconciled, that the worst of sins were of the tongue, and the other spirits would leave those who[m] they were punishing.

On the twenty-eighth day of the exorcism, Lucifer left, bringing a sign during the fainting spell of María Trujillo inside the church. He caused a great deal of anxieties and movements, having expelled through her mouth the tooth of a horse with such effort that it became necessary to repeatedly place the stole on her back. Finally, forced by the dominion of the Word of God, she spit it out and remained at my feet. Her body was not injured. The spirit also said that it had entered her in the summer on the plains close to her house and at that place and home there were a legion of spirits. . . . [María Trujillo] was successfully delivered of the evil spirit.

Within two days of its leaving this sick woman at this place there was a continuing pathetic lament outside of the church and during the whole Mass and exorcism. So that she would not forget, María Trujillo also said that all those named, at all times and occasions, while in their evil and depraved state, spit on the Cross, the *Agnus Dei*, relics, holy water, and on the rosary. They seized the rosary and broke it to pieces, and those same women also removed the relic, etc. The third sick woman, the sister of Francisca Barela named María Agueda, was left by the spirit on another day than that of María Trujillo's and it said its name was the devil Cojuelo. She said it entered her the previous year at Chimayo in order to abuse her, and although it was leaving, there remained another three spirits in all.

This same day, there was not much rest. Immediately after the sun went down, one of the possessed women began to stretch out her hands and catch stones. When she took nourishment, she warned that what they put on the plate of food and the supper was blessed with a special benediction. We removed from that plate splinters, stones, pieces of adobe, etc. María de Chávez and María Rosalía, since the fifteenth of January, have been calm, without giving signs as to when the spirit would leave, which is why I continued with the exorcism, returning to María Trujillo, who, as I said has remained well two days. On the third day, over what displeasure with her husband I did not know, in a house of the Pueblo, she was found standing for the benefit of the exorcism. She invoked the devil for a long time while enraged and deranged, as the devil who was not made deaf, came, bringing as signs the shaking of the house. This was declared by those who were present.

María Trujillo's face and body started to make various grimaces and forceful gestures, as she wanted to break free from the hands of those who held her. She blasphemed and apostatized verbally, and her lips were black like coal. This lasted more than two and a half hours. Many people who went and saw this remarkable occurrence came to call me. . . . After I had succeeded in the execution of the exorcism, María proved to me the spirit was not inside her body by reciting the divine oath. As I was over her head, she advised me of the danger of certain people, so as to publicly announce the goodness of their souls, etc. She revealed things of a personal nature about many who were present. Because so many people saw these signs, they were reconciled through the sacrament of penance by me, asking for pardon. Finally, the spirit withdrew, leaving María's sanity in good condition, and her coloring returned. However, she was very maimed.

The next day, María Trujillo returned at the same hour and declared herself to be ecstatic. She gave helpful advice for souls. On the third day, she returned. With the alcalde mayor present, she advised him as to what he should do to cleanse this land of so much impurity. She did this by giving signs, from place to place, and by advising the Indian discoverer not to fail or cover up a thing, because it was the will of the Creator that so much adoration of the devil should stop and, instead, such actions should be given to our Creator. She finished, referring to me what she had said to the alcalde mayor.

There is not a mind that can comprehend this situation, for as in a battle, where the leader cannot lose faith, I am assisting without getting caught up again. . . . I am certain that, although I have jurisdiction, am healthy, and I have He who is Our Lord Jesus Christ, and while I am a very sinful man, I have nevertheless struggled with the idea that these women are tormented by the devil. Through the exorcism I performed and by the signs the authors of the manuals of exorcism present, it is evident there are very few signs of possession these creatures are lacking. The possessed have had frightful experiences in their dreams, as well as outside of them, in their judgment a tingling sensation issued forth through their bodies. With the exorcism, they became deaf, they understood Latin, and their coloring changed at the hour of these bad events. When the spirit withdrew, their good coloring came back, they declared that which was within their soul, and their major goal was to make sins public.

These they have not carried out, for they admit that they are subjects of the Minister of the Church and the Lord, who has ordered them not to reveal the sins of others. They have chanted in the Tewa language, chants they do not know in the Taos language. In her evil state, one declared to have been taken to Sandia, Isleta, and Belen. Another said the spirits take her to Chimayo, while another said she was taken to Pojoaque, Nambe, and Tesuque. Besides all this, the most significant sign, which is when they are free and using their own judgment, they do not remember the things that they have said. Being violent when they were ordered to be silent, they did not obey many times. This was outside of the exorcism. If devout prayers were said for them, or some prayed, those who were prayed for would get furious. Many other times, whoever would enter, they would call by their name, even though they did not know that person. To all those present, including myself, they say "son of a whore" and other disgraceful words. . . .

I am also remitting the list of those who have been accused of sorcery without being questioned. All this has been done before the public, since there has been no shortage of people to help. They lie about whom they desire. It is not my motivation or intention to place the blame on them because I know, through the practice of exorcism, that it is not licit for me to discover this crime, when it is only to the exorcist that the devil will reveal it. It has not been revealed only to me, nor questioned by me alone. Rather, other people have voluntarily given this information. Nevertheless, I do not ignore that the devil, the father of lies, has attemped to excuse all of this information. But I am not ashamed, nor afraid to use all the means necessary to remove all obstacles and give adoration to the Highest. This is advised for the alcalde mayor, the Indian discoverer, and myself. As I told the alcalde mayor, so I say to the Governor vocally: May the majesty of all powerful God illuminate our senses and hearts. May your Lordship be granted much health and may God protect you many years. From this Pueblo of Abiquiu, 22 of January 1764

> Your assured servant and chaplain kisses the hand of Your Lordship
> fray Juan José Toledo

Notes

1. How art thou fallen from Heaven, O Lucifer, who did rise in the morning? From the Manual of Exorcism.

2. The word made flesh

Source: Robert D. Martínez, "Fray Juan José Toledo and the Devil in Spanish New Mexico: A Story of Witchcraft and Cultural Conflict in Eighteenth-Century Abiquiu" (M.A. thesis, University of New Mexico, 1997), 56–59, 60–64, 66–71, 72–73.

Outbreaks

This section focuses on two major outbreaks, the first at Salem, Massachusetts, in 1692, and the second a series of witch hunts launched by Tenskwatawa, also known as the Shawnee Prophet, in the early nineteenth century in the Ohio River valley. The Salem documents, selected from a massive archive of available material, illustrate the range of people (English, Indian, and African) ensnared in the witch hunts, and also suggest the fears people around Salem had about witch attacks. Several of the documents contain confessions, one of the unusual features of Salem's outbreak, and the documents also permit us to see how the possessed accusers shaped court proceedings.

The second outbreak is the series of witch hunts that took place in the early nineteenth century, when Tenskwatawa put witches—and their extirpation—at the center of his campaign for Indian revitalization. One document articulates the Prophet's code, a second contains short excerpts from a similar code by the Seneca leader Handsome Lake, and the third is an account from a pair of Moravian missionaries about the executions of several witches among the Delaware Indians along the White River in the U.S. territory of Indiana. This final document takes us full circle, back to the first documents in this book, also generated by religious observers of indigenous

society, and back to the theme of witchcraft as a way of looking at intersections and transformations as cultures met and clashed, both for the first time
and over centuries of contact.

19. The Examinations of Tituba
and Sarah Good, Salem, March 1, 1692

*Sarah Good, Tituba, and Sarah Osborne were the first three people in Salem,
Massachusetts, to be accused of witchcraft. Tituba was a slave owned by Samuel
Parris, the minister of Salem Village, whose daughter and niece were the first possessed victims. Sarah Good, aged thirty-eight when she was named, was a woman
whose neighbors harbored long-time suspicions of witchcraft. She was a marginal
member of the community, in some respects the prototypical English witch.*

*Tituba soon confessed, naming both Good and Osborne as witches in her testi-
mony, and both Good and Osborne denied the charges, although Good implicated
Osborne. Tituba provided confessions on two different days; the first confession is
included here. All three women were found guilty. Sarah Osborne died in prison
on May 10. Sarah Good was executed on July 19, 1692. Tituba recanted in the
fall of 1692, as enthusiasm for trials and executions waned. In April 1693, she
was finally released from jail when an unknown person paid her fees. What made
these women likely witches, as far as you can tell from these legal documents? Why
did Tituba confess? Why didn't Good do the same? What does the content of the
confession tell you about witch beliefs in Salem in 1692—and whose witch beliefs,
Tituba's or her accusers?*

Salem Village, March 1, 1691

The Examination of Titibe

(H) Titibe what evil spirit have you familiarity with
(T) none
(H) why do you hurt these children
(T) I do not hurt them
(H) who is it then
(T) the devil for ought I know
(H) did you never see the devil.
(T) the devil came to me and bid me serve him
(H) who have you seen
(T) 4 women sometimes hurt the children
(H) who were they?

(T) goode Osburn and Sarah good and I doe not know who the other were Sarah good and Osburne would have me hurt the children but I would not shee furder saith there was a tale man of Boston that shee did see

(H) when did you see them

(T) Last night at Boston

(H) what did they say to you they said hurt the children

(H) and did you hurt them

(T) no there is 4 women and one man they hurt the children and then lay all upon me and they tell me if I will not hurt the children they will hurt me

(H) but did you not hurt them

(T) yes, but I will hurt them no more

(H) are you not sorry you did hurt them.

(T) yes.

(H) and why then doe you hurt them

(T) they say hurt children or wee will doe worse to you

(H) what have you seen a man come to me and say serve me

(H) what service

(T) hurt the children and last night there was an appearance that said Kill the children and if I would no go on hurting the children they would do worse to me

(H) what is this appearance you see

(T) sometimes it is like a hog and some times like a great dog this appearance shee saith shee did see 4 times

(H) what did it say to you

(T) the black dog said serve me but I said I am a fraid he said if I did not he would doe worse to me

(H) what did you say to it

(T) I will serve you no longer then he said he would hurt me and then he lookes like a man and threatens to hurt me shee said that this man had a yellow bird that keept with him and he told me he had more pretty things that he would give me if I would serve him

(H) what were these pretty things

(T) he did not show me them

(H) what else have you seen

(T) two rats, a red rat and a black rat

(H) what did they say to you

(T) they said serve me

(H) when did you see them

(T) Last night and they said serve me but shee said I would not

(H) what service

(T) shee said hurt the children

(H) did you not pinch Elizabeth Hubbard this morning

(T) the man brought her to me and made me pinch her

(H) why did you goe to thomas putnams Last night and hurt his child

(T) they pull and hall me and make goe

(H) and what would have you doe Kill her with a knif Left. fuller and others said at this time when the child saw these persons and was tormented by them that she did complain of a knif that they would have her cut her head off with a knife

(H) how did you go

(T) we ride upon stickes and are there presently

(H) doe you goe through the trees or over them

(T) we see no thing but are there presently

(H) why did you not tell your master

(T) I was a fraid they said they would cut off my head if I told

(H) would not you have hurt others if you could

(T) they said they would hurt others but they could not

(H) what attendants hath Sarah good

(T) a yellow bird and shee would have given me one

(H) what meate did she give it

(T) it did suck her between her fingers

(H) Did not you hurt mr Currins child

(T) goode good and goode Osburn told that they did hurt mr Currens child and would have had me hurt him two but I did not

(H) what hath Sarah Osburn

(T) yesterday shee had a thing with a head like a woman with 2 leggs and wings Abigail williams that lives with her uncle mr Parris said that shee did see this same creature and it turned into the shape of goode osburn

(H) what else have you seen with g osburn

(T) an other thing hairy it goes upright like a man it hath only 2 leggs

(H) did you not see Sarah good upon elisebeth Hubbar last Saturday

(T) I did see her set a wolfe upon her to afflict her the persons with this maid did say that shee did complain of a wolf

(T) shee furder said that shee saw a cat with good at another time

(H) what cloathes doth the man go in

(T) he goes in black clouthes a tal man with white hair I thinke

(H) how doth the woman go

(T) in a white whood and a black whood with a tup knot

Figure 19.   English witches with their familiars.
Source: From *The Wonderful discoverie of the witchcraft of Margaret and Phillip Flower, daughters of Joan Flower neere Bever Castle: executed at Lincolne, March 11, 1618* (London, 1619). This item is reproduced by permission of *The Huntington Library, San Marino, California.*

(H) doe you see who it is that torments these children now

(T) yes it is goode good she hurts them in her own shape

(H) & who is it that hurts them now

(T) I am blind noe I cannot see

The Examination of Sarah Good

(H.) Sarah Good what evil spirit have you familiarity with

(S G) none

(H) have you made no contract with the devil,

(g) good answered no

(H) why doe you hurt these children

(g) I doe not hurt them. I scorn it.

(H) who doe you imploy then to doe it

(g) I imploy no body,

(H) what creature do you imploy then,

(g) no creature but I am falsely accused

(H) why did you go away muttering from mr Parris his house

(g) I did not mutter but I thanked him for what he gave my child

(H) have you made no contract with the devil

(g) no

(H) desired the children all of them to look upon her, and see, if this were the person that had hurt them and so they all did looke upon her and said this was one of the persons that did torment them — presently they were all tormented.

(H) Sarah good doe you not see now what you have done why doe you not tell us the truth, why doe you thus torment these poor children

(g) I doe not torment them,

(H) who do you imploy then

(g) I imploy nobody I scorn it

(H) how came they thus tormented,

(g) what doe I know you bring others here and now you charge me with it

(H) why who was it.

(g) I doe not know but it was some you brought into the meeting house with you

(H) wee brought you into the meeting house

(g) but you brought in two more

(H) Who was it then that tormented the children

(g) it was osburn

(H) what is it that you say when you goe muttering away from persons houses

(g) if I must tell I will tell

(H) doe tell us then

(g) if I must tell I will tell, it is the commandments I may say my commandments I hope

(H) what commandment is it

(g) if I must tell you I will tell, it is a psalm

(H) what psalm

(g) after a long time shee muttered over some part of a psalm

(H) who doe you serve

(g) I serve god

(H) what god doe you serve

(g) the god that made heaven and earth though shee was not willing to mention the word God her answers were in a very wicked, spitfull manner reflecting and retorting aganst the authority with base and abusive words and many lies shee was taken in. it was here said that her housband had said that he was afraid that shee either was a witch or would be one very quickly the worsh mr Harthon asked him his reason why he said so of her whether he had ever seen any thing by her he answered no not in this nature but it was her bad carriage to him and indeed said he I may say with tears that shee is an enimy to all good.

Source: Paul Boyer and Stephen Nissenbaum, eds., *The Salem Witchcraft Papers* (New York: Da Capo Press, 1977), v. 3, 747–49; v. 2, 356–57.

~ ~ ~

20. Nathaniel Cary's Account of His Wife's Examination, May 1692

Captain Nathaniel Cary was a wealthy merchant who lived in Charlestown, Massachusetts. He and his wife Elizabeth traveled to Salem in May 1692 after hearing rumors that she had been accused of witchcraft. To both Carys' dismay, Elizabeth was accused, arrested, and put in chains in the Cambridge jail. Nathaniel watched the trials closely, saw the ominous trend, and arranged his wife's escape from jail first to Rhode Island and then to New York. How did Nathaniel Cary account for the events at Salem? Why do you think the Carys traveled to Salem to confront the accusations against Elizabeth Cary?

I having heard some days, that my Wife was accused of Witchcraft, being much disturbed at it, by advice, we went to Salem-Village, to see if the afflicted did know her; we arrived there, 24 May, it happened to be a day appointed for Examination; accordingly soon after our arrival, Mr. Hathorn and Mr. Curwin, etc., went to the Meeting-house, which was the place appointed for that Work, the Minister began with Prayer, and having taken care to get a convenient place, I observed, that the afflicted were two Girls of about Ten Years old, and about two or three other, of about eighteen, one of the Girls talked most, and could discern more than the rest. The Prisoners were called in one by one, and as they came in were cried out of, etc. The Prisoner was placed about 7 or 8 foot from the Justices, and the Accusers between the Justices and them; the Prisoner was ordered to stand right before the Justices, with an Officer appointed to hold each hand, least they should therewith afflict them, and the Prisoners Eyes must be constantly on the Justices; for if they look'd on the afflicted, they would either fall into their Fits, or cry out of being hurt by them; after Examination of the Prisoners, who it was afflicted these Girls, etc., they were put upon saying the Lords Prayer, as a tryal of their guilt; after the afflicted seem'd to be out of their Fits, they would look steadfastly on some one person, and frequently not speak; and then the Justices said they were struck dumb, and after a little time would speak again; then the Justices said to the Accusers, "which of you will go and touch the Prisoner at the Bar?" then the most courageous would adventure, but before they had made three steps would ordinarily fall down as in a Fit; the Justices ordered that they should be taken up and carried to the Prisoner, that she might touch them; and as soon as they were touched by the accused, the Justices would say, they are well, before I could discern any alteration; by which I observed that the Justices understood the manner of it. Thus far I was only as a Spectator, my Wife also was there part of the time, but no notice taken of her by the afflicted, except once or twice they came to her and asked her name.

But I having an opportunity to Discourse Mr. Hale (with whom I had formerly acquaintance) I took his advice, what I had best to do, and desired of him that I might have an opportunity to speak with her that accused my Wife; which he promised should be, I acquainting him that I reposed my trust in him.

Accordingly he came to me after the Examination was over, and told me I had now an opportunity to speak with the said Accuser, viz . Abigail Williams, a Girl of 11 or 12 Years old; but that we could not be in private at Mr. Parris's House, as he had promised me; we went therefore into the Alehouse, where an Indian Man attended us, who it seems was one of the afflicted [Parris's slave, John Indian]: to him we gave some Cyder, he shewed several Scars, that seemed as if they had been long there, and shewed them as done by Witchcraft, and acquainted us that his Wife, who also was a Slave, was imprison'd for Witchcraft. And now instead of one Accuser, they all came in, who began to tumble down like Swine, and then three Women were called in to attend them. We in the Room were all at a stand, to see who they would cry out of; but in a short time they cried out, Cary; and immediately after a Warrant was sent from the Justices to bring my Wife before them, who were sitting in a Chamber near by, waiting for this.

Being brought before the Justices, her chief accusers were two Girls; my Wife declared to the Justices, that she never had any knowledge of them before that day; she was forced to stand with her Arms stretched out. I did request that I might hold one of her hands, but it was denied me; then she desired me to wipe the Tears from her Eyes, and the Sweat from her Face, which I did; then she desired she might lean her self on me, saying, she should faint.

Justice Hathorn replied, she had strength enough to torment those persons, and she should have strength enough to stand. I speaking something against their cruel proceedings, they commanded me to be silent, or else I should be turned out of the Room. The Indian before mentioned, was also brought in, to be one of her Accusers: being come in, he now (when before the Justices) fell down and tumbled about like a Hog, but said nothing. The Justices asked the Girls, who afflicted the Indian? they answered she (meaning my Wife) and now lay upon him; the Justices ordered her to touch him, in order to his cure, but her head must be turned another way, least instead of curing, she should make him worse, by her looking on him, her hand being guided to take hold of his; but the Indian took hold on her hand, and pulled her down on the Floor, in a barbarous manner; then his hand was taken off, and her hand put on his, and the cure was quickly wrought. I being extreamly troubled at their Inhumane dealings, uttered a hasty Speech (That God would take vengeance on them, and desired that God would deliver us out of the hands of unmerciful men.) Then her Mittimus was writ. I did with difficulty and charge obtain the liberty of a Room, but no Beds in it; if there had, could have taken but little rest that Night. She was committed to Boston Prison; but I obtained a Habeas Corpus to remove her to Cambridge Prison, which is in our County of Middlesex. Having been there one Night, next Morning the Jaylor put Irons on her legs (having received such a command) the weight of them was about eight pounds; these Irons and her other Afflictions, soon brought her into Convulsion Fits, so that I thought she would have died that Night. I sent to intreat that the Irons might be taken off, but all intreaties were in vain, if it would have saved her Life, so that in this condition she must continue. The Tryals at Salem coming on, I went thither, to see how things were there managed; and finding that the Spectre-Evidence was there received, together with Idle, if not malicious Stories, against Peoples Lives, I did easily perceive which way the rest would go; for the same Evidence that served for one, would serve for all the rest. I acquainted her with her danger; and that if she were carried to Salem to be tried, I feared she would never return. I did my utmost that she might have her Tryal in our own County, I with several others Petitioning the Judge for it, and were put in hopes of it; but I soon saw so much, that I understood thereby it was not intended, which put me upon consulting the means of her escape; which thro the goodness of God was effected, and she got to Road Island, but soon found her self not safe when there, by reason of the pursuit after her; from thence she went to New-York, along with some others that had escaped their cruel hands; where we found his Excellency Benjamin Fletcher, Esq; Governour, who was very courteous to us. After this some of my Goods were seized in a Friends hands, with whom I had left them, and my self imprisoned by the Sheriff, and kept in Custody half a day, and then dismist; but to speak of their usage of the Prisoners, and their Inhumanity shewn to them, at the time of their Execution, no sober Christian could bear; they had also tryals of cruel mockings; which is the more, considering what a People for Religion, I mean the profession of it, we have been; those that suffered being many of them Church-Members, and most of them unspotted in their Conversation, till their Adversary the Devil took up this Method for accusing them.

Source: Robert Calef, *More Wonders of the Invisible World* (London: Nath. Hillar and Joseph Collyer, 1700), 95–98.

~ ~ ~

21. The Examination of Candy, July 4, 1692

Candy was a slave owned by Margaret Hawkes who, like Samuel Parris, had moved from Barbados to Salem. Candy was indicted on two charges of bewitching Ann Putnam and Mary Walcott, but the jury found her not guilty of each. Why do you think the jury doubted her confession?

SALEM, Monday, July 4, 1692. The examination of Candy, a negro woman, before Bartholomew Gedney and John Hawthorne Esqrs. Mr. Nicholas Noyes also present.

Q. Candy! are you a witch?

A. Candy no witch in her country. Candy's mother no witch. Candy no witch, Barbados. This country, mistress give Candy witch.

Q. Did your mistress make you a witch in this country?

A. Yes, in this country mistress give Candy witch.

Q. What did your mistress do to make you a witch?

A. Mistress bring book and pen and ink, make Candy write in it.

Q. What did you write in it?—She took a pen and ink and upon a book or paper made a mark.

Q. How did you afflict or hurt these folks, where are the puppets you did it with?—She asked to go out of the room and she would shew or tell; upon which she had liberty, one going with her, and she presently brought in two clouts, one with two knots tied in it, the other one; which being seen by Mary Warren, Deliverance Hobbs and Abigail Hobbs, they were greatly affrighted and fell into violent fits, and all of them said that the black man and Mrs. Hawkes and the negro stood by the puppets or rags and pinched them, and then they were afflicted, and when the knots were untied yet they continued as aforesaid. A bit of one of the rags being set on fire, the afflicted all said they were burned, and cried out dreadfully. The rags being put into water, two of the aforenamed persons were in dreadful fits almost choaked, and the other was violently running down to the river, but was stopped.

Source: Thomas Hutchinson, *The History of the province of Massachusetts-Bay, from the charter of King William and Queen Mary, in 1691, until the year 1750* (Boston: Jeremiah Condy, 1767), 33–34.

~ ~ ~

22. The Petition of John Proctor, July 23, 1692

Immortalized in Arthur Miller's play, The Crucible *(1953), John Proctor is one of the most familiar names associated with Salem witchcraft. His servant, Mary Warren, was one of the first possessed accusers, and the Proctors were named early in the proceedings. They were arrested in April. Both John and Elizabeth Proctor were found guilty of witchcraft. John petitioned several prominent ministers on July 23, and was executed on August 19. Elizabeth Proctor survived only because she was pregnant and the court would not hang her. Her son was born in prison in January 1693, and she was released in May. How did Proctor make sense of his plight? How did he explain his neighbors' confessions?*

SALEM-PRISON, July 23, 1692. *Mr. Mather, Mr. Allen, Mr. Moody, Mr. Willard, and Mr. Bailey.*
Reverend Gentlemen.
The innocency of our Case with the Enmity of our Accusers and our Judges, and Jury, whom nothing but our Innocent Blood will serve their turn, having Condemned us already before our Tryals, being so much incensed and engaged against us by the Devil, makes us bold to Beg and Implore your Favourable Assistance of this our Humble Petition to his Excellency, That if it be possible our Innocent Blood may be spared, which undoubtedly otherwise will be shed, if the Lord doth not mercifully step in. The Magistrates, Ministers, Jewries, and all the People in general, being so much inraged and incensed against us by the Delusion of the Devil, which we can term no other, by reason we know in our own Consciences, we are all Innocent Persons. Here are five Persons who have lately confessed themselves to be Witches, and do accuse some of us, of being along with them at a Sacrament, since we were committed into close Prison, which we know to be Lies. Two of the 5 are (Carriers Sons) Youngmen, who would not confess any thing

till they tyed them Neck and Heels till the Blood was ready to come out of their Noses, and 'tis credibly believed and reported this was the occasion of making them confess that they never did, by reason they said one had been a Witch a Month, and another five Weeks, and that their Mother had made them so, who has been confined here this nine Weeks. My son William Procter, when he was examin'd, because he would not confess that he was Guilty, when he was Innocent, they tyed him Neck and Heels till the Blood gushed out at his Nose, and would have kept him so 24 Hours, if one more Merciful than the rest, had not taken pity on him, and caused him to be unbound. These actions are very like the Popish Cruelties. They have already undone us in our Estates, and that will not serve their turns, without our Innocent Bloods. If it cannot be granted that we can have our Trials at Boston, we humbly beg that you would endeavour to have these Magistrates changed, and others in their rooms, begging also and beseeching you would be pleased to be here, if not all, some of you at our Trials, hoping thereby you may be the means of saving the shedding our Innocent Bloods, desiring your Prayers to the Lord in our behalf, we rest your Poor Afflicted Servants,

JOHN PROCTER, etc.

Source: Calef, *More Wonders*, 104–5.

~ ~ ~

23. The Examination of Mary Toothaker, July 30, 1692

Mary Toothaker lived in Billerica, Massachusetts. Her husband, Roger, was accused on May 18; ten days later Mary, along with her daughter, Margaret, and her sister, Martha Carrier, was accused. Roger died in prison in Boston in June. Two days after Mary Toothaker confessed, Indians attacked Billerica, killing all of the residents of two homes near her own. Toothaker was acquitted in 1693, along with her nephew Richard; her sister hanged on August 19, 1692. Toothaker never retracted her confession. What does Toothaker's confession tell you about the conditions in which she lived? How did the proximity of Indians shape her experience and her confession? How does her depiction of the Devil compare with his image in other documents from Salem? Do you think that Toothaker believed that she was a witch?

30 July 92 The Examination and confession of widow Toothaker Taken before Major Gidney Mr Hauthorn Mr Corwin & Cap'n Higginson.

After many questiones and negative answers returned and her Stricking Down of severall of the afflicted persons with her looks, she was Desyred to tell the truth in this matter She then said that this May last she was under great Discontentednes & troubled with feare about the Indians, & used often to dream of fighting with them. Being asked what was the Devils temptation under her discontentment she said she would confess if she could But that there was something at her breast that hindered her. she said she had often prayed but thought she was the worse for praying and knows not but that the Devil has tempted her not to pray, for her breath has been often Stopt as it was just now; Being asked if the Devil did not Desier her to renounce her baptisme, she answered that she had thoughts she was rather the worse for her baptisme and has wished she had not been baptised because she had not improved it as she ought to have done she saith she used to get into a corner alone and Desryed to prey but her mouth would be Stopt but sometymes she had been helped to say Lord be merce full to me a sinner. Being again asked how far she had yeilded to Satan she said the Devil promised her she should not be discovered and if she was discovered & brought down that she should goe home Innocent & cleare but now find he has deluded her. Being again asked how long it is since saten furst wrought with her in this manner she said she could not well tell how long but thinks it is not two years. And confesses that she went In her Spirit [to Timo' Swans] and did often think of him & her hands would be clinched, and that she would grip the dishclout or anything else and so think of the person; And by this & afflicting of others since She came down she is convinced she is a witch—she saith now, the Devil appeared to her in the shape of a Tawny man and promised to keep her from the Indians and she should have happy dayes with her sone—she was asked if she did not signe the Devills book; answered he brought something which she [took] to bee a piece of burch bark and she made a mark with her finger by rubbing off the whit Scurff. And he promised if she would serve him she should be safe from the Indians (she was then a litle stopt again & believed it was the Devil that did it). Being asked if the Devil did not say she was to serve him Answered Yes, and signed the mark upon that condition and was to praise him with her whole heart, and twas to that appearance she prayed at all tymes for he said he was able to delyver her from the Indians And it was the feare of the Indians that put her upon it. she confesses she hurt Timothy Swan and thinks she was twice at salem Village witch meeting and that Goody Bridges was one of her company—she said as she came along in order to examination she promised herself twenty tymes by the way (but [seald] it was to the Devil) That if she should Dye upon the Gallowse yet she would not say any thing but that she was Innocent. & rejoyced In the thought of it that She Should goe home Inocent—she saith that Goody Green and Goody Broomage were also her companions and that Broomage afflicted Swan by squeezing his arms, And is afrayd that she the said Toothaker squeezed his throat—she said further that when Goody Bridges (who had confessed before) urged her also to confess she had then no remembrance of this but with the justices Discourse and the help of god it came into her mind. she saith she thought that that appearance was God her creator & being asked if she did not know otherwise answered The Devil is so subtel that when she would confess he stops her and deludes also by scripture and being asked what scripture he made inser of to her she mentioned that in the Psalmes where it is said Let my enemies be confounded, And so she had wished them all Destroyed that raised such reports of her she confesses that her sister was with her at all the meetings & particularly at Salem Village & there went with her Goody Bridges Goody foster Goody Green & Goody Broomage Several afflicted persons said they saw the black man before her in the tyme of her examination And she now, her self confesses she saw him upon the table before her. She sayes further there was a minister a litle man whose name is Burroughs that preached at the Village meeting of witches, and she heard that they used read & write at these meetings And, that they did talk of 305 witches in the country. she saith their discourse was about the pulling down the Kingdom of Christ and setting up the Kingdom of satan, and also Knew Goody How emong the rest. Being asked if there was not a woman that stirred them up to afflict Swan Answered yes there was a pretty [Elderly] woman that was most busie about him and encouraged the rest to afflict him. she thinks she set her hand to that book at Salem Village meeting. And thinks the [End] of all their setting their hand to that book was to come in, and afflict & set up the Devils Kingdome. she being asked if her husband did not speak to his daughter to Kill one Button a reputed witch answered yes, and that they used to read many historyes, especially one book that treated of the 12 signes, from which book they could tell a great Deale.—she saith she never knew her daughter to be in this condition before this summer, But that she was at Salem Village meeting once with her, she cannot tell that her daughter did then signe the book but a great many did. Being asked how many were of her Society she said Goody Broomage, foster, green, the two Mary Laceyes older and younger, Richard Carrier, her sister Carryer and another aged woman—she saith she heard the Beating of a drum at the village meeting And think also heard the sound of a trumpet.

Source: *Salem Witchcraft Papers*, v. 3, 767–69.

~~~

24. The Examinations of Abigail Faulkner, August 1692

Abigail Faulkner of Andover, Massachusetts, along with several members of her family, was accused in August. At first she denied her guilt, but after William Barker accused Faulkner and her sister of drawing him to witchcraft, she confessed, and her sister did as well. Faulkner was found guilty. She languished in prison for several months, and petitioned for her release on December 3, 1692. How did the behavior of the possessed affect the trial proceedings, and why did Faulkner confess?

August 11, 1692

Mr Hauthorn; Mr Corwin: & Cap: Higginson pressent when she was brought into the room: the afflicted persons fell down Mr Ha: You are:heare: aprehended:for:witchcraft: but Answ'd: I know nothing of it with: the cast of her eye: mary:walcot: & the rest afflicted: mary waren and others fell down: it was said to her do you not see: she said yes but it is the devill dos it in my shape: mary Walcot said she had seen her 2 monthes a good while agoe but was not hurt by her till last night: An Putnam sayd she had seen said falkn'r but was not hurt by her till last night & then she pulld me off my hors: mary warin said she had seen her in company with other witches: but was not hurt by her till lately

Mary Warin & others of the afflicted: were struck down into: fitts & Helped up out of their fitts by a touch of Abig'l folkn'rs hand: she was urged to confes the truth:for the creddit of hir Town: her CouzEliz Jonson urged her: with that: but: she refused to do it saying god would not: require her to confess that: that she was not gilty of Phelpses daughter complayned her af-flicting her: but: she denyed: that she had any thing to doe with witchcraft she said falkn'r had a cloth in her hand: that when she squeezed in her hand the afflicted; fell into greevous fits: as was observed: the afflicted sayd Dan'll Eames & Capt floyd was upon that cloth when it was upon the table

She sayd she was sorry they were afflicted: but she was told & it was ob-servd she did not shed a tear: mary waren was pulld und'r the table & was helpd out of her fitt by a touch of said faulkn'r she said she had looked on some of these afflicted: when they came to Andov'r & hurt them not: but she was told it was before she had began to afflict them: she was told that it was reported she used to Conjure with a seiv: but she said it was not so that story:was cleared up:

August 30: 92: Abig'l Fokner: before: their Majestt's Justices at first denyed witchcraft as she had done before: but afterward: she owned: that: she was

Angry at what folk s:d when her Couz Eliz. Jonson was taken up: & folk laught & said her sister Jonson would come out next: & she did look with an evil eye on the afflicted persons & did consent that they should be afflicted: becaus they were the caus of bringing her kindred out: and she did wish them ill & her spirit being raised she did:pinch her hands together: & she knew not but that the devil might take that advantage but it was the devil not she that afflicted them: this she said she did at Capt Chandlers garison: the Night after: Eliz Jonson had bin examined before Capt Bradstreet in the day.

Source: *Salem Witchcraft Papers*, v. 1, 327–28.

~ ~ ~

25. Thomas Brattle's Skepticism, 1692

Born in Boston in 1658, Thomas Brattle was educated at Harvard College and traveled and studied abroad before becoming the treasurer of Harvard in 1693. He wrote this letter to an unknown minister about the legal procedures that were followed in Salem and the phenomenon of the confessing women. His letter conveys considerable skepticism about the course of events in Salem. What was the basis of his skepticism? Was he more troubled by violations of legal procedure or by the belief system exposed in the trials? How did he explain confession? How does his explanation for confession compare with your own, based on your analysis of documents 19, 21, 23, and 24?

October 8, 1692.

. . . whether you expect such freedome from me, yea or no, yet shall you find, that I am very open to communicate my thoughts unto you, and in plain terms to tell you what my opinion is of the Salem proceedings.

First, as to the method which the Salem Justices do take in their examinations, it is truly this: A warrant being issued out to apprehend the persons that are charged and complained of by the afflicted children, (as they are called); said persons are brought before the Justices, (the afflicted being present.) The Justices ask the apprehended why they afflict those poor children; to which the apprehended answer, they do not afflict them. The Justices order the apprehended to look upon the said children, which accordingly they do; and at the time of that look, (I dare not say by that look, as the Salem Gentlemen do) the afflicted are cast into a fitt. The apprehended are then blinded, and ordered to touch the afflicted; and at that touch, tho' not by the touch, (as above) the afflicted ordinarily do come out of their fitts. The afflicted persons then declare and affirm, that the apprehended have afflicted them; upon which the apprehended persons, tho' of never so good repute, are forthwith committed to prison, on suspicion for witchcraft. One of the Salem Justices was pleased to tell Mr. Alden,[1] (when upon his examination) that truly he had been acquainted with him these many years; and had always accounted him a good man; but indeed now he should be obliged to change his opinion. This, there are more than one or two did hear, and are ready to swear to, if not in so many words, yet as to its natural and plain meaning. He saw reason to change his opinion of Mr. Alden, because that at the time he touched the poor child, the poor child came out of her fitt. . . .

I cannot but condemn this method of the Justices, of making this touch of the hand a rule to discover witchcraft; because I am fully persuaded that it is sorcery, and a superstitious method, and that which we have no rule for, either from reason or religion. The Salem Justices, at least some of them, do assert, that the cure of the afflicted persons is a natural effect of this touch; and they are so well instructed in the Cartesian philosophy, and in the doctrine of effluvia, that they undertake to give a demonstration how this touch does cure the afflicted persons; and the account they give of it is this; that by this touch, the venemous and malignant particles, that were ejected from the eye, do, by this means, return to the body whence they came, and so leave the afflicted persons pure and whole. I must confesse to you, that I am no small admirer of the Cartesian philosophy; but yet I have not so learned it. Certainly this is a strain that it will by no means allow of.

I would fain know of these Salem Gentlemen, but as yet could never know, how it comes about, that if these apprehended persons are witches, and, by a look of the eye, do cast the afflicted into their fitts by poisoning them, how it comes about, I say, that, by a look of their eye, they do not cast others into fitts, and poison others by their looks; and in particular, tender, fearfull women, who often are beheld by them, and as likely as any in the whole world to receive an ill impression from them. This Salem philosophy, some men may call the new philosophy; but I think it rather deserves the name of Salem superstition and sorcery, and it is not fitt to be named in a land of such light as New-England is. I think the matter might be better solved another way; but I shall not make any attempt that way, further than to say, that these afflicted children, (as they are called,) do hold correspondence with the devill, even in the esteem and account of the S. G.[Salem Gentleman]; for when the black man, i. e. (say these gentlemen,) the Devill, does appear to them, they ask him many questions, and accordingly give information to the inquirer; and if this is not holding correspondence with the devill, and something worse, I know not what is. . . .

Secondly, with respect to the confessours, (as they are improperly called,) or such as confesse themselves to be witches, (the second thing you inquire into in your letter), there are now about fifty of them in Prison; many of which I have again and again seen and heard; and I cannot but tell you, that my faith is strong concerning them, that they are deluded, imposed upon, and under the influence of some evill spirit; and therefore unfitt to be evidences either against themselves, or any one else. I now speak of one sort of them, and of others afterward.

These confessours, (as they are called,) do very often contradict themselves, as inconsistently as is usual for any crazed, distempered person to do. This the S. G. do see and take notice of; and even the Judges themselves have, at some times, taken these confessours in flat lyes, or contradictions, even in the Courts; By reason of which, one would have thought, that the Judges would have frowned upon the said confessours, discarded them, and not minded one tittle of any thing that they said; but instead thereof, (as sure as we are men,) the Judges vindicate these confessours, and salve their contradictions, by proclaiming, that the Devill takes away their memory, and imposes upon their brain. . . .

But now, if, in the Judges' account, these confessours are under the influence of the Devill, and their brains are affected and imposed upon by the Devill, so that they are not their own men, why then should these Judges, or any other men, make such account of, and set so much by, the words of these Confessours, as they do? In short, I argue thus:

If the Devill does actually take away the memory of them at some times, certainly the Devill, at other times, may very reasonably be thought to affect their fancyes, and to represent false ideas to their imagination. But now, if it be thus granted, that the Devill is able to represent false ideas (to speak vulgarly) to the imaginations of the confessours, what man of sense will regard the confessions, or any of the words, of these confessours? . . .

Now for the proof of the said sorcery and witchcraft, the prisoner at the bar pleading not guilty.

1. The afflicted persons are brought into Court; and after much patience and pains taken with them, do take their oaths, that the prisoner at the bar did afflict them: And here I think it very observable, that often, when the afflicted do mean and intend only the appearance and shape of such an one, (say G. Proctour [John Proctor]) yet they positively swear that G. Proctour did afflict them; and they have been allowed so to do; as tho' there was no real difference between G. Proctour and the shape of G. Proctour. This, methinks, may readily prove a stumbling block to the Jury, lead them into a

very fundamental errour, and occasion innocent blood, yea the innocentest blood imaginable, to be in great danger. . . .

2. The confessours do declare what they know of the said prisoner; and some of the confessours are allowed to give their oaths; a thing which I believe was never heard of in this world; that such as confesse themselves to be witches, to have renounced God and Christ, and all that is sacred, should yet be allowed and ordered to swear by the name of the great God! . . .

4. They are searched by a Jury; and as to some of them, the Jury brought in, that [on] such or such a place there was a preternatural excrescence. And I wonder what person there is, whether man or woman, of whom it cannot be said but that, in some part of their body or other, there is a preternatural excrescence. The term is a very general and inclusive term.

Some of the S. G. are very forward to censure and condemn the poor prisoner at the bar, because he sheds no tears: but such betray great ignorance in the nature of passion, and as great heedlessnesse as to common passages of a man's life. Some there are who never shed tears; others there are that ordinarily shed tears upon light occasions, and yet for their lives cannot shed a tear when the deepest sorrow is upon their hearts; and who is there that knows not these things? Who knows not that an ecstasye of Joy will sometimes fetch teares, when as the quite contrary passion will shutt them close up? Why then should any be so silly and foolish as to take an argument from this appearance? But this is by the by. In short, the prisoner at the bar is indited for sorcery and witchcraft acted upon the bodyes of the afflicted. Now, for the proof of this, I reckon that the only pertinent evidences brought in are the evidences of the said afflicted.

It is true, that over and above the evidences of the afflicted persons, there are many evidences brought in, against the prisoner at the bar; either that he was at a witch meeting, or that he performed things which could not be done by an ordinary natural power; or that she sold butter to a saylor, which proving bad at sea, and the seamen exclaiming against her, she appeared, and soon after there was a storm, or the like. But what if there were ten thousand evidences of this nature; how do they prove the matter of inditement! And if they do not reach the matter of inditement, then I think it is clear, that the prisoner at the bar is brought in guilty, and condemned, merely from the evidences of the afflicted persons.

I am very sensible, that it is irksome and disagreeable to go back, when a man's doing so is an implication that he has been walking in a wrong path: however, nothing is more honourable than, upon due conviction, to retract and undo, (so far as may be,) what has been amiss and irregular. . . .

There are two or three other things that I have observed in and by these afflicted persons, which make me strongly suspect that the Devill imposes upon their brains, and deludes their fancye and imagination; and that the Devill's book (which they say has been offered them) is a mere fancye of theirs, and no reality: That the witches' meeting, the Devill's Baptism, and mock sacraments, which they oft speak of, are nothing else but the effect of their fancye, depraved and deluded by the Devill, and not a Reality to be regarded or minded by any wise man. And whereas the Confessours have owned and asserted the said meetings, the said Baptism, and mock Sacrament, (which the S. G. and some others, make much account of) I am very apt to think, that, did you know the circumstances of the said Confessours, you would not be swayed thereby, any otherwise than to be confirmed, that all is perfect Devilism, and an Hellish design to ruine and destroy this poor land: For whereas there are of the said Confessours 55 in number, some of them are known to be distracted, crazed women, something of which you may see by a petition lately offered to the chief Judge, a copy whereof I may now send you; others of them denyed their guilt, and maintained their innocency for above eighteen hours, after most violent, distracting, and draggooning methods had been used with them, to make them confesse. Such methods they were, that more than one of the said confessours did since tell many, with teares in their eyes, that they thought their very lives would have gone out of their bodyes; and wished that they might have been cast into the lowest dungeon, rather than be tortured with such repeated buzzings and chuckings and unreasonable urgings as they were treated withal.

They soon recanted their confessions, acknowledging, with sorrow and grief, that it was an hour of great temptation with them. . . .

What will be the issue of these troubles, God only knows; I am afraid that ages will not wear off that reproach and those stains which these things will leave behind them upon our land. I pray God pity us, Humble us, Forgive us, and appear mercifully for us in this our mount of distress: Herewith I conclude, and subscribe myself,

Reverend Sir, your real friend and humble servant,

T. B.

Note

1. John Alden was examined at Salem on May 28, 1692, arrested on May 31, and incarcerated in the Boston jail, from which he escaped.

Source: Burr, ed., *Narratives*, 170, 171–72, 173–76, 186, 188–89, 190.

~ ~ ~

26. Ann Putnam's Confession, 1706

Ann Putnam was a thirteen-year-old possessed accuser in Salem in 1692 whose testimony was central to the conviction and executions of most of the people accused and hanged in that year (see documents 21 and 24). Fourteen years later, she stood before the church at Salem Village and made the following confession before she joined the church. What exactly did she confess to?

1706. Aug 25. Received Ann Putnam to full communion.

The confession of Anne Putnam when she was received to communion: 1706

I desire to be humbled before God for that sad and humbling providence that befell my fathers family in the year about 92; that I then being in my childhood should by such a providence of God be made an instrument for that accuseing of severall persons of a grievous crime, wherby their lives were taken away from them, whom now I have just grounds and good reason to believe they were innocent persons; and that it was a great delusion of Satan that deceived me in that sad time, whereby I justly fear I have been instrumental with others tho' ignorantly and unwittingly to bring upon myself & this land the guilt of innocent blood Though what was said or done by me against any person I can truly and uprightly say before God & man I did it not out of any anger, malice, or ill will to any person for I had no such thing against one of them; but what I did was ignorantly being deluded by Satan. And particularly as I was a chief instrument of accuseing of Goodwife Nurse and her two sisters I desire to lye in the dust & to be humbled for it in that I was a cause with others of so sad a calamity to them & their families, for which cause I desire to lye in the dust & earnestly begg fforgiveness of God & from all those unto whom I have given just cause of sorrow & offence, whose relations were taken away or accused.

[Signed]
Anne Putnam

Source: Danvers Church Records, *The New England Historical and Genealogical Register and Antiquarian Journal* 12 (July 1858), 246.

~ ~ ~

27. The Code of Handsome Lake

Handsome Lake (1735–1815) was a Seneca prophet and religious leader. In the 1790s, during a serious illness, he had a series of revelations which crystallized as a new and enduring religious movement. He produced a massive code of laws for his followers. It contains 130 sections, covering all facets of conduct. The two excerpts here focus on his concerns about witches. What did witches do and why were they such a threat? Who were the witches? How do the depictions of witches that emerge in documents 27 and 28 compare with the descriptions of seventeenth-century witch beliefs among the Iroquois and their neighbors in the Jesuit Relations (documents 2 and 3)?

The Great Message

Section 2

Now spoke the beings and said, "We now speak of the second word. This makes the Creator angry. The word is Got'go^n?. [witch]

Witches are people without their right minds. They make disease and spread sickness to make the living die. They cut short the numbered days, for the Creator has given each person a certain number of days in which to live in this world.

Now this must you do: When you have told this message and the witches hear it they will confess before all the people and will say, "I am doing this evil thing but now I cease it forever, as long as I live." Some witches are more evil and can not speak in public so these must come privately and confess to you, Handsome Lake, or a preacher of this Gai'wiio`. Now some are most evil and they must go far out upon an abandoned trail and there they must confess before the Creator alone. This course may be taken by witches of whom no one knows.

Now when they go they must say:
"Our Creator, O listen to me!
I am a miserable creature.
I think that way
So now I cease.
Now this is appointed
For all of my days,
As long as I live here
In this earth-world.
I have spoken."

In this manner all must say and say truly, then the prayer will be sufficient.

So they said and he said. Eniaiehuk [It was that way].

Section 72

Now another message.

Now we think that a time will come when a woman will be seen performing her witch spells in the daylight. Then will you know that the end is near. She will run through the neighborhood boasting how many she has slain by her sorcery. Then will you see how she who refused to believe in Gai'wiio' will suffer punishment.

So they said and he said. Eniaiehuk.

Source: Arthur C. Parker, *The Code of Handsome Lake, the Seneca Prophet, New York State Museum Bulletin* 163 (1912), 27–29, 58.

~ ~ ~

28. The Code of the Shawnee Prophet, circa 1812

This account of the code of Tenskwatawa, the Shawnee prophet, comes from a letter written by an Indian agent named Thomas Forsyth to General William Clark, dated December 23, 1812. The Prophet's code comes to us at best third hand. What kind of social critique did this code contain? How would you compare the Prophet's vision with those articulated by Indian leaders in documents 4 and 5? How did witchcraft fit within the Prophet's vision for a new social order?

1st Spiritous liquors was not to be tasted by any Indians on any account whatever.

2nd No Indian was to take more than one wife in future, but those who now had two three or more wives might keep them, but it would please the Great Spirit if they had only one wife.

3d No Indian was to be runing after the women; if a man was single let him take a wife.

4th If any married woman was to behave ill by not paying proper attention to her work, etc., the husband had a right to punish her with a rod, and as soon as the punishment was over, both husband and wife, was to look each other in the face and laugh, and to bear no ill will to each other for what had passed.

5th All Indian women who were living with whitemen was to be brought home to their friends and relations, and their children to be left with their fathers, so that the nations might become genuine Indians.

6th All medicine bags, and all kinds of medicine dances and songs were to exist no more; the medicine bags were to be destroyed in presence of the whole of the people collected for that purpose, and at the destroying of such medicine, etc., every one was to make open confession to the Great Spirit in a loud voice of all the bad deeds that he or she had committed during their lifetime, and beg for forgiveness as the Great Spirit was too good to refuse.

7th No Indian was to sell any of their provision to any white people, they might give a little as a present, as they were sure of getting in return the full value in something else.

8th No Indian was to eat any victuals that was cooked by a White person, or to eat any provisions raised by White people, as bread, beef, pork, fowls, etc.

9th No Indian must offer skins or furs or any thing else for sale, but ask to exchange them for such articles that they may want.

10th Every Indian was to consider the French, English, and Spaniards, as their fathers or friends, and to give them their hand, but they were not to know the Americans on any account, but to keep them at a distance.

11th All kind of white people's dress, such as hats, coats, etc., were to be given to the first whiteman they met as also all dogs not of their own breed, and all cats were to be given back to white people.

12th The Indians were to endeavour to do without buying any merchandise as much as possible, by which means the game would become plenty, and then by means of bows and arrows, they could hunt and kill game as in former days, and live independent of all white people.

13th All Indians who refused to follow these regulations were to be considered as bad people and not worthy to live, and must be put to death. (A Kickapoo Indian was actually burned in the spring of the year 1809 at the old Kickapoo Town for refusing to give up his medicine bag, and another old man and old woman was very near sharing the same fate at the same time and place).

14th The Indians in their prayers prayed to the earth, to be fruitful, also to the fish to be plenty, to the fire and sun, etc., and a certain dance was introduced simply for amusement, those prayers were repeated morning and evening, and they were taught that a diviation from these duties would offend the Great Spirit. There were many more regulations but I now have forgot them, but those above mentioned are the principal ones.

Source: "The Code of the Shawnee Prophet, Tenskwatawa," in Emma Helen Blair, *The Indian Tribes of the Upper Mississippi Valley and Region of the Great Lakes* (Cleveland: The Arthur H. Clark Company, 1912), v. 2, appendix 2, 274–78.

~ ~ ~

29. The Witch Hunt at the White River Mission, 1806

This account of the Shawnee prophet's witch-hunting activities comes from the pen of two Moravian missionaries, John Peter Kluge (1768–1849) and Abraham Luckenbach (1777–1854), who lived with Kluge's family (he had a wife and children) and a small number of Delaware Indian converts at the Moravian mission on the White River in Indiana Territory. Kluge was born in Prussia and came to the United States after serving as a missionary in Suriname. Luckenbach was born in Pennsylvania.[1]

The Moravians were a Christian denomination that emerged in the eighteenth century in Germany. Moravians had settled in Pennsylvania and North Carolina in the eighteenth century, and were active missionaries to Indians in the northeast. Kluge and Luckenbach first established their mission at White River in 1801. They abandoned their mission in September 1806, not long after the tumultuous events described here. How did Kluge and Luckenbach make sense of what was happening at the White River mission in 1806? Can you read their account carefully to understand what Indian participants might have thought? How did the Moravians and the Delawares understand witches? Compare this document to the seventeenth-century accounts by missionaries (documents 1 through 5). What strike you as important changes or continuities in Christian missionaries' perceptions of Indian religious and cultural practices?

March 13, 1806

On the afternoon of this day, seven wild Indians with faces painted black came to us and took our last remaining brother Joshua away by force. The reason for this, according to them, was this: The Indians had resolved to abolish poison and all sorcery among them, as we mentioned in our record of February. To this end the young people had banded together, deposed their chiefs, and at the instigation of the heathen teacher guarded those who had come together as captives, especially the older people, and appointed a great day on which to sit in judgment upon all who were suspected of dealing out poison. These suspects were to be brought to confess through fire. Old Chief Tedpachsit was the first one whom they accused of having poison with which he had brought about the death of many Indians. When the poor old man would not confess, they bound him to stakes and actually began to burn him. In his distress he said he had stored poison in our Indian Br. Joshua's house. This was what they desired to hear, for it gave them a pretext to draw our poor Joshua into their terrible upheaval. They had called him a number of times before this but he had not gone, answering that he was a believer and had nothing to do with their matter; that they should do what they pleased but that they should let us alone. But the savages were not satisfied and were only too happy to get him in their midst through deceit and, as mentioned before, took him away by force so that he might tell Chief Tedpachsit to his face that he had nothing like that in his house, after which he might return home. In spite of everything, Joshua had to go with the savages to the Indians gathered at Woapicamikunk. And now we were quite alone with our Sr. Theresa. As mentioned in the record of February, the recently baptized Hannah had been impelled by fear and superstition to go to the assembled savages. How we felt under the circumstances cannot be described, especially so, because we could not tell what their object really was in regard to our poor Joshua. In our trouble we prayed to God our Saviour that He should have mercy upon us and upon our poor Joshua who was in the hands of the wild ones. In this time of trouble the text for the day was a great comfort to us.

15th. At last an Indian from Woapicamikunk came and told us that when Joshua was led before the old Chief and declared to him that his statement had been false, the old Chief confessed that he had lied from fear, in order to quiet somewhat the wrought-up savages; that he knew well enough that he had nothing of the kind and much less had he anything stored in Joshua's house. Joshua was then declared free of the charge, but they would not allow him to return home on the ground that he had to wait until their prophet, the Schawano [Tenskwatawa], had arrived.

N.B. This Schawano is the greatest teacher among the savages because he not only pretends to have had visions of God who had told him how the Indians should live, but also to have been given the power to know all that is concealed and to uncover even the thoughts of people; he pretends that he can look into a man's heart as well as into his face, and knows all that is going on in it. He lays claim to many other foolish things.

This fellow, a well-known evildoer, was to tell the Delaware nation, who among the people had poison or possessed the unallowed gift of sorcery to bring about the death of Indians. They made it very easy for the arch-deceiver. They were so full of their superstition that they would tell him beforehand whom they suspected. This instrument of the Devil had nothing to do but to confirm their suspicions, then they were satisfied because it was in accordance with their own ideas. For this reason we were quite uncertain how poor Joshua would fare, for the visiting Indian's report did not set our hearts at rest. We were therefore very glad when, on the afternoon of the 16th, a well-known Indian arrived who could talk English fluently and who had not gone to the assembled savages. Imagine our horror when we heard that the expected Schawano had come to the assembled Indians the day before. All Indians of both sexes formed a circle about this miscreant so that he might point out those who had poison or other supernatural gifts which relate to their superstition. After a great many ceremonies he accused a number of having poison with which they brought about the death of Indians in all sorts of ways. The two old chiefs, Tedpachsit and Hackingpomska, were accused of having poison, the first named being especially charged with the death of a large number of Indians. Now they had heard what they desired. The wild young people took all these unjustly condemned captives and guarded them closely. We also heard that the raging savages had burned alive an old woman named Caritas, who had been baptized by the Brethren in olden times, and that our poor Joshua was likewise a captive. How we felt when we heard this sad news may be better imagined than described. Although we had been told that they would not murder him, we had no rest day or night and from anxiety we could neither eat nor sleep, because we distrusted the superstition and rage of the wild ones, especially so because we know that they hate the believing Indians.

17th. Our worry and perplexity over the fate of our Joshua increased. We were overcome with terror and fright when all of a sudden we saw ten Indians with their faces painted black, some on foot, others on horseback, coming into our village with old Chief Tedpachsit. Soon after these barbarians built a large fire near our place, struck the old Chief on the head with the hatchet and threw him half-alive into the fire. Meanwhile they stood near and rejoiced over the pitiful cries and movements of the unfortunate one. The plain south of our village and the woods caught fire so that our village was full of smoke and fumes. Our feelings under this trial cannot be described. We realized that we were in the midst of a band of murderers, without human help, and all the while were tortured by the uncertain fate of our poor Br. Joshua.

After the murder the monsters, quite wild, came into the house, boasted of the awful deed, put on a hypocritical front and demanded something to eat and tobacco to smoke. We gladly gave them both so as to get rid of them. We summoned up courage as well as we could and asked what had become of our Joshua. They immediately began to accuse him of their abominable superstition and said that it was not for nothing that he was a prisoner; that they knew full well that he was familiar with the black art and could destroy the lives of Indians or cause them to become lame; that he merely pretended to be a believer of our teaching, etc. We did our best to show them that their charge was groundless, but in vain. To calm us, they assured us that they would not put him to death. We therefore sent with them a message to the captain of the savages admonishing them to be careful what they should do and saying that Joshua was an old believer and had nothing to do with the things they accused him of, for he belonged to God and has nothing to do with the works of the Devil, that in addition to this he was a Mohican, and as they well knew had come with us as our interpreter; that we requested therefore that they should release him at once, for what they did to him they might consider as being done to us, etc. Here again the hypocrisy of the savages becomes apparent. Though they knew that Joshua was murdered the same day (we learned of it afterwards), they never said a word about it and promised to deliver our message. They left with wild yells. . . .

Though we had heard that the savages suspected us and all teachers of the believing Indians of taking away the poison of all Indians who were converted, and of keeping it so that white teachers might use it to put the Indians to death or make them sick if they would not do as they were told, and though for this reason, we could not know to what the Devil might lead them and what our fate would be in consequence, especially since the savages had threatened to put to death anyone who should say the least against their actions, the burden of our hearts led us to resolve that we would make a speech to the assembled wild ones. Our hope was that we might do something toward having Joshua released, or, if that were impossible, at least talk with him once more. This we were ready to do even though we should have to suffer for it. Since it was impossible for us to leave Sr. Kluge all alone with the children under such circumstances, Br. Luckenbach felt it his duty to go alone. His object was to look up a French trader on the way and take him along.

18th. With high courage he left here early in the morning. He had hardly gone half way when he was met by an Indian who gave him the terrible news that, on the day before, our poor Joshua had become a victim of their cruelty. They likewise had struck the hatchet into his head two times and then burned him. With this terrible news Br. Luckenbach came back in the afternoon. This was the severest blow that could be given us. We were filled with terror and the horror of it all robbed us of all thought. We could do nothing but sigh and weep. As soon as we recovered somewhat our first thought was to sell everything and flee from here to Goshen as soon as possible. All preparations had been made when cold weather set in and put the difficult journey, on account of the children, out of the question, for the time being. After several days we heard that Joshua had said a great deal at the place of murder that the savages could not understand. It is quite likely that he prayed to the Saviour in German, for he was in an encouraging state of heart when the savages took him away. On the 22d we also heard that the wild ones had thrown our poor Joshua into a terribly large fire, which they constantly replenished, but that Joshua's body had been hardly singed after two hours. This made them all the more savage, consequently they built a still hotter fire but even then his body was not burned to ashes before the following morning.

23d. A French trader sent a man to us to inform us that the Indians had told him to tell us that they would not hurt us, but that we should go away from here as soon as possible. . . . But we resolved to go to them to inquire whether they really meant what they said in their message to us through the Frenchman mentioned above; [we would say] that we wanted to hear direct from them, because they, the chiefs, had invited us to come here. As soon as we should hear this from them, then we would believe and would gladly leave here, for it depended on them whether they wanted us here any longer with the Word of God; we had no desire to force ourselves on them, because, as they knew, we had no other object in view than to be of service to them and bring them salvation, etc. With these words Br. Luckenbach rode away on the 25th to learn what the savages had to say. They did not want to admit that they had tried to send us away, at the same time they said, "You can go whenever you please; we do not need you here. In olden times the Indians did not know how to live aright, but now we ourselves know how to live and need no one to teach us. None of us will come to hear your Word, for you are white people and we are Indians. You have another color than we, also another teaching; your teaching is good for white people but not for us. But if you want to remain anyway, you may do so. We will not tell you to go away, neither will we ask you to remain. You can do as you please, and we will do as we please." With this answer Br. Luckenbach returned on the 26th. From this we could see clearly that they were setting us aside entirely and that we could expect no protection from them.

27th. On this and the following days we continued to hear of all sorts of the most terrible murders and burnings. . . .

April 1. We heard again that the savages had taken one of their numbers, a peaceable Indian, hacked him to pieces and burned him up, and that 7 others were held as prisoners. The general supposition is that these will meet a similar fate. . . .

9th and 10th. We heard that the savages were about to put to death their last remaining chief, old Hockinpomsga, besides the Chief of the Nanticokes and 6 other Indians of both sexes, and burn them. Just as they laid hands on the unfortunate victim, the friends of the Chief took their weapons, sprang in the midst of the people and threatened to kill anyone who should take part in this murder. This put a check on further slaughter. Nevertheless, those who had been set apart for the brutal sacrifice did not feel themselves safe before the rage of the young people. For this reason the most well-to-do among them secretly sent the Indian teacher or lying prophet several hundred strings of wampum, besides gifts of silver and cows, with the request that their lives might be spared. This pleased the instruments of the Devil. The result was that the unfortunate victims who had been condemned to death were released under all sorts of pretexts. It was announced that they had bought their release as prisoners. . . .

13th. We passed the day quietly, for we could have no public service both from lack of an interpreter and hearers. The heathen no longer care to hear anything of the Word of God. Yes, it has come so far that they immediately fly into a rage when one tells them that they are not on the right path and should be converted to the Saviour of mankind, and forsake all their evil ways. For the time being we can do nothing more than pray, weep, and debate what should be done further. . . .

15th and 16th. We heard that there was a famine among the assembled Indians in Woapicamikunk. On this account they intend to have a sacrificial festival and pass a number of nights and days with dancing. With this, their supposed worship of God is brought to a close.

Note

1. Harry Emilius Stocker, *A History of the Moravian Mission Among the Indians on the White River in Indiana* (Bethlehem, PA, 1917), 25–26.

Source: Lawrence Henry Gipson, ed., and Harry E. Stocker, Herman T. Frueauff, and Samuel C. Zeller, trans., *The Moravian Indian Mission on White River: Diaries and Letters, May 5, 1799, to November 12, 1806* (Indianapolis: Indiana Historical Bureau, 1938), 412–421.

Index

About the Author

Alison Games is the Dorothy M. Brown Distinguished Professor of History at Georgetown University, where she has taught since 1995. She is the author of *Migration and the Origins of the English Atlantic World* (1999), which won the Theodore Saloutos Prize in Immigration and Ethnic History, and *The Web of Empire: English Cosmopolitans in an Age of Expansion, 1560–1660* (2008), which won the Roland H. Bainton Book Prize in History. She is coauthor, with Douglas R. Egerton, Kris Lane, and Donald R. Wright, of *The Atlantic World: A History*, the first textbook to be written in the field of Atlantic History (2007), and coeditor, with Adam Rothman, of *Major Problems in Atlantic History* (2008). Her articles have appeared in the *American Historical Review, William and Mary Quarterly, Itinerario, Shakespeare Studies,* and *Slavery and Abolition.*